The Novel Histories of Galdós

THE

Novel Histories of Galdós

Diane Faye Urey

Princeton University Press
Princeton, New Jersey

Copyright © 1989 by Princeton University Press
Published by Princeton University Press
41 William Street, Princeton
New Jersey
08540
In the United Kingdom:
Princeton University Press, Guildford, Surrey

Library of Congress Cataloging-in-Publication Data
Urey, Diane F.
The novel histories of Galdós / Diane Faye Urey.
p.   cm.   Bibliography: p.   Includes index.
ISBN 0-691-06777-5 (alk. paper)
1. Pérez Galdós, Benito, 1843-1920—Criticism and interpretation.
2. Historical fiction, Spanish—History and criticism.
3. Spain—History—19th century.
4. Spain in literature.
I. Title.   PQ6555.Z5U74 1989   863'.5—dc19   88-27626   CIP

This book has been composed in
Linotron Aldus

Clothbound editions of
Princeton University Press books
are printed on acid-free paper, and binding
materials are chosen for strength and durability.
Paperbacks, although satisfactory for personal collections, are not usually
suitable for library rebinding

Printed in the United States of America
by Princeton University Press
Princeton, New Jersey

For
Matthew
and
Benjamin

Contents

Acknowledgments   ix
Introduction   3

Chapter One: The Search for Meaning in the Third Series   16
    The Individual and History in *Zumalacárregui*   19
    Networks of Character, Plot, History, and Art in
       La campaña del Maestrazgo   30
    Translating Fernando Calpena   47
    Fernando as the Word between History and Fiction in *Vergara*   53
    The Confusion of Letters and the Fusion of Texts   60
    Documenting the Origin   67
    Generative Degeneration in *Bodas reales*   74
    Rewriting History through the Narration of Isabel II's Marriage   87
    The Procession of History through Marriage, Adultery, and
       Death in Conclusion to the Third Series   91

Chapter Two: Women and Writing in the Fourth Series   101
    The Sovereign Contradiction of Isabel II   102
    The Interpenetration of History and Fiction through the
       Mysterious Truths of *Narváez*   111
    Tracing Lucila in the Original Words of History   118
    Names for Things in *O'Donnell*   123
    Politics and Signification   126
    The Presence and Absence of Food   130
    Theory and Practice of the "Desamortización"   137
    The Rhetoric of Sexuality   140
    Inconclusions   142

Chapter Three: Strategies of Reading in the Fifth Series   147
    Naming   153
    Constructs of Personality   160
    Organizing Plot Sequences   170
    Organizing Histories   173
    Temporal Organizations   179
    Writing and Blindness   188
    The Repetition of History   193
    Seeking Symbols   206
    Forming Allegories   219

Conclusion   228
Notes   237
Bibliography   255
Index   261

Acknowledgments

I wish to express my gratitude to the American Council of Learned Societies for providing me with a fellowship in 1983 that allowed me to write a substantial portion of this volume. I also wish to thank the National Endowment for the Humanities for the Travel to Collections Grant that aided my investigation of the Galdós manuscripts in the Biblioteca Nacional. Thanks also to the five summer research grants from Illinois State University, I was able to complete the project.

I am deeply indebted to the many friends and colleagues who have given me so much support in my studies of the *Episodios nacionales* over the last several years. Without the helpful critiques of my work by fellow galdosistas, and especially their encouragement to continue with the project, this book would never have been completed. I owe the opportunity to do the extensive reading and annotation that Galdós's novels require to the tranquil infancies of my sons Matthew and Benjamin. Above all, I wish to thank my husband Stephen for his thoughtful advice during the process of revision and for so carefully proofing the typescript. Finally, I wish to thank Vivian Hauser and Janis Swanton for their invaluable aid in typing the manuscript.

This study contains revised versions of the following articles: "Isabel II and Historical Truth in the Fourth Series of Galdós' *Episodios nacionales,*" *Modern Language Notes* 98 (1983): 189–207; "Linguistic Mediation in the *Episodios nacionales* of Galdós: *Vergara,*" *Philological Quarterly* 62 (1983): 263–71; "The Confusion and the Fusion of Fiction and History in the Third Series of Galdós' *Episodios nacionales,*" *Philological Quarterly* 64 (1985): 459–73; "Words for Things: The Discourse of History in Galdós' *O'Donnell,*" *Bulletin of Hispanic*

Studies 63 (1986): 33–46; "From Monuments to Syllables: The Journey to Knowledge in *Zumalacárregui*," *Anales galdosianos* 21, in press; "La historia como revisión: el caso de *Bodas reales*," *Galdós y la historia*, Ottawa Hispanic Studies 1, edited by Peter Bly, 113–30 (Ottawa: Dovehouse Editions, 1988).

The Novel Histories of Galdós

Introduction

Novelists and historians alike inevitably confront fundamental problems when they endeavor to describe real life in words. These problems have occupied writers since Aristotle, but our sensitivity to them has become especially acute in modern times because objectivity and realism have been, for at least a century and a half, normative modes of historical and literary writing. Contemporary attempts to supersede literary realism symbolically or surrealistically and plans to define more precisely the objective or subjective methods of historical inquiry are all symptoms of the pervasive concern with the exact relationship between reality and the language that describes it.

One measure of the lasting appeal of the most valued writers of the nineteenth and twentieth centuries is their evident concern with these same issues. Benito Pérez Galdós (1843–1920), the foremost modern Spanish novelist, is no exception in this regard. In the history of Spanish literature Galdós stands second only to Cervantes in the development of the novel. Though not universally acknowledged as Spain's greatest modern novelist, the last decade has seen his stature rise, both in Spanish and in international letters. In his 1978 book, *The Realists*, C. P. Snow places Galdós alongside Dostoevski and Balzac as a leader in the development of the realist novel.[1] However, Galdós still remains an obscure figure for many scholars of the epoch. In 1979 James Stamm writes of the "enormous novelist creativity" of Galdós, "which can transform the banal, the sordid, even the saccharine into the texture of human experience." Yet, he continues, "It is indeed a mystery why Galdós remains almost unknown outside of Spain as a major literary genius, comparable in his creativity to any literary figure the Western world has produced."[2] Martin Seymour-Smith writes in 1980 that Galdós

> is probably a better and more consistent novelist than Balzac, yet he has been astonishingly neglected. . . . His two

early influences were Charles Dickens and Balzac, but he had greater psychological insight than either. . . . His historical significance is that in his encyclopedic work may be found all the kinds of novel written in the nineteenth and twentieth centuries. Once his numerous works have been made available in English, which they almost certainly will be in the 1980s, he will become one of the major sources of pleasure and wisdom in the next decade.[3]

Galdós's seventy-eight novels, twenty-four plays, and numerous occasional pieces, written between 1867 and his death in 1920, made him one of the most prolific writers in Europe and assured his indelible impression on nineteenth- and twentieth-century Hispanic writers. The relative boom in the translation of some of his better known works in the last few years should begin to correct the glaring omission of Galdós in comparative critical studies of the novel.[4]

Although Galdós is finally coming to earn recognition as one of the world's great novelists, there are still major portions of his work that incur serious critical neglect even among Galdós scholars. One of the most obvious areas is that which constitutes the largest part of Galdós's literary production, his forty-six historical novels called the *Episodios nacionales*. The *Episodios nacionales*, or "Episodes in the Nation's Life," constitute five series. Each series contains ten volumes except the last, which contains six. The first twenty *Episodios* were written at the beginning of Galdós's career, between 1873 and 1879, and the last twenty-six toward the end, between 1898 and 1912. They form a unique kind of "historical novel," treating near-contemporary Spanish history from 1805 and the battle of Trafalgar through the Bourbon Restoration and the 1880s. Because they deal with almost contemporary historical events, the *Episodios nacionales* offer direct insight into how Galdós sought to turn the world he perceived around him into words. They are particularly relevant, therefore, to the fundamental questions that concern any writer of history or fiction.

Despite their inherent relevance to the basic functions of realist literature, the *Episodios nacionales* continue to be the least read and least studied of Galdós's work. Few editions of these novels were available until recently, when the establishment of democratic government in Spain and the elimination of press censorship revived some popular interest in them as a corrective or alternative to previous official histories of Spain's political, social, and economic troubles in the nineteenth century. The main obstacle to adequate study and appreciation of the *Episodios*, however, has undoubtedly been the critical bias that prefers Galdós's more well-recognized contemporary novels, the thirty-one *Novelas contemporáneas*. The *Novelas contemporáneas* have been the chief focus of Galdós scholarship during this century. They are usually considered to be works of superior literary value because they are seen as more "fictional" than the *Episodios*. Yet this critical value judgment has not always been universal, and it obscures the crucial place that the *Episodios* hold in Spanish literary history.

Alfred Rodríguez has shown in *An Introduction to the "Episodios nacionales" of Galdós* (1967), that it is not because of the *Novelas contemporáneas*, but rather because of the twenty volumes of the first two series, that Galdós was known all his life as "el autor de los *Episodios nacionales*." Galdós transformed Spain's reading public from consumers of cheap translations and serials to loyal followers of his literary revitalization of the nineteenth-century novel. He "raised the living language of the Spaniard to a literary function, and thus re-vitalized—on contact—the overly staid academic expression of his epoch."[5] Part of the contemporary bias against the *Episodios* reflects an a priori judgment of the historical novel as an inferior artistic product in which any problems of technique or method have been arbitrarily and narrowly answered in advance. Their "historical" subject matter is frequently seen as hindering their "literary" value. Many of the existing scholarly studies of the *Episodios nacionales* adopt a limited view of them: they treat the works either as simple historical records, which should be judged by their faithfulness to real events, or as literary expressions of Galdós's personal views of Spanish history, which should be judged by their sensitivity to political, social, or cultural issues. Even Rodríguez maintains that the five series of novels display a single philosophy of history and an unvarying approach to the problem of representing reality in language (e.g., 30). This assessment must appear immediately suspect when one considers that the forty-six volumes occupied Galdós's attention over virtually the entire course of his career and that during these years the techniques and methods employed in his other writings changed dramatically, as scholars have effectively demonstrated. But Galdós's innovations and developments in narrative are perhaps even more obvious in his historical novels. It is that designation itself which poses the largest obstacle to a critical appreciation of their artistic worth. As Stephen Gilman writes in his seminal study, *Galdós and the Art of the European Novel* (1981), "Galdós' generic innovations modify profoundly both terms of the hybrid, or perhaps it would be better to say redundant, classification 'historical novel'."[6]

The notion that works of literature can be classified into distinct types or genres—short story, novel, lyric, epic, etc.—is a traditional principle of literary criticism. There are, needless to say, many works of literature that resist easy classification according to genre, and this is surely the case with this special kind of historical novel, the *episodio nacional*. The critical judgments that such difficult-to-classify works receive may range from "brilliantly original" to "hopelessly confused." Both assessments have befallen Galdós's works, but too often some version of the latter. The *Episodios* demand to be treated as literary creations in themselves. While it would be impossible to deny that they provide striking social commentary, this study will investigate the style of their historical narrative apart from preconceived notions of their political or social message. Those social and political aspects have been perhaps too zealously examined before, at the expense of artistic qualities of the texts that are, to say the least, worthy of equal consideration. The following chapters attempt to understand what is meant by the terms and categories of history and novel as they are practiced by this highly experimental, not naively realistic author.

Galdós's novels, though generally labeled realist, range in technique from historical, naturalistic, dialogic, or epistolary, to modes that today are called self-conscious, metafictional, and self-referential. This "self-conscious" aspect of Galdós's work was not recognized until relatively recently, in spite of the overdetermined value of the designation in literary criticism. While Robert Alter, in *Partial Magic: The Novel as a Self-Conscious Genre*, goes to great lengths to define the term, his often provocative analyses and categorizations leave no room for a writer like Galdós. Alter maintains there is

> an ultimate dividing line between self-conscious and other kinds of novelists. . . . The self-conscious novelists are always simultaneously aware of the supreme power of the literary imagination within its own sphere of creation and its painful or tragicomic powerlessness outside that sphere. The great nineteenth-century imaginists, on the other hand are impelled by a deep inner need to confuse the two realms.[7]

Later he writes of the "modernist revival of self-conscious fiction" in authors like Unamuno and Gide. This revival takes the form, to a great extent, of parody in the Cervantine tradition:

> The parodistic novel, exploding the absurdities of previous literary conventions as it unfolds, effects a kind of dialetical refinement and correction of lying, edging us toward the perception of certain truths about the manipulation of language, about character, about human nature, perhaps even about the kind of social world we inhabit. (158)

Galdós obviously cultivated parody, as many of his *Novelas contemporáneas* reveal, and as this study of the *Episodios* will clearly demonstrate. Perhaps many of his works written at the turn of the century, such as the last three series of *Episodios nacionales*, form part of the "modernist revival." But many of Galdós's much earlier works are self-conscious, too, in part because of his Cervantine heritage, if one continues in Alter's terms.

Beyond the Metafictional Mode, Robert Spires's examination of the genre in Spanish literature, shows how one of Galdós's first stories, "La novela en el tranvía" (1871) is metafictional.[8] The self-conscious techniques he identifies in this early work are displayed throughout the *Episodios* from the first series to the last. It is not only the lack of translations of Galdós's work that has prohibited his inclusion in so many treatments of nineteenth-century literature from Lukács to Alter (C. P. Snow and J. P. Stern being lonely, if excellent, exceptions), but also that very tendency, repeatedly demonstrated, to categorize and define movements and genres. Galdós resisted this tendency in theory, as in the prologue to *El Abuelo*, and consistently in practice, in works like the *Episodios nacionales*. Gilman writes of Galdós's

> calculated and radical modifications of the traditional shape of historical novels. The "episodios" differ from the Scottian model not only in being "agreeable" and "brief," although both qualifications are correct, but in their very conception. Today we would term them "nouveaux romans" and expect from their author an appropriate amount of polemical self-display. Galdós, as usual, preferred to let what he had written speak for itself. (*Art*, 54–55)

John W. Kronik's discussions of Galdós's self-consciousness or metafiction provide useful correctives to Alter's categories. As he writes in "Feijoo and the Fabrication of Fortunata,"

> Evidently Alter is unfamiliar with Galdós, for anyone who can say that the realistic novelist avoids the paradoxes of the relationship between fiction and reality cannot be writing about Galdós. . . . Not only in *El amigo Manso*, where the concern is obvious, but in all his writing he puts into play the dynamics of what the book is and what the book does.[9]

While I believe that the later *Episodios* challenge Professor Kronik's statement that "*Misericordia* is Galdós' most trenchant demonstration of artistic self-consciousness,"[10] I thoroughly agree with his observations that

> Galdós, able heir to Cervantes, sensed in his own time the rich potential in using art as an instrument for commentary on art, and he did so througout his career. . . . Galdós as a writer of fiction also functions as a critic of fiction because he is interested in displaying how fiction works. His creative endeavor bears a double result: a creation and an investigation of the mystery that caused that creation to be. (*"Misericordia,"* 37)

Many of the contemporary authors of self-referential fiction in Spain and Latin America today cannot deny their debt to Galdós. Even his virulent critics of the Generation of 1898 owe some of their most acclaimed achievements to Galdós; the historical novels of Baroja, Valle-Inclán's *Tirano Banderas*, Azorín's *Doña Inés*, and Unamuno's *Niebla* testify to this, as Ricardo Gullón, among others, has illustrated.[11] Galdós's realism was always much more than any simple definition of the term can imply. Just as writers today attempt to describe their reality through unrealistic techniques, so too did Galdós always define, in practice if not in theory, the real in the broadest of terms.

Thus, the misconception that somehow Galdós's historical novels can be studied differently from his fictional novels is gradually being superseded by those critics who treat the historical novels as the literary texts that they indeed are, rather than as historical records or ideological manifestos. As early as 1972, Ricardo Gullón observed that

> más de una vez se olvida el hecho obvio de que la obra de arte es un sistema de signos, y que en entenderlos consiste la operación intelectual encomendada al lector. La calidad del descifrado—y aún la variación cuantitativa representada por los diferentes niveles de penetración a que cada lector alcance—dependerá de la aptitud de éste para captar esos signos y para comprender su significado.[12]

Whether labeled historical or contemporary novels, Galdós's art is still a system of language and must be studied as such. The interpretations that ignore the linguistic structure of Galdós's work, while offering valuable insights into many aspects of the *Episodios*, reveal an inability to fully appreciate what was, from the beginning, an amazing artistic virtuosity. This study seeks to bring to the attention of modern scholars that virtuosity through which Galdós poses basic questions about historical knowledge and truth in language, topics of widespread critical debate today.

The ambiguous status of the historical novel suggests an oxymoronic union of fact and fiction. In spite of the long-acknowledged difficulty of this designation, the paradox remains unavoidable in critical examinations of the genre. The label historical novel exposes the representational limits inherent in language itself, limits that contemporary strategies of literary interpretation can never ultimately transcend. Modern structuralist linguistics, beginning most notably with Saussure, recognizes this dilemma when it posits that language does not recreate things in words, but rather creates a structure of verbal differences in which no signifying or signified element can maintain its identity without reference to the other elements of the system. The mutually interdependent relations of terms establish their values, making them subject to constant and inescapable association with each other in such a way that the value of one always implies and embraces that of another. Even in the simplest system of opposing binary terms, one of these always has the potential to take on the significance of the other. Galdós's *Episodios nacionales* are remarkable for their awareness and exploitation of the representational limits of, and potential for structural play in, language.

The *Episodios nacionales* constantly call into question both the value of representation and the existence of historical truth in discourse and in the world. Yet such distinctions between truth and falsehood or between the general categories of fiction and history are ultimately unimportant since, as Hayden White has argued in *Tropics of Discourse*, these distinctions of classical historicism are grounded in the structure of language itself:

any given linguistic protocol will obscure as much as it reveals about the reality it seeks to capture in an order of words. This *aporia* or sense of contradiction residing at the heart of language itself is present in *all* of the classic historians. It is this linguistic self-consciousness which distinguishes them from their mundane counterparts and followers, who think that language can serve as a perfectly transparent medium of representation and who think that if one can only find the right language for describing events, the meaning of the events will display *itself* to consciousness.[13]

Galdós can hardly be classified among those "mundane counterparts" who see language as a "perfectly transparent medium of representation." The linguistic self-consciousness of his works is evident everywhere, perhaps most obviously in the *Episodios nacionales*. It is this awareness of the inherent contradiction residing in language and of the problematical relationships between language and reality that conditions Galdós's definitions of history and of meaning and opens his works up to conflicting interpretations and to disagreement over his purported aims. Galdós does not pretend that his narrative can display real events in anything but a paradoxical way, because this is all that the nature of language itself allows. Hence, as White observes, "It does not matter whether the world is conceived to be real or only imagined; the manner of making sense of it is the same" (98). Whether one labels a narrative history or fiction, or a novel realist or historical, the language that composes it is the same in every case.

As historical novels, the *Episodios nacionales* confront directly the relationship of man to history and to language. Nonetheless, as Lukács and others have claimed for the novel in general, and as Peter Bly has recently claimed for Galdós in particular, narrative need not be entitled historical in order to be so in numerous implicit and explicit ways.[14] It is precisely the term historical that is called into question in the *Episodios*. Galdós's brilliant manipulation of language could surely only be

11

achieved by a keen perception of its intrinsic and inseparable role in every aspect of life, including what is called history.

The present study does not intend to be in any way comprehensive, but rather to offer new insights into some of the narrative strategies that constitute the *Episodios nacionales*, and to better understand the relationships between their historical consciousness and literary form. The five series of forty-six novels provide a still largely untouched resource for criticism on Galdós and on the novel in general. Their sheer volume often proves daunting, especially when the *Novelas contemporáneas* are themselves virtually inexhaustible ground for illustration and interpretation. But the *Episodios* are by no means Galdós's "second best" novels. In many ways they allow the reader to appreciate Galdós's stylistic virtuosity even more fully than his contemporary novels because of their variety of technique and form and because of the artistic development they display over the immense span of time in which they were written. They also offer a reevaluation of the reader's and the writer's relationships with literature and history as they inevitably call into question the definitions of those perspectives and those discourses themselves.

Due to the vast quantity of material that could be addressed, I have chosen to treat only the last three series here, reserving a study of the early *Episodios* for a separate volume. The last three series, all written after 1898, display Galdós's most sophisticated, complex, and problematical narrative strategies and contain some of his most provocative texts. Since the focus of this study is on narrative strategy, the reader interested in more referential, explanatory and systematic explorations of the *Episodios nacionales* can refer to the fine studies offered by Brian Dendle, Alfred Rodríguez, Hans Hinterhäuser, Antonio Regalado García, or José Montesinos. Their works have been of great value in the preparation of this volume.

The three chapters offered here employ ostensibly different tactics for analyzing the *Episodios*. Chapter 1 treats most of the ten novels of the third series. The initiation of the third series coincides with the completion of the major fictional novels on

which Galdós's contemporary reputation rests. This series examines the years 1834 to 1846 in Spain through its two chief
topics, civil war and romanticism. These two movements in history and literature are both, interchangeably, manifestations of
the motif of the journey. The diverse journeys of these *Episodios* illustrate the constant weaving and unraveling of literary
and historical discourse.

Chapter 2 makes reference to several of the novels of the
fourth series, but examines principally *Narváez* and *O'Donnell*
as exemplary of its focus on women characters. This series addresses the years 1848 to 1868, the adult reign of Isabel II, which
culminates in the overthrow of the Bourbon monarchy. These
works, published after 1900, are about events whose reality was
already resembling fiction: financial frauds, religious quackery,
cover-ups of royal scandals, hyperbolic political propaganda, and
social double standards. The fictional treatment of these some-
what unreal events illustrates well the ambiguous relationships
between literary invention and historical truth.

The last chapter deals with all of the fifth series, arguing that
it overtly displays the problematical relationships between text
and reader. These six volumes address the period of 1869 to
1882, when Spain suffered the upheavals of revolution, civil
war, a short-lived experiment in republican government, and
the restoration of the monarchy. Galdós recounts these events
by constructing fantastic, supernatural, or unreal storylines
concerning almost perversely grotesque or repugnantly banal
characters and situations. Scholars' widely varying reactions to
these novels have largely ignored the texts' deliberate challenge
to any notion of representational language.

Each chapter of this study ultimately serves to establish the
conclusion that novel and history are interchangeable and indistinguishable modes of discourse because they both necessarily
rely on the same narrative strategies. However diligently the
reader may pursue some absolute point of reference, some sure
knowledge of the past in the novel or in history, in Galdós's
novel histories this effort is constantly undermined. While the
Episodios nacionales may give us a better understanding of

many aspects of Spain's past, they also always tell us that the past they create is still an illusion.

I append a list of the *Episodios nacionales* for the reader's convenience. Each volume was written in the same year that it was published.

PRIMERA SERIE
spans 1805 to 1813

1. *Trafalgar* (1873)
2. *La Corte de Carlos IV* (1873)
3. *El 19 de marzo y el 2 de mayo* (1873)
4. *Bailén* (1873)
5. *Napoleón, en Chamartín* (1874)
6. *Zaragoza* (1874)
7. *Gerona* (1874)
8. *Cádiz* (1874)
9. *Juan Martín "el Empecinado"* (1874)
10. *La batalla de los Arapiles* (1875)

SEGUNDA SERIE
spans 1813 to 1834

1. *El equipaje del rey José* (1875)
2. *Memorias de un cortesano de 1815* (1875)
3. *La segunda casaca* (1876)
4. *El Grande Oriente* (1876)
5. *El 7 de julio* (1876)
6. *Los cien mil Hijos de San Luis* (1877)
7. *El terror de 1824* (1877)
8. *Un voluntario realista* (1878)
9. *Los apostólicos* (1879)
10. *Un faccioso más y algunos frailes menos* (1879)

TERCERA SERIE
spans 1834 to 1846

1. *Zumalacárregui* (1898)
2. *Mendizábal* (1898)
3. *De Oñate a La Granja* (1898)

4. *Luchana* (1899)
5. *La campaña del Maestrazgo* (1899)
6. *La estafeta romántica* (1899)
7. *Vergara* (1899)
8. *Montes de Oca* (1900)
9. *Los Ayacuchos* (1900)
10. *Bodas reales* (1900)

CUARTA SERIE
spans 1848 to 1868

1. *Las tormentas del 48* (1902)
2. *Narváez* (1902)
3. *Los duendes de la camarilla* (1903)
4. *La Revolución de Julio* (1904)
5. *O'Donnell* (1904)
6. *Aita Tettauen* (1905)
7. *Carlos VI, en la Rápita* (1905)
8. *La vuelta al mundo en la "Numancia"* (1906)
9. *Prim* (1906)
10. *La de los tristes destinos* (1907)

QUINTA SERIE
spans 1869 to 1882

1. *España sin rey* (1908)
2. *España trágica* (1909)
3. *Amadeo I* (1910)
4. *La primera República* (1911)
5. *De Cartago a Sagunto* (1911)
6. *Cánovas* (1912)

The Search for Meaning
in the Third Series

Historical truth, romantic idealism, the journey—these are some of the diverse concerns of the third series of Galdós's *Episodios nacionales*. Written between 1898 and 1900, these ten historical novels examine the literary, social, economic, and political transformations in Spain from 1834 to 1846. These years see the zenith of romanticism, the first Carlist war over the heir to the throne (Fernando VII's infant daughter Isabel or his reactionary brother don Carlos), the regencies of María Cristina and Espartero, and the beginning of Isabel II's reign. The *Episodios'* treatment of these times and events can be viewed as a temporal projection that establishes relationships of cause and effect. Symbolic relationships among the various historical and fictional elements of the novels supplement and clarify the stories. Yet the conventional types of relations that seem to produce meaning also break down and undo meaning in the series, so that cause and effect become an infinite tracing of effects whose hypothetical causes are forever absent. Symbolic structures like metaphor and analogy give way to irony and antithesis; relations of identity become relations of difference in their constant fluctuation. Such ceaseless and often contradictory movements are, of course, inherent in the mode called historical fiction. These two apparently different, yet fundamentally similar, manifestations of meaning in temporal, or historical, and symbolic, or fictional, projections are both functions of the same relationship among words. Thus both temporal and symbolic projections are similar interpretive constructs. The reader's journeys into the past through historical reconstruction or the many and varied journeys undertaken by fictional characters in the novels are all equally journeys through words. As we seem to travel back in time to 1834, forward through love and war to 1846, and through each volume to our interpretations of character and epoch, we journey only through the relations among signs. Fiction is about images, significative processes, signs. The *Episodios nacionales* are about the fictions of fiction and the fictions of history. More than anything else, these works are concerned with the signifying processes that produce the illusion of meaning.

There are many moments in the third series where it can be seen that the temporal, structural, thematic and symbolic organizations of these novels are themselves unstable processes inviting varying interpretations. Such moments demythify the logics of history, romanticism, and the journey. Each of these relations can provide an explanation of one system of signs in terms of another, but not of the founding order itself. This is the case for any explanatory tactic, as Lévi-Strauss perceived. In "How I Became an Anthropologist," he writes of finding his models in the geologist, in Freud, and in Marx, and observes: "At a different level of reality, Marxism seemed to me to proceed in the same way as geology and psycho-analysis (in the sense in which its founder understood it). All three showed that understanding consists in the reduction of one type of reality to another; that true reality is never the most obvious of realities, and that its nature is already apparent in the care it takes to evade our detection."[1] The third series constantly exchanges one reality or perspective for another, that is, one explanation for another, as it exchanges words for words. Yet each explanation is only one more interpretation, translation, symbolic or temporal projection, in an open series of relationships among signifying systems. This is the logic and the process of the interpretive enterprise of Galdós's historical novels, and of history itself. As Jean Baudrillard writes, "Thus, to be logical, the concept of history must itself be regarded as historical, turn back upon itself, and only illuminate the context that produced it by abolishing itself. . . . To be rigorous the dialect must dialectically surpass and annul itself." Where this does not occur, as with many nineteenth-century interpretations of history that assume universal explanations, the explanation itself becomes the ultimate meaning: it is "transhistoricized."[2] By revealing its own status as signifying process, the third series undermines the

17

notion of a transcendentally significant meaning in history or in any other interpretive projection. It is thus about itself as process, not just an interpretation. The following pages will examine some of the ways in which these ten novels demythify and demystify their own novel histories.

The third series is about the illusions involved in the temporal pursuit of meaning in multiple ways. First, if labeled historical reconstruction, these volumes can be read as explanations of past causes and effects which might serve as lessons for future generations.[3] Such a reading entails a dual temporal projection or interpretation. This duality corresponds to the two great movements in nineteenth-century philosophy of history—that there is a force or logic that can be objectively observed, and that this logic then can be projected into its future evolution and/or ultimate meaning. In this way the historical pursuit appears to move in two directions, revealing truth in both cases. Second, the dominant literary code of the series, romanticism, also invokes a dually temporal projection: it is the cultivation and idealization of a past coupled with a desire for its return. This romantic urge is demonstrated in the characters' emotions and activities throughout the series. Third, in the formal structure of the series there is an emphasis on narrative discontinuities which conflicts with a more conventional illusion of a linear storyline and reading process. The series begins in medias res and ends with a retracing of events that began before the first volume opens. The reader must often wait for the end of one story sequence until several volumes have elapsed, then backtrack in order to find out what "occurred." The reader's distance from characters and events is usually mediated by many narrators, just as the characters remain at geographical or epistolary distances from each other. Fourth, the characters are involved in journeys that, while seeming to carry them forward, often lead them backward—emotionally or geographically. Their paths are frequently unknown, random, or sidetracked. Correspondingly, as they consciously search for their past, their ideal or their identity, they find instead emptiness, disillusion, or, ultimately, the separated self of the schizophrenic.

18

Each one of these temporal aspects in the third series relies on multiple symbolic relationships among words and readers. Each textual process ultimately reveals how all interpretations of history, fiction, self, and other break down, just as do the textual structures upon which these interpretations rely. Such an undermining motivates a reevaluation of conventional modes of perceiving history, of reading literature, and of constructing meanings for the self and the world. As we journey through the third series, we come to rethink our ways of reviewing the past and of reading signs, just as the characters reread themselves in the search for an absent ideal. The journeys of the characters of these novels reflect on all the other elements of the series. These *episodios* fully exploit the metaphors of life and literature as journey or voyage and ultimately reevaluate that metaphor as metaphor. Thus they consider the status of language as image or sign. This study analyzes these processes in the three separate plots contained in *Zumalacárregui, La campaña del Maestrazgo,* and *Bodas reales,* and in the unifying plot revolving around Fernando Calpena, thus incorporating detailed reference to *Mendizábal, La estafeta romántica, Vergara,* and *Los ayacuchos,* and passing reference to *De Oñate a la Granja, Luchana,* and *Montes de Oca.*

THE INDIVIDUAL AND HISTORY IN *ZUMALACÁRREGUI*

José Fago, the soldier-priest protagonist of the first volume of the third series, *Zumalacárregui,* is, as Alfred Rodríguez writes, "an anguished being, withering under the strain of an unbearable inner contradiction." This contradiction arises from his "confused effort to segregate an obsessive past . . . from a present that demands a very different pattern of behavior."[4] His libertine past haunts him when his emotional and military energies become focused on the futile pursuit of Saloma Ulibarri, the woman he seduced, before becoming a priest, three years before the novel opens in 1834. The first chapter finds Fago sent to confess Saloma's father, a village mayor condemned to the firing squad by the Carlist general Zumalacárregui. He ends up, rather, confessing to Ulibarri. This fictional introduction is a counterpart to the historical beginning: In *Galdós: The Mature Thought*, Brian Dendle writes that "No historical background is given; the novel begins, in medias res, with Zumalacárregui's invasion of the Ribera de Navarra."⁵ Like Fago's inconclusive emotional and geographical journeys are the random record of military skirmishes and the "wandering, inconclusive nature of the military campaign" (*Mature Thought*, 40). Both the story and the history take place over a wide geographical area and seem to follow no logical sequence of events. Fago's crisis of conscience, a chance word about Saloma, or his hallucinations direct his course. Dendle observes that this serves to provide an "impressionistic vision of the nature of the [Carlist] movement" (40). Indeed, this impressionism seems a most appropriate format for depicting events of the past, if they are without logic.

References to the role of chance as opposed to logic in human affairs abound in this volume and throughout the series. For example, chapter 24 describes Fago as he begins one of his many searches for Saloma:

> Toda la noche anduvo por desolados campos, sin dirección fija, adoptando el acaso por guía único de su andar vagabundo, y creyendo que los senderos desconocidos suelen conducirnos a donde deseamos. Renegaba de la previsión, del método, de todo el fárrago de prescripciones por que se guían los hombres, y que comúnmente resultan de menor eficacia que los dictados de la fatalidad. Somos unos seres infelices que creemos saber algo y no sabemos nada, que inventamos reglas y principios para engañar nuestra impotencia; vivimos a merced de la Naturaleza y de las misteriosas combinaciones del tiempo. Iba, pues, entregado a lo que el espacio y el tiempo, ministros de Dios, quisieran disponer en su tiránico dominio.⁶

Whether he is confronting time, space, fatality, chance, nature or God, man is powerless to know or alter his mysterious, indecipherable course; so a lack of direction or a vagabond path is as effective as method or foresight. The repetition of Fago's opinions by the narrator ("somos unos seres infelices . . .") in this and many other passages, or their echo through the voices of other characters in the novel, makes this question not idiosyncratic to Fago, but pertinent to the larger concerns of the series. In this case, both those loyal to the pretender don Carlos, the "carlistas," and those loyal to the throne and the regent María Cristina, the "cristinos," believe that God is on their side and thus directs their actions. The Carlists go so far as to refer to the Virgin as "Generalísima" (2:852). But even this hyperbolic faith in a divine logic does not spell victory for don Carlos:

> Pero aquel Dios, que muchos suponían tan calurosamente afecto a uno de los bandos, dispuso las cosas de distinta manera, y pasó lo que según unos no debió pasar, y según otros, sí. Estas sorpresas, que nada tienen de sobrenaturales, obra de la divina imparcialidad, son tan comunes, que con ellas casi exclusivamente se forma un tejido de variados hechos que llaman Historia, expresando con esta voz la que escriben los hombres, pues la que deben tener escrita los ángeles no la conocemos ni por el forro (2:832).

The right or wrong of history is a matter of opinion; its truth is forever hidden from men. Rather, what is called History is merely the written weave of assorted events, ordered according to the writer's impressions and perspective. Whether Zumalacárregui, the Carlists, the Cristinos, or Fago believe their course directed by God or chance makes no difference, since the directing hand, should it exist, is forever unknown.

The desire to judge right and wrong in war is a search for an ultimate meaning, a transcendental truth, just as is the search for the correct interpretation of the written texts of the novel or history. *Zumalacárregui* illustrates how the knowledge of and judgment about history are necessarily derived from written documents that have already been interpreted and thus always removed from the origin of the event itself—its cause—which can never be present. The meanings offered in histories as to causes may be rather an ordering of effects. In *The Use and*

Abuse of History Nietzsche identifies this effort, which he calls "monumental history," as one type of error that can be made in historical interpretation:

> Its object is to depict effects at the expense of the causes "monumentally," that is, as examples for imitation; it turns aside, as far as it may, from reasons, and might be called with far less exaggeration a collection of "effects in themselves" than of events that will have an effect on all ages. The events of war or religion cherished in our popular celebrations are such "effects in themselves." . . .
>
> As long as the soul of history is found in the great impulse that it gives to a powerful spirit, as long as the past is principally used as a model for imitation, it is always in danger of being a little altered and touched up and brought nearer to fiction. Sometimes there is no possible distinction between a "monumental" past and a mythical romance, as the same motives for action can be gathered from the one world as the other.[7]

These remarks are particularly suited to this first volume of the third series, just as Nietzsche's other categories—"antiquarian" and "critical"—offer insights into subsequent volumes. The cultivation of great men and deeds and the forgetting or hating of all else (Nietzsche, 15–16) appear to be the follies of don Carlos, of Fago in his admiration and emulation of Zumalacárregui, of Zumalacárregui's concept of his own historic mission (2:789), and of posterity's exaltation of him. The first chapter exclaims: "¡Zumalacárregui, página bella y triste! España la hace suya, así por su hermosura como por su tristeza" (2:789). Yet this monument of Spain's history is perhaps not a fit object for emulation, the volume will suggest.

The two-paragraph apostrophe to the Carlist general in chapter 1 depicts him as a valiant military strategist who puts "los deberes militares sobre todo sentimiento de humanidad" (2:789). Correspondingly, the first view of Zumalacárregui in action has him mercilessly whipping the women who resisted his siege at Villafranca (2:801). The narrator's comments about the necessity of this tactic to strengthen the soldiers' resistance are conveyed in part through the free indirect style, as were the opening two paragraphs of the novel. The free indirect style implicates the narrator, and consequently the reader, in this epic brutality.[8] Thus Zumalacárregui's behavior—including his "heroism"—is presented in an ambiguous light from the outset. Fago cannot understand the necessity for this public display of cruelty, which provides another dissenting point of view in an equivocally "epic" characterization (2:801). Such contradictory interpretations of this "monument of history" serve to undermine unilateral definitions of greatness, right, and wrong. This is most obvious in the physical description of the General, through Fago's eyes:

> Era el General de aventajada estatura y regulares carnes, con un hombro más alto que otro. Por eso, y por su ligera inclinación hacia delante, efecto sin duda de un padecimiento renal, no era su cuerpo tan garboso como debiera. En él clavó sus ojos Fago, examinándole bien la cara, y al pronto se desilusionó enteramente, pues se lo figuraba de facciones duras, abultadas y terroríficas, con hermosura semejante a la de algunas imágenes de la clase de tropa, como los guerreros bíblicos Aarón, Sansón y Josué. . . . [Zumalacárregui] era un tipo melancólico, adusto, cara de sufrimiento y meditación. (2:800–801)

Thus Fago's illusion of the historic figure compares him to legendary monuments; the reality of Zumalacárregui pales by comparison.

The divergent codes which traverse Zumalacárregui's character make any interpretation of him subject to reversal. Not only does monumental history easily become confused with a mythical romance, as Nietzsche writes, but "monumental history lives by false analogy; it entices the brave to rashness, and the enthusiastic to fanaticism by its tempting comparison" (16). The dangers signaled here can be observed in Fago and in modern interpreters of this novel as well. Dendle, for instance, although acknowledging certain weaknesses in his character, writes that

> Zumalacárregui is presented in epic terms. . . . It would not . . . be rash to see in Zumalacárregui a warning note that Galdós is sounding in the early months of 1898 to his fellow countrymen. . . . [Fago] represents in his instability, his quest for an ever-elusive meaning for his existence, his inability to see clearly into his own nature—Galdós's projection onto the past of the Spain of 1898, of a Spain rent in two, unable to set firm goals in the future and vainly seeking a past made impossible by the very violence of the methods used to pursue it. (40–41)

Dendle's pursuit, however provocative, is of an "ever-elusive meaning" as well, since whether one chooses to read into this volume the Spain of 1898 or of 1834, what remains are still only the interpretations of those elusive times. As the passage from the novel cited above suggests, the reader and interpreter can never be certain of cause and effect; all we have is our own written weave (2:832). This open, indeterminate textuality—a concept that involves a constant movement from a never-recuperable past towards an always out-of-reach future—in *Zumalacárregui* is most poignantly illustrated by Fago's physical search for Saloma.

Fago's valiant fighting for the Carlists (chapter 16) gives way to hallucination and self-recrimination after shooting someone he believes to be the already-dead Ulibarri. After his wanderings of subsequent days, triggered by this specter from his past, he finally takes refuge in a hut whose occupants have heard of a Saloma or Salomé. This Salomé/Saloma both is and is not identifiable with Fago's memory/idealization of her (2:844–45). He also learns that his "double" is sighted with her. The next morning, as he journeys back to his unit, "empezó a ser atormentado por una idea." He recalls "una carta olvidada" (2:845) that fell out of the jacket given him by an old woman. Before she tore it up, he believes he read the "sílaba *Mé*, abreviatura de Salomé, con que de niña la nombraba su abuela." This syllable of a signature of the nickname (Salomé) of Saloma Ulibarri, this trace, inscribes itself in a goat's bleat, which then directs his course: "por todo el camino, sobre la blancura inmaculada de la nieve, fue viendo algo, como huellas de una cabra, un signo que evidentemente decía: *Mé, Mé, Mé* . . ." (2:846). The grammatical symbolism of this syllable is obvious: this "Mé" is the objective projection of Fago's subjective self, his "yo." The narrative thus becomes the story of the wanderings of the divided self.

This passage identifies the journey with the book, the white snow with the blank page. Fago pursues an elusive meaning that is only the syllable "Mé," not the woman herself, as he thinks. Yet this syllable is not really written; it is "algo, como huellas," "un signo," whose meaning is imagined. Only when the signifying "huellas" are given the status of the signified "Mé" do they become a complete sign and thus evidence, meaning. Yet the identification is not a stable sign, since "Mé" is another signifier, not a signified idea or woman. Fago pursues this trace of meaning, this signifier of a signifier, for three days, "durante los cuales iba viendo el *Mé, Mé,* ya representado por la huella de cabras, ya por los letreros diferentes, trazados con negro en esquinazos de iglesias o en tapiales de caserones" (2:846). The instability of the sign is underlined further as the signified signifier "Mé" slips from one signifier—"huellas"—to others—"letreros diferentes." Fago sees his meaning wherever he looks. His search is guided by a preconceived vision of his goal; thus the snow and the road write what he wishes to read. Moreover, he only thinks he remembers the syllable that he pursues; he is not even certain of his memory:

Y yo digo, ¿esto de creer recordar es como recordar verdaderamente? Si vi pasar la palabra *Mé* por el aire, ¿cómo no me causó la impresión que ahora me causa el querer recordarlo? Luego no hubo tal palabra . . . ¿Y no podría suceder que viera la sílaba sin darme cuenta de lo que significaba? (2:846)

Like the historical documents that seem to signify the remembered memory of the event itself, this syllable signifies the absolute elusiveness of the woman as text.

In his illuminating essay, "The Infinite Text," Manfred Frank connects the literary tradition of life as a journey to the infinite journey of the written text. In classical and early Christian literature there was usually a happy return at the end of a journey, but "this changes upon the threshold of the new era. Here doubts about the 'immanence of meaning in life' . . . disturb the economy of the successful homecoming." This era is marked by the romantic period; thus "Our historical interest in ideas and motifs encounters the problem of losing one's way only, of course, at the thematic level. In fact, one can observe that modern literature—since Coleridge and Brentano—has identified the aimless passage with the fate of poetic speech."[9] Fago's chance-determined travels and particularly his fruitless pursuit of Saloma, "Mé,"—black marks on a white background—clearly corollate travel with writing in *Zumalacárregui*. Fago never reaches his goal—neither his own identity as priest, soldier, or man, nor the syllable "Mé," or the woman Saloma. As Frank writes, "The endlessness of the trip clearly becomes a problem in the interminability of writing itself. Literature reflects its own condition when it de-limits (*ent-grenzt*) the metaphor of the journey with life" (72). Fago's endless journey is one of the many ways in which the series describes its own textual process.

When Fago finds his way back to his unit, he is at first accused of spying, since he was sighted with Salomé—a case of mistaken identities never resolved in the novel. He is sent on a mission to capture her, since she is believed to be a Cristinist spy. He first resists this disorienting pull of his past, then agrees after his manhood is challenged: "No se le exige ciencia militar ni teología dogmática. Esta no es empresa de guerrero ni de sacerdote. —¿Pues de qué?— De hombre . . . , simplemente de hombre, señor Fago" (2:854). He falls almost fatally ill—"sin ganas de vivir" (2:854), however, before he can begin his search. When he recovers and undertakes the mission, he follows only false clues or chance sightings of the plural identities of Salomé, "ama de cura . . . clériga—mujer virtuosa" (2:845), "monja domínica, . . . aldeana rústica o ama de cría" (2:853). His jour-

ney, like his life and subsequent death, is without logic, a series
of discontinuous movements toward an objective whose various
aspects like "ama de cura" and "ama de cría" cannot be reconciled.

Two important episodes precede Fago's death, again marked
by a fever, convulsions, and unexplainable mental images
(2:887), suggesting his lack of both physical and mental control
of his identity. Every day, as he goes to Zumalacárragui's house,
he observes the washerwomen in the creek: "Apoyado los codos
en el pretil del puente, se pasaba allí el hombre largos ratos,
viendo a las mujeres con media pierna dentro del agua" (2:885).
The reader can deduce from the final words of the novel that one
of these women is Salomé, since she says of Zumalacárregui,
"Bien muerto está. . . . Mandó fusilar a mi padre" (2:889).
These lines are as close as the novel comes to presenting Salomé,
since the character who speaks these words is not named. The
signifying process that relates the final words of the novel to
Fago's first confession to Ulibarri and the main plot of the *episodio* is a complicated series of substitutions and connections.
An association is established between the washerwoman and Salomé Ulibarri, between the end of the novel and the beginning,
through the words "padre," "fusilar," and "Zumalacárregui."
But just as the daughter, the object of Fago's relentless search,
is absent in the first scene, so the name Ulibarri is not literally
identified with "padre" in the last scene, although one readily
assumes the substitution. These substitutions and associations
through which the reader unifies the plot of the novel, names its
characters, and instills it with meaning are arbitrary and ultimately unstable in the ceaseless signifying process. The various
functions of substitution will be discussed throughout this
study, particularly in chapter 2.

The gaps between words are bridged by imagined associations, just as Fago gazes down upon the women, unable, however, to reach them. Yet those gaps can never really be bridged,
just as Fago does not reach Salomé here or anywhere in the
novel, nor can he bridge the distance between himself and his
past, a meaningful life, or a stable identity. Shortly after his

glimpse of the women, he dies. Fago's death, which leaves his search unended, his story as incomplete as it began, coincides with Zumalacárregui's, in the midst of the unresolved war. These two seekers of an unattainable past, which in Zumalacárregui's case is both heroic and reactionary, perhaps illustrate Nietzsche's thesis that " 'only strong personalities can endure history; the weak are extinguished by it.' History unsettles the feelings when they are not powerful enough to measure the past by themselves" (32). Fago's search is also for his own identity in his pursuit of the syllable/woman/meaning/memory/text/ "Mé." He continually fluctuates among his roles of "guerrero," "sacerdote," and his past as "seglar desalmado y libertino" (2:853), unable to find a settled association of these signifiers, which cannot logically substitute for each other. His dilemma is most melodramatically illustrated when he dreams of interrupting mass to exterminate "cristinos" (2:841–42). It is the challenge to this unsettled or unstable identity that makes him take up the search for his history labeled Salomé. He is told that "un hombre muy listo, muy despierto, buena estampa, aficionadillo a las aventuras," who has not "recibido más que la primera tonsura [del estado eclesiástico], y parece inclinado a seguir carrera muy distinta" (2:856) will be "competidor suyo en la comisión de atrapar a la volandera *Mé*" (2:859). Unable to endure his task, however, Fago is extinguished by it, just like his historical model.

Before Zumalacárregui and Fago die, however, they have a conversation. In spite of the General's encouragement and praise, Fago insists upon denying his ability, and likewise his identity, by remarks such as "no soy apto para nada" (2:886); "Y aquí me tiene usted sin vocación ninguna, pues todas las he perdido, y con toda verdad le digo que no sé adónde han ido a parar"; "¡Mi vida es tan poco útil!" (2:887). He dies without confession, so the end of his journey is up to God: "a Dios toca darle su merecido" (2:889). Dendle observes that "Fago's own identity is as much a mystery, both for himself and others, as that of Saloma" (40). For Rodríguez he "is the oddest characterization in the Series" (125). Fago's mysterious, unsettled identity, like that of "Mé," signals the indeterminacy not only of his personality, in its past and present manifestations, but of his temporal and personal journeys. Fago seeks in "Mé" what he might have had in the past—a reconciliation of his own warring facets. But as seen in his confession to Ulibarri, he never possessed a stable identity in the first place; he has always led an erratic life: "Mi carácter violento, mis hábitos de disolución y desorden de mi conducta, fueron causa de que, a los tres meses de aquella vida errante, Saloma y yo pareciéramos enemigos" (2:792). Fago's dilemma suggests the romantic notion of "yearning for the Infinite" as Schlegel expresses it. Frank discusses Schlegel's concept of "Infinite" and writes that it

> presupposes the loss of an "original meaning" and feels "driven" to seek it just the same. The self finds itself in a substantially negative relation to its Other. This negativity nowhere allows the self to achieve "self-identity. . . . The result is that the 'existence' of the self becomes the 'greatest secret,' the unsolvable 'riddle'." (78–79)

These remarks are applicable to the search of Fago's "yo" for his "Mé," to the details of his personality, to his journey, and to the concepts of historical recuperation and textuality in *Zumalacárregui*. They are also pertinent to the third series as a whole, which will become particularly obvious in Fernando Calpena, the "greatest secret" of the series.

José Fago's secret, his identity, is never discovered; his journey is endless. Frank observes that "the indeterminacy of personality reflects the loss of an absolute meaning of Man" (79). If the past is forever absent—only an illusion, a fiction, a remembered memory—then its pursuit in the self or in books is a self-destructive endeavor, since the goal is always out of reach, if it ever existed in the first place. This is the fate of Fago's journey, of the Carlist war, of the text of the first *episodio* of the third series: "The endless deferral of the goal which our texts relate thus corresponds to an endless deferral of sense within the structure of the texts themselves" ("Infinite Text" 78). Any sense of character, of history, or of the novel that the reader creates is only one among a continual chain of signifying relations that can be fabricated in the open-ended process of historical fiction.

Just as *Zumalacárregui* begins in the middle of a journey and ends without completing it, so the third series travels from scene to scene, plot to plot, character to character, *episodio* to *episodio*. Like the episodic structure of each novel, plots and characters are frequently only partially developed in a given volume, so the sense that can be made of them there is incomplete. The weave of each volume extends to *episodios* that precede and succeed it, and not always in their first order of reading. In this way the meaning of each novelistic element is deferred, often endlessly, as when Fago never reaches his goal, when he dies without explanation or confession. These incomplete meanings rest, however, on other textual elements even for their incompleteness, itself a value. The realization of Fago's goal relies on the presence/absence of the text "Mé," his death on his identification with Zumalacárregui and difference/distance from the washerwomen, and his final destiny on the absence of confession and God's unknown judgment. The text Fago is thus a function of the other military, sexual, and religious texts of *Zumalacárregui*, "Mé," and the Church. And the functional value of these other texts for the deferred meaning of Fago—or any other element—is often inversely proportionate to its presence in the series.

The absence of Salomé Ulibarri in *Zumalacárregui*, for example, motivates most of the plot and the characterization of Fago. The trace of a syllable of her name marks the importance of her absence. Salomé appears, finally, in *Luchana*, the fourth volume of the series, as the wife of Baldomero Galán. Yet in this novel Salomé has little significance in herself; she serves chiefly to facilitate the identification of Baldomero Galán with Espartero. Her function is thus a catalyst for that series of resemblances and differences between the historical and fictional Baldomeros. Her appearance in the fifth novel, *La campaña del Maestrazgo*, is even more obviously functional. It is through her eyes, in the first chapter, that one reads of don Beltrán de Urdaneta, the protagonist of the *episodio*: "la atención de Saloma, se apartó de la mesa. Mirando casualmente hacia la escalera del parador, vio que por ella descendía un caballero anciano" (2:1262). Such deceptively "casual" moments direct the course of reading, of seeking an order or sense from diverse episodes and characters. *La campaña del Maestrazgo* is connected to the separate plot of *Zumalacárregui* through Saloma, and to both *Luchana* and the main plot of Fernando Calpena through Beltrán, since Beltrán appears in *Luchana* as Calpena's advisor. This mostly independent volume is traversed by the names Calpena, Beltrán, and most prominently, Aurora Negretti, Calpena's first love, now the object of conquest by the protagonist of *Luchana*, Zoilo Arratia.[10] In this way one syllable—"Mé"— or one name—Salomé, Beltrán, or Aurora—can set off numerous chains of relationships, which in turn create the plots and characters of the third series. In the case of "Mé," the term is virtually the only fictional element that travels from the first to subsequent volumes. Through the contiguity of syllable to syllable, word to word, name to name, then, the various networks of identity and difference, of signification, are woven. These relationships are in constant movement: Fago's identity is in a continual and unresolved state of flux; Baldomero Galán and Baldomero Espartero are and are not alike; history and fiction are the same, yet as language they are both always processes of deferral.

In *La campaña del Maestrazgo* the weaving and unraveling of the narrative network is most obviously discernible in the strangely parallel journeys of the volume's two protagonists, don Beltrán de Urdaneta and Manuel Santapau (Nelet). Beltrán's quest, the main plot of the novel, and his character are defined by and define those of Nelet. Such definitions, though, are of course only partial, if not arbitrary, since Beltrán signifies equally through his relationships with other characters. Correspondingly, Nelet acquires significance through his relationships of identity and difference to various characters in addition to Beltrán, characters that likewise signify through their relationships with others. Not only does each character function through relationships with characters in the third series, but naturally, with characters from other texts as well. Nelet is a Carlist regiment commander serving under the ruthless General Cabrera. A former libertine and sporadically repentant sinner, Nelet is visited by visions of saints and demons, subject to bouts of violence (in this, like Cabrera) and sentimentality. Thus romantic literature and specifically the Don Juan motif are codes affecting his characterization.[11] Moreover he is easily identifiable in these alternating codes with the "libertino," "guerrero," "sacerdote" José Fago. Yet in Nelet's excesses these identifications, whether with don Juan, Fago or Cabrera, become distorted, hyperbolic, not merely metaphorical.

Like Fago, Nelet pursues a woman, Marcela Luco. His obsession with her reflects his obsession with his past and a desire to expiate his sins (2:1313). Thus Nelet is also on a journey whose goal is at once a woman, a past, and a reconciliation of dueling codes of behavior. Marcela is both similar to and different from the phantom "Mé." She is physically present to Nelet, where Salomé is always absent, yet she is a nun, which would seem to place her sexually beyond his reach. Salomé's function as the endlessly deferred goal was signaled not only by her absence, but by the series of mistaken identities between the two Salomés in *Zumalacárregui*. Fago, thinking he was tracing Ulibarri's path, would encounter her double as often as her absence. In this way Salomé served a multiple and indeterminate function in the oscillations presence/absence, self/other, woman/syllable, past/present, Saloma/Salomé. Marcela's function as indeterminate goal is similar in some of these respects, but notably different as well. She is a sexual hybrid, the lengthy and detailed description of her emphasizes: "es un muchacho amujerado o mujer hombruna"; "una figura híbrida"; "Los ojos grandes . . . parecían de hombre; de la nariz para abajo representaba cara fina y graciosa de hembra"; "era como de muchachón tierno"

(2:1287). As a nun and a hybrid, Marcela is a woman who is not; she is different from herself. The ever-sliding signifiers that weave the character of Marcela question the possibility of meaning, of making sense, of naming. Her unresolved sexual difference epitomizes the impossibility of resolving difference into identity.

Where Fago's woman was a syllable, Nelet's goal is not a woman either. Both "Mé" and Marcela, by their unwomanliness, unapproachability, and indeterminate identities, demythify the notion of referentiality. They are not in themselves complete signs, having neither stable conceptual nor material identities. The reinscription of Marcela's textuality, while more conventional, serves the same function as that of the syllable "Mé" in *Zumalacárregui*. It connects the codes of woman, journey, and writing, and reveals their common reliance on and inability to escape from the processes of language. From the moment her name appears in the text, it is obvious that Marcela is modeled on Cervantes's creation.[12] So the reader's pursuit of the meaning of Marcela also involves a journey, into the text of *Don Quijote*, not into the material world. Marcela's irreducible textuality therefore poses questions about representation and originality, as does that of "Mé."

Don Beltrán de Urdaneta, an aged aristocrat fleeing from what he perceives as a restrictive and parsimonious life imposed by his nephew Rodrigo, pursues Marcela, too. He seeks in her the restoration of his past wealth and with it his nobility and freedom. He first receives news of her whereabouts from "El epístola" (2:1276-78), the messenger, spy, and intermediary who greatly complicates Calpena's plot in *Vergara*, as will be seen. Beltrán believes that Marcela possesses buried pots of money that were originally his, since he lent money to her father. Both Beltrán and Nelet journey to capture a fullness they believe they have lost; but their desires are never realized since they seek what exists only as illusion. Their efforts, like those of so many characters in the series, are commentaries on the epoch. Casalduero has observed that the third series,

Junto a los acontecimientos político-militares, presenta la transformación económico-social y la evolución ideológico-sentimental de estos años. La lucha que se entabla en España en un plano militar (esto es lo característico español y lo que da un tono tan arcaico a nuestro siglo XIX), se dispone en Europa en un plano económico, aunque no sea ni menos dura, ni menos cruel, ni menos bárbara, ni menos inmoral, ni menos fratricida. Diferenciar estas luchas, sin embargo, es algo muy importante. En Europa se está luchando por tomar posesión del nuevo mundo industrial, por adueñarse de esta nueva dimensión del mundo. La lucha es algo creador. En España, en cambio, estamos en plena Edad Media. Son los pretendientes a la corona los que pelean, y por eso los generales adquieren en seguida los rasgos de señores feudales, medievales.[13]

La campaña del Maestrazgo describes such a medieval, regressive, elusive and illusory pursuit in many ways: its settings; its plots of war, love, and greed; the literary, social, moral, and sexual identities of its characters; its self-conscious cultivation of certain types of historicism; and its romantic pursuit of the past.

The attempt to recapture or restore the past is in some ways like trying to preserve—mummify—the dead. The emphasis on death in this novel, through the extensive narration of bloody battles and countless executions, is a realistic counterpoint to the romantic idealization of the war: "La guerra, el país, la raza, renovaban en todo los tiempos medievales. La vida tomaba esplendores poéticos y risueñas tintas que se mezclaban con el rojizo siniestro de la sangre, tan sin medida derramada" (2:1314 and elsewhere). As in *Zumalacárregui*, a journey into the past extinguishes life. This is exemplified in Marcela and Nelet: in the final scene, Beltrán and two other ancients must bury the murder/suicide of the would-be lovers. When Nelet is unable to reconcile his own warring facets of violence and humanity he destroys his other—Marcela—and therefore himself (2:1365). With Marcela, Beltrán's pots of gold and his illusions of restored glory are also buried forever.

Beltrán's pursuit of original riches, his past way of life, ends in the ultimate impossibility of such a recuperation. Along with the realization of his forever unattainable goal comes an awareness that the identity he journeys to find exists only as an idealized memory (see his "confession" in chapters 23 and 24). Like Fago and Nelet, Beltrán led the life of a Don Juan. He seems to represent nobility—urbanity, generosity, liberality, yet this representation is clearly a myth. If he is a symbol of Spain's noble past, then he is profligate dissipation, egotism, corruption, lies, and deceit. He forces the near union of Marcela and Nelet, knowing that it is ill-starred and immoral, for his own selfish gain. No longer capable of being a Don Juan himself, he has become a Celestina:

> El corazón de la mujer no tiene secretos para mí: ciencia dolorosa, amigo mío, porque los maestros no llegamos a este doctorado sino a fuerza de amarguras y sufrimientos. En mi tendrá usted un asesor desinteresado. . . . yo le aconsejaré lo más eficaz para conquistar el corazón y la voluntad de esa doncella (2:1314).[14]

Even after Beltrán's religious confession, when he is saved from execution, he returns to his devious, selfish ways. Learning that Nelet, in a "furor de matanza" after a battle, killed Marcela's already wounded and helpless Cristino brother (2:1351), Beltrán encourages him to suppress the truth and to proceed with the marriage:

> Como a continuación expresa el ladino viejo la idea de que bien podía Marcela ignorar siempre quién había sido matador de su hermano, se remontó Nelet de la tristeza lúgubre a la ira, diciendo: ". . . En el estado de mi conciencia es imposible el disimulo. . . . Si usted me aconseja que le oculte la verdad, no es usted tan completo caballero como creí: no, no lo es." (2:1352)

Beltrán's seemingly noble identity must be reexamined in relation to Nelet, who, despite his passions and irrationality, has a more conventional code of honorable behavior. The description of Beltrán in the final chapter refers several times to "la mentira venial a que le obligaban las circunstancias" (2:1361). He lacks the sort of "valor" that gives Nelet the capacity to confess his crime (2:1364). Even his final acts are deceitful and cowardly; his novel ends unromantically, without his moral or even his material redemption. Beltrán's trajectory reveals his inability to escape the reality of corruption, deceit and immorality, not the restoration of an ideal past that never existed.

Nelet's trajectory is also deceptive at first, seeming to move toward stability: "habiéndose trocado, por virtud de su amorosa llama, de feroz en benigno y humanitario" (2:1321). But his newfound emotional identity is at odds with his military duty: "es lástima que las obligaciones militares me separen de la divina Marcela" (2:1322). Torn between these two roles, his movements are often erratic, directionless, even unconscious: "me encontré, sin saber cómo" (2:1321). Like Fago he suffers illness and hallucination, culminating in a fantastic underground journey that prefigures almost precisely that of Tito in the fifth series, as will be discussed in chapter 3. Nelet's hopes of resolving the dualities of fantasy and reality, warrior and lover, are forever banished when he kills Marcela's brother. Finally, he kills himself after murdering Marcela. The violence of this ending precludes even the moral and theological ambiguity of Fago's death and ultimate destination.

La campaña del Maestrazgo displays the progressively negative tone of the series in other aspects. Cabrera's tactics are more brutal than Zumalacárregui's, the battle scenes are more vivid, and the descriptions of executions more numerous and bloody. Nelet's search for a stable identity reiterates the pattern of the endless journey. He is condemned by God, he says, never to be loved by Marcela (2:1311), to suffer "una sed no saciada" (2:1313). Rodríguez writes of him: "A downtrodden Don Juan, his self-image broken by failure, Nelet strives to refurbish a shattered self-image" (123). But he cannot refurbish what he does not possess in the first place. His life has always been on the wrong path, he says of himself in a curious passage of free indirect speech: "sus padres no supieron enderezarle desde niño por los buenos caminos. . . . desde los diez y seis años, escandalicé la villa en que vivíamos" (2:1310). Nelet cannot return to a place or to an identity he never knew. Both he and Beltrán describe the yearning "which presupposes the loss of an 'original meaning' and feels 'driven' to seek it just the same" (Frank, 78). *La campaña del Maestrazgo* makes clear that in neither case did this original meaning exist.

Nelet seeks to cast off his old identity and find another, but he succumbs to even more violent behavior than in the past. Beltrán seeks to maintain his past and is confronted with the hollowness of that idealized identity. Thus, while seeming to travel in opposite psychological and temporal directions, Beltrán and Nelet actually journey on paths that are more than just geographically parallel. Their courses converge in an extinction for which both characters are culpable. The Carlist Nelet and the Cristinist sympathizer Beltrán, the youth and the old man, the farm boy and the aristocrat, suffer similar fates, just as the Carlist war works to extinguish the future of Spain by its entrenchment in behaviors that should have been cast off.

Beltrán daydreams of medieval grandeur for himself and Spain. Upon awakening he exclaims, "¡Oh tiempo, o fin de fines!" According to him, time is "insaciable, que va devorando, y no siempre crea cosas nuevas con que sustituir a las pasadas" (2:1327). In both of these passages Beltrán laments the loss of a great and noble past, a better past, especially for him:

> Pues si las mudanzas de los tiempos y las revoluciones no hubieran hecho escombros de todo aquel orden social, tu amigo don Beltrán de Urdaneta sería hoy quizás gran maestre. . . . Figúrate. . . . Nadie nos tosía en estos valles y montes; con mi gente armada y esta red de castillos . . . haríamos aquí lo que nos diera la gana; a ti te nombraría bailío para que me gobernaras todo mi territorio; elegiríamos prior a un clérigo sumiso que a nuestro gusto nos gobernara todo lo espiritual. (2:1327)

This view of the past is singularly egotistical and idealized, though not so different from that of the Carlist leaders, or government officials and "caciques." In Beltrán one can see the stifling excess of a historical sense that Nietzsche calls "antiquarian":

> the things of the past are never viewed in their true perspective or receive their just value; but value and perspective change with the individual or the nation that is looking back on its past.
>
> There is always the danger here that everything ancient will be regarded as equally venerable, and everyone without this respect for antiquity, like a new spirit, rejected as an enemy. (19)

Beltrán, romanticism's idealization of the Middle Ages, and the nineteenth-century Spain described by Casalduero all display such a valuation of the excesses of the past.

Nietzsche offers an alternative, though not in itself sufficient, to monumental and antiquarian views of the past, a necessary "critical" vision: "Man must have the strength to break up the past, and apply it, too, in order to live. He must bring the past to the bar of judgment, interrogate it remorselessly, and finally condemn it. Every past is worth condemning" (20–21). The uncritical idealization and romantic poetization of the past by characters like Beltrán lead to the dead end so dramatically depicted in the final scene of the novel. Beltrán, the antiquarian, sacrifices Nelet and Marcela to his own vain illusion of restored grandeur. Instead of directing the misguided Nelet on a morally and emotionally stable course, he is an inadvertent accomplice in the deaths of the youths, and thus in the death of his own ideal. His judgment is too selfishly narrow to see the consequences of his actions. Nietzsche writes:

> If the judgment of a people hardens in this way, and history's service to the past life is to undermine a further and higher life; if the historical sense no longer preserves life, but mummifies it, then the tree dies unnaturally, from the top downward, and at last the roots themselves wither. Antiquarian history degenerates from the moment that it no

longer gives a soul and inspiration to the fresh life of the present. (20)

The wholesale extermination resulting from the Carlist war, Nelet's romantic delusions and Beltrán's selfishness are equally implicated in this warning. All the elements of this *episodio*—destructive characters, historical and fictional plots of violence and death, the medieval landscape, the romantic aspects of melodrama, the supernatural, and tragedy—create a total vision of a world stifled under the weight of the past. Rodríguez concludes his discussion of the third series by observing that "the cumulative effect in *La campaña del Maestrazgo* is one of artistic distortion by anachronism. The impressionistic world of the Episodio, geographically, and even historically medieval, is peopled with protagonists who provide, despite their realistic integration, an additional residue of anachronism" (138). Anachronism and antiquarianism characterize the morbid pursuit of the past in *La campaña del Maestrazgo*. In these pursuits, the novel everywhere invokes the motif of the endless journey. This is true even in the oddest passages, those which seem to resist incorporation or naturalization with the text's other elements.

During Nelet's fantastical journey in chapter 20, for example, he is carried from one geographical location to another without accounting for time. His literal transposition belies Beltrán's explanation that it was a dream. Nelet describes his experience

en una caverna cuyo techo parecía la bóveda de una catedral; en el fondo de ella varios hombres cavaban la tierra . . . les vi sacar del suelo un objeto largo y pesado, de color de tierra. "¿Es eso una momia, amigos?", les pregunté. Y ellos respondieron: "Mojama es de un muerto de metales, que agora sacamos y resucitamos por orden de la sacra señora, para mayor grandeza de Dios e de su Religión." (2:1326)

What at first appears to be an isolated, perhaps nonsensical, episode discloses a network of diverse narrative elements that suggest the motifs and characters of the main plot. The excavators bring to mind the buried treasure that Beltrán seeks—"'los fines de su viaje no eran otros que proveerse del precioso metal" (2:1278); the passage seems to describe Carlism, which fights for the greater glory of religion and God; Marcela is a nun and thus a holy woman; the war dead are implied in the terms "muerto de metales"; and even Nietzsche's mummified past can be recalled through the archaic language of the excavators and the specific word "mojama." These lines are also an absurd prefiguration of the novel's final burial scene. Just as the other textual codes traverse this fantastic scene, so the fantastic traverses even the most apparently real episodes, like the war. Beltrán listens to the shooting,

> que por esta y la otra encañada de este y el otro monte venía; ignorante de quién perdiera o ganara en aquellos combates, a su parecer fantásticos y aéreos, sostenidos en las alturas o en los desfiladeros por bandadas de aves más que por hombres. Eran las guerras de fábula, entre animales de pluma o pelo, veloces, y que prontamente corrían de un punto a otros, sin dejar rastro. (2:1324)

This description of the movements of the war is immediately preceded by a remarkably similar description of a fantastical character, another prefiguration of the fifth series. Malaena is the messenger between Nelet and Marcela, and like Tito's "Efémeras" in the fifth series, she is "una ave discreta y solícita," "un puro espíritu." "Frecuentaba los bosques. . . . En ligereza para pasar de un valle a otro salvando las más altas muelas y los puertos pedregosos, no la igualaban más que los pájaros" (2:1323). The war and the movements of characters are erratic, illusory, often fantastic journeys back and forth. A spirit who speaks only Valencian thus enables communication (2:1327). The codes of realism and fantasy, of the journey, translation, and interpretation are interwoven in moments like these.

Nelet seeks to rationalize his fantastic journey with the tradition that such subterranean passages existed in feudal times (2:1326). Beltrán rejects this explanation, saying that "la tradición era una vieja loca, que había sido poetisa, pero que ya, con la edad, chocheaba" (2:1327). The same characteristics that Beltrán gives tradition can be attributed to him, since indeed he seeks to recapture it. Moreover, his vision of past tradition as poetic, and the present as senile, represents an idiosyncratic perspective on both the past and the present, which recalls Nietzsche's warning about mummification and degeneration.[15] Beltrán is also a degenerated, if not a senile, relic of tradition that lives on. It is not he who dies at the end of the novel, but rather the youths who attempted to escape traditional patterns of behavior, but could not.

Beltrán thinks that he sees more clearly than Nelet, but no perspective on tradition or history sees anything but the illusion of the past, memories of memories. The opening paragraph of the novel implies this:

> En la derecha margen del Ebro y a cinco leguas de la por tantos títulos esclarecida Zaragoza existe la villa de Julióbriga, fundación de romanos, según dicen libros y rezan lápidas desenterradas, la cual, en tiempos remotos, mudó aquel nombre sonoro por el de Fuentes de Ebro, con que la designaron cien generaciones aragonesas. (2:1261)

Like the knowledge and value accorded to the ancient Aragonese nobleman, don Beltrán de Urdaneta, an appreciation of this village relies on tradition—here books and unearthed tombstones. These two written documents have particular import for this *episodio*'s statements about the ability to know the past.

First, the history of this town is based on other written documents, underlining its status as the writing about writing; historical discourse is always based on previous texts. In *The Savage Mind*, Lévi-Strauss illustrates this with respect even to the selection of dates or "facts." The choice of what is to be deemed historical fact is as much a selective, interpretive process as the narrative that explains it: "historical facts are no more given than any other. It is the historian, or the agent of history, who constitutes them by abstraction and as though under the threat of an infinite regress."[16] The dates have already been grouped into "classes of dates," which are prearranged, then, for interpretation as classes. The historical code, that which historical knowledge employs "to analyse its object," is the chronicle (258). But this code consists not of the dates alone: "a historical date, taken in itself, would have no meaning, for it has no reference outside itself. . . . The code can therefore consist only of classes of dates, where each date has meaning in as much as it stands in complex relations of correlation and opposition with other dates" (259). This system of relations is like that of writing itself, an endless text, which is not meaning, but process:

> In fact history is tied neither to man nor to any particular object. It consists wholly in its method. . . . It is therefore far from being the case that the search for intelligibility comes to an end in history as though this were its terminus. Rather, it is history that serves as the point of departure in any quest for intelligibility. As we say of certain careers, history may lead to anything, providing you get out of it.
>
> This further thing to which history leads for want of a sphere of reference of its own shows that whatever its value (which is disputable) historical knowledge has no claim to be opposed to other forms of knowledge as a supremely privileged one. (262–63)

The quest for an ultimate knowledge of Julióbriga in the opening paragraph of *La campaña del Maestrazgo* illustrates just such a process of correlation and opposition with other texts, through the codes of history. The fantastical elements and the romantic plots of the novel only reinforce a definition of history as method, as one more type of fabulation. History is no more an objective, ultimately intelligible view of the past than is romanticism; the reader's inability to surmount or get beneath its linguistic processes reveals that history is as much of an endless text—with no origin or end—as any myth.

Second, the documents of history in the first paragraph of the novel—the "lápidas desenterradas"—also correlate historical knowledge with death. Unearthing these stones here, as with the "mojama . . . de un muerto de metales," is only the obverse of the burial of soldiers, and of Nelet and Marcela. The connection between these present deaths and those of the past is further reinforced as the paragraph goes on to describe the Gothic churchyard "donde yacen, en desmoronados sepulcros, multitud de condes de Fuentes, que rabiaron o hicieron rabiar al pueblo" (2:1261). War and the passions of men bring death now as they did then. Even Beltrán's daydream includes this feudal savagery (see above). The carnage of the past was no less than that of the present.

The novel's opening scene marks the convergence of the codes of history as writing and history as death. Moreover, the village is most famous for its "parador de Viscarrués," whose food has always attracted all types of people traveling in many directions (2:1261). There also Beltrán and Salomé meet, initiating the network of connections between novels, characters and plots. Likewise historical and fictional paths cross: "Fue causa de tan desmedida aglomeración la coincidencia de dos caravanas de pasajeros, la una que venía de Oriente, huyendo de la guerra; la otra, de Occidente, que hacia la guerra iba" (2:1262). The war, the fictional and historical characters and plots, life and death, past and present traverse this inn and the opening chapter of *La campaña del Maestrazgo*, describing the textual process. Food enters this convergence of codes as well, in a way that laces the pseudoserious historical chronicle with anticlimactic humor: "Un solo dato pudo arrancar el historiógrafo a la empedernida memoria de Mateo Guasa [criado y después dueño del parador]: era que aquel día fue el primero del año en que se agregaron al cocido las habas verdes" (2:1262). This detail prefigures the confusion of codes in subsequent passages, where scenes of savage and careless execution take place while the victorious Carlists revel in food and drink.[17]

The reinscription of history in the first paragraph of the novel can be observed in other passages as well, most notably in chapter 18. Nelet's regiment, with Beltrán prisoner, rests at a famous Cistercian monastery, successively devastated by three wars: "Daba pena ver su noble arquitectura mutilado por bárbaras manos . . . y el claustro, en fin, con sólo tres costados, más triste que todo lo demás y más poético y ensoñador" (2:1321). Beltrán and Nelet are at peace in this personified and romantic ruin of noble architecture. Beltrán "se extasiaba recorriendo los venerables restos de la construcción medieval . . . y tan dulce encanto encontró en aquella paz y en el poético lenguaje de las nobles y tristes piedras, que habría deseado permanecer allí todo el tiempo que su prisión durase" (2:1321). The venerable ruin, Beltrán, feels at home in this ruin of art and history. The romantic Nelet also feels at ease here, composing poetry for Marcela: "Nelet se sentía muy a gusto en el monasterio, que perfectamente cuadraba a su espíritu en aquella ocasión" (2:1321). Yet the monastery, this ruin of time and war, reflects the devastation that age and dissipation have wreaked upon Beltrán, and also that which excessive passion has wreaked upon Nelet.

Like a good antiquarian, "no era lego en Arqueología el buen aragonés," Beltrán finds in the architecture a poetic and noble language that he is no longer able to read himself. "Urdaneta rogaba a su amigo que *le leyese el claustro*, esto es, que examinara uno por uno los capiteles y el simbolismo que representaban, para poder él juzgar de obra tan bella como si con sus propios ojos la deletreara" (2:1321). This passage is a description of a type of historiographical method that seeks to pronounce judgment on the past. However, such judgments are necessarily mediated by the distance of time and interpretation. Even though the historical document is visibly present, its evaluation or categorization is still subjective. Words like "simbolismo," "representaban," "juzgar" and "deletreara" place this inevitably interpretive process in the foreground. The distance between Beltrán and the object of interpretation becomes greater still since he must rely on another's eyes to read and decipher for him. Such reduplicated interpretation describes the multiple constitutive and selective processes of historical discourse. Such selections, classifications, interpretations, and judgments inevitably involve preconceived standards for the historical value of beauty (as in this case), or heroism (as in others), or merely standards of choice about which elements are to be included in the interpretive field.

These preconceived standards are particularly obvious when

Nelet becomes enthusiastic while reading what he deems his own story. Anticipating its denouement, he looks for certain types of capitals and excludes the others from interpretation:

> Yo no estoy aquí . . . parece como si me hubiera ido. . . .
> Debo de estar más allá. . . . Déjame ver. . . . Aquí no es-
> toy; forman el adorno unos como perritos o leoncitos, y
> luego sigue otro con cabezuelas de ángeles, entre las púas
> retorcidas de cardos borriqueros. . . . ¡Ah!, ya parecí . . .
> aquí estoy, en este otro capitel. (2:1322)

This passage illustrates Nietzsche's description of the antiquarian historian: "The history of his town becomes the history of himself; he looks on the walls, the turreted gate, the town council . . . as an illustrated diary of his youth, and sees himself in it all—his strength, industry, desire, reason, faults and follies" (18). Nelet exclaims: "¡Ay, aquí veo mi propia historia! . . . No, no se ría; es mi historia, que aquí representaron aquellos artífices algunos siglos antes de que yo viniera al mundo . . . veo un guerrero que adora a una penitente. . . . ofrece gran semejanza con Marcela" (2:1321–22). He provides extensive analogies of these images to his own life, replete with moral evaluations. Beltrán is skeptical, until Nelet describes "un caballero con cruz en el pecho" (2:1322). Soon convinced that he, too, is inscribed in stone, Beltrán states: "No me niegues que puedo ser yo" (2:1322). However, the story in the capitals does not correspond to his idealized history. Noting the absence of a noble lady in this picture, he rationalizes: "puede que el tiempo haya desgastado la otra figura. Dama ilustre debe de haber, que me acompaña en el noble ejercicio de la caza; y si no es así, no soy yo el que miras, Nelet" (2:1322). If the documents do not read as Beltrán imagines they should, then he reinterprets or discards them. Beltrán's historical fallacy is particularly evident here, since he has always been a bachelor. He wants history to read the way he desires, not the way it occurred. Their examination of the cloister ends with Nelet saying: "Créalo usted o no lo crea, yo sostengo . . . que vivimos en estos pedruscos. Esto que aquí nos rodea no es cosa muerta; esto tiene alma, como la tienen los montes, el viento, las cavernas y los torrentes que cantan y rezan en las profundidades" (2:1322). Seeking life amid the ruins of an imagined past or a medieval landscape is as futile as searching for it in a fantastic cavern or through civil war. The very last scene of the novel restates this poignantly. Witnessing Nelet's fatal acts are Beltrán and two "pobres sepulteros, a quienes el estupor y su propia debilidad senil paralizaron en la fugaz duración de la tragedia" (2:1365). After Nelet kills Marcela and himself, one of the gravediggers asks Beltrán if the survivors are alive or dead. Beltrán responds: "nosotros, tristes despojos de la vida, aún respiramos. . . . ¿Y para qué? El siglo no quiere soltarnos" (2:1365). These living relics of the past serve the same function as the gravestones of Julióbriga: to bury the dead. Unable to relinquish his search for an imagined past— his buried pots of gold—Beltrán must now bury this illusion and the future with it.

The passage describing Nelet and Beltrán's reading of themselves in the monastery capitals illustrates another aspect of the novel's process of reinscription. As a historical novel, *La campaña del Maestrazgo*, like all the *Episodios*, invokes conventions of historical and artistic image-making. Here art and history are interchangeable for Beltrán and Nelet, as they were essentially since Hegel and the romantics.[18] In his critique of the notion of historical objectivity, Nietzsche writes,

Might not an illusion lurk in the highest interpretation of the word "objectivity"? We understand by it a certain standpoint in the historian who sees the procession of motive and consequence too clearly for it to have an effect on his own personality. We think of the aesthetic phenomenon of the detachment from all personal concern with which the painter sees the picture and forgets himself, in a stormy landscape, amid thunder and lightning, or on a rough sea; and we require the same artistic vision and absorption in his object from the historian. But it is only a superstition to say that the picture given to such a man by the object really shows the truth of things. Unless it be that

objects are expected in such moments to paint or photo-
graph themselves by their own activity on a purely passive
medium! (37)

Whether they be the strictest realism, the most scientific historiography, the egotistical ravings of a Beltrán, or the deluded
sentimentality of a Nelet, the processes that govern the different
modes of expression in history or in art are inevitably the same.
An absolute truth, the immediate presence of the past, a sure
knowledge of the future are impossible, mere yearnings for an
infinite, for an indissoluble sign, that are never to be realized.

TRANSLATING FERNANDO CALPENA

Beltrán and Nelet's efforts to read the images of stone as passions of the flesh, to make art into history and to see the individual in the universal, describe the processes of translation.
One definition of translation, for example, that describes their
situation is "the expression or rendering of something in another medium or form, e. g., of a painting by an etching."[19] The
term translation encompasses multiple functions that can be observed throughout the third series. To translate implies a transference of meaning, in other words, metaphor. It is also a physical movement: "to bear, convey, or remove from one person,
place or condition to another . . . to transport." To translate is,
specifically, "to turn from one language into another . . . retaining the same sense." More generally it is "to interpret, explain; to expound the significance of . . . to express (one thing)
in terms of another." At the same time it is also "to change in
form, appearance, or substance, to transmute; to transform, alter." These definitions describe a process which is perceived as
both altering and retaining the same sense; translation is thus
an emblem of the process of repetition and difference. The definition of translation, including the process of definition, is obviously pertinent to many facets of the series already discussed:
the journey motif, the text as metaphor, the physical, emotional, or fantastical alterations in characters' identities, and so

on. These aspects and others can all be seen traversing simultaneously the protagonist of the third series, Fernando Calpena.

Calpena's trajectory spans nine *episodios*—*Mendizábal* to *Bodas reales*—and the years 1835 to 1846. His roles range from protagonist in *Mendizábal, De Oñate a la Granja, Vergara,* and *Los Ayacuchos,* to supporting character in *Luchana* and *La estafeta romántica,* to mere mention in *La campaña del Maestrazgo* and *Montes to Oca,* and finally to significance only through absence in *Bodas reales.* The last chapter of the last volume of the series relates that Calpena and his friends and family are virtual political exiles in France. Their absence from Spain is a final commentary, or "sarcasm" as Dendle phrases it, on the new epoch which begins with Isabel II's marriage.[20] Calpena's final journey to France is the inverse of his entrance to the series. In the first paragraph of *Mendizábal,* he comes to Madrid in a coach from France (2:891). *Mendizábal,* again like *Zumalacárregui,* begins in medias res. But whereas Fago's encounter with Ulibarri spurs his erratic search for and flight from his past, Fernando Calpena's course is not even directed by the erratic impulses of his memories, since he has no certain knowledge of his past nor plans for his future.

Calpena's total anonymity is emphasized from the beginning:

> Entre tantos viajeros, sólo uno no tenía quien le esperase: nadie se cuidaba de él ni le decía "por ahí te pudras." . . . Era el tal un joven de facciones finas y aristocráticas. . . . Su talle sería sin duda airoso cuando cambiara el anticuado y sucio vestidito. . . . ¡Pobrecillo! Solo y sin maestro ni amigo a quien arrimarse, se lanzaba en aquel confuso laberinto; sin duda entraba gozoso y valiente, con la generosa ansiedad del mozuelo de veinte años . . . como . . . los que empiezan a vivir. (2:891)

This confused young stranger seems unknown even to the narrator, the reader is to deduce from his repeated use of "sin duda." He is literally without direction: "embobado . . . estaba el hombre contemplando el ir y venir de vagos bien vestidos" (2:891). He is a traveler suspended in his course or a blank page upon which nothing is yet written. His name is revealed not by the narrator, but by another character who shouts: "¡Don Fernando Calpena! ¿Quién es don Fernando Calpena?" (2:891). As he receives a linguistic identity, so is he given a course to follow when the messenger who names him takes him to his new, prearrranged residence. Thus Calpena is transported from France to Madrid, from the station to a boarding house, from a handsome, unknown, and condescendingly described youth ("vestidito," "pobrecillo," "mozuelo") to the protected "don" Fernando Calpena, from a suspended journey to a new leg of it, which is its beginning.

The fortuitous events of Calpena's first day in Madrid are a mystery to him: "ignoraba de dónde y de quién le venían tantas dichas." He believes he is dreaming:

> "Pues, señor, . . . sin duda estoy soñando, o me equivoqué de camino, y en vez de ir a Madrid, me he metido en Jauja. Porque esto de que le reciban a uno desconocidos emisarios del diablo o de las mimísimas hadas, . . . no le ha pasado a ningún nacido. . . . Mucho ojo, Fernando, y trata de sondear al patrón, que tal vez posea la clave del acertijo." (2:893)

The enigma that Fernando seeks to solve becomes more complex as subsequent days bring him money, tailors, theater tickets, a position in Mendizábal's office, and finally, in chapter 9, letters from the unknown benefactor who watches and seeks to guide his every movement. So the first clues to the guiding force in Calpena's plot/life are written texts. The letters advise and direct him throughout the series and gradually reveal to him the secret of his enigmatic identity and history. In other words, they write his plot and his character as they seem to write a double story—Calpena's past and his future. His course in the third series will entail extensive travels back and forth through Spain and to knowledge of himself. He displays numerous emotional and even physical transformations, as he changes from classic to romantic styles and attitudes (2:983), or takes on disguises for his activities in the war (especially in *Vergara*). All of these transformations are part of the answer to that first question about his identity, "¿Quién es don Fernando Calpena?" Like this moment of naming in the first chapter of his story, Calpena's identity and his journey are inseparable from his function as text.

The interpretation that Calpena seeks of himself, like that the reader seeks of him and the series, is a process of successive transformations or translations of the unintelligible into an intelligible, sense-making expression. Translation seeks to express, name, explain, or interpret one element in terms of another. It is a process of moving from signifier to signifier in an attempt better to grasp a signified idea. Yet this idea or signified is always out of reach, since the processes of interpretation and translation in this novel and in the series are always open-ended, having neither original meaning nor final definitive expression. Calpena's search for "la clave del acertijo" will not find a satisfactory resolution here, for its answer lies in another text, not in the world.[21] As the letters gradually explain more of Calpena, they also eventually identify themselves as from his origin—his aristocratic mother, Pilar de Loaysa. But Pilar never appears in the series except in her letters. This epistolary kinship underlines the infinite and inescapable textuality of Calpena himself.

Calpena's uncertain destination parallels his uncertain origin. He believes he is an orphan, and when Padre Hillo, his friend and advisor, asks if he has relatives in Madrid, Fernando responds: "No lo sé. . . . Creo que no . . . , creo que sí" (2:897). His linguistic and national identities are just as indeterminate as his family ties: "—Pero es usted español, seguramente. —Creo que sí . . . , digo, sí: español soy. —Habla usted nuestra lengua con gran corrección. —Lo mismo hablo el francés" (2:897). He is as uncertain of his nationality and of his mother tongue as he is of his own mother. Fernando's equivocal identity rests on apparently distinct, yet fundamentally similar processes. The absence of an original signified—mother, nation—permits the fluctuation of signifiers—no/yes, Spanish/French. Also, a conventional hierarchy among primary and secondary languages or nations gives way to their equation. If Calpena speaks both languages equally well, then he can make no qualitative nor originary distinctions among them, no conventional translation.

Avital Ronell, a translator of Derrida, describes many of the problems of translation when he writes of the translated text: "It is neither itself nor its other: unable to make authoritative claims for its autonomy—for instituting its *own name*—it is also prohibited by an implicit limit from drawing too closely to its origin, to the ever engendering Urtext." He calls this form of text a "hybrid form of non-identity." In addition, "it is only after the 'second' text ['the translation'] has been produced that the first acquires its aura of originality."[22] Calpena emblemizes these contradictory functions of the translated text. As a French Spaniard or a Spanish Frenchman, he is a hybrid; lacking knowledge of his past, his is a non-identity. His inability to privilege Spanish or French has its counterpart in his inability to draw too near his origin, his mother, since the series allows Pilar only a textual identity. She is present only through her own letters, her mention in others' letters, or the occasional narratorial reference to her. Pilar is the "Urtext" that Calpena cannot approach too closely. In the same way that the woman Salomé is the text "Mé," and that Marcela Luco seeks her identity in *Don Quijote*, this series reiterates constantly the notion of the woman as text.[23]

At the same time that Fernando Calpena is unable to draw near his mother, the Urtext, he is severely limited by that text. Although he appears to be alone and autonomous when he arrives in Madrid, his every movement is directed by an unseen hand. He seems free, yet is not, he complains to Hillo:

> no acepto la protección en esa forma despótica, altanera. Se obedece ciegamente a una madre, a un padre . . . pero ¿quién puede exigir que sacrifiquemos libertad, dignidad, vida, a los caprichos de un fantasma? ¿Que no es fantasma dice usted? Pues que se quite la gasa, el capuchón. . . . Abandonado estuve, abandonado estoy. . . . ¿Qué me ha dado el fantasma? ¿Me ha dado un nombre? (2:985)

The phantom is indeed his mother, the original, yet always elusive text that he cannot escape. This invisible, yet restrictive bond approaches caricature at the end of *Mendizábal* when the still unnamed Pilar orchestrates Calpena's imprisonment so he will not elope with his romantic love, Aurora Negretti, or commit suicide should he fail (2:1008–9). Nevertheless, in spite of such all-engendering limits imposed by the mother-text Pilar, she is indeed unable to give him a name. Fernando as translated text is that "non-identity" without his "own name" that Ronell describes. Fernando is and is not the name on a baptismal certificate (2:915). He is separate from Pilar—another text, another name—yet at the same time engendered by her.

In the same way that Calpena epitomizes the translated text, he exemplifies other functions of translation. Just as he is transported to Madrid at the beginning of *Mendizábal*, and thus his plot begins, throughout most of the major plot movements of his trajectory he plays the role of a transporter. First, he transports a package of jewels and a beautiful fan (replete with its own history) from France to the avaricious jewel merchant, Jacoba Zahón. In her house he meets her ward, Aurora. Calpena's instant, all-consuming love for the beautiful orphan motivates his emotional and geographical movements through much of the series, and also initiates his transformation from a neoclassical into a romantic man (2:983). Then, in *De Oñate a la Granja*, as Calpena travels north in search of Aurora, he encounters Demetria and Gracia Castro-Amézaga. Demetria appeals to him to free her quixotic father, don Alonso, from a Carlist prison. Thus he changes geographical direction as he heroically aids the dying Alonso and his daughters. Wounded while protecting them, he recuperates in La Granja under Demetria's care, and so begins his emotional movement toward the noble heiress. His love for Demetria and the tempering of his romantic impulses eventually succeed his passion for Aurora during the course of *Luchana*, *La estafeta romántica*, and *Vergara*. But before he can marry Demetria, before he can end his own journey, Fernando must transport his friend, Santiago Ibero, back to his betrothed, Gracia, in *Los Ayacuchos*. That novel, too, concludes without a conclusion, as will be discussed below.

FERNANDO AS THE WORD

BETWEEN HISTORY AND FICTION IN *VERGARA*

Fernando Calpena's movements rely not only on transporting people and things, but most notably on words. In *Vergara*, he attempts to return Zoilo Arratia to his wife Aurora (e.g., 3:140, 189–90), serving as mediator of that emotional relationship. His trajectory also becomes more "historical" as he takes on the role of Espartero's emissary in the peace negotiations at Vergara. As a mediator or conciliator of fictional and historical passions, Fernando occupies a strategic position between conflicting forces of love and war, all the while vacillating between his attractions to, and oscillating in his movements toward, Aurora and Demetria. The novel itself occupies a mediate position; it is where many of the series' plots and characters (e.g., Santiago Ibero, Beltrán, Arratia, Calpena) come together. Fernando is that third term between Zoilo and Aurora, peace and war, Espartero and Maroto, which is necessarily invisible in itself, but without which their various reconciliations would not take place. As the "in-between," Fernando inscribes the function of the word itself in any text. The word is necessarily already a translation, since it is and is not itself, a signifier marking the place of an absence.

Vergara epitomizes in many ways the various processes of linguistic mediation that are at work throughout the forty-six *Episodios nacionales*. This seventh volume of the third series summarizes the mediation that characterizes the romantic movement, the Carlist war, the universal themes in literature and the world—such as love, death, liberty, religion, war, and peace—as well as the mediation inherent in language, whether in the service of supposedly historical or merely fictional narration. Attention is repeatedly called to these functions again through letters and translation. As a letter writer, and later as a narrator, Fernando Calpena specifically invokes the interchanging relationship between history and fiction at various points in

53

the novel. In one of his letters to Pilar, he relates his process of discovering (from various illiterate intermediaries) information about "Churi." "Churi" is a minor character who indirectly links Fernando Calpena to Aurora, the object of his romantic idealization and disillusionment. This love, incidentally, parallels the history of the rise and disintegration of the Carlist cause. Fernando writes: "Ya comprenderá usted, querida madre, que con los datos que me da la señora *Seda* con su rudo y deslavazado estilo compongo yo la historia, procurando la mayor fidelidad en lo sustancial. Sigo, con el recelo de que usted verá, en lo que escribo, antes la novela que la historia. Lo mismo da, adelante" (3:117). Fernando, on a mission of peace for Espartero, is sidetracked from his historical to his fictional journey because of his curiosity about Aurora and her precipitous marriage to Zoilo Arratio. Zoilo's cousin, "Churi," now serves unknowingly as the source of Fernando's information, just as he had deliberately intervened in the earlier *episodios*, *Luchana* and *La estafeta romántica*. The informational process is further complicated since "Churi," who was previously deaf and inarticulate, is now almost completely dumb and borders on the imbecilic. Through his friend "Seda," Fernando learns of "Churi's" own ludicrously parodic love affairs, and how they touch, in a novel manner, on his own once again. The information he receives solves an enigma about Aurora from the previous *episodio*, *La estafeta romántica*.

Fernando was introduced to this group of camp followers by a parasitic intriguer, nicknamed "el Epístola," who sowed discontent among the Carlist troops. His name appropriately marks the mediation inherent in the epistolary form used in the first ten chapters of *Vergara* and throughout the third series. The subjectivity of the epistolary form underscores the process of mediation of events and ideas inherent in letter writing and reading. Rodríguez observes that "in effect, letters are employed to express a striking relativism, with diametrically opposed perceptions of a single reality being expressed simultaneously" (110). The epistolary form emphasizes that there is never only one perspective, one meaning, but rather any number of verisimilar interpretations of a given situation. The use of letters brings to the foreground the interpretive process involved in reading the *Episodios*. Just as the letter writers read the same world in different ways, so each reader approaches a novel in always diverse circumstances. Furthermore, according to Rodríguez: "the very use of letters gives an impression of documentation; but what is more important, Galdós hit upon the technique of novelization that best expresses the well-nigh ineffable subjectivity of Romanticism" (110). The appearance of documentation or historicism, contrasting with the unmistakable subjectivity of the letter, epitomizes the conflict, opposition and irony involved in any narration. As Fernando writes to Pilar, "lo mismo da," novel or history. The passage, of course, applies to the historical novel, a term that seems to form an oxymoron, an ironic hybrid of antithetical genres, yet is merely a translation of alternate and equivocal terms. The historical novel as "between" history and fiction is both history and fiction interchangeably.

Ironically, it is the very process of mediation that contributes to the illusion of either history or fiction. For while one usually chooses to attribute either a fictionality or a historicity to given characters, it is easy to forget that the narrator—the mediator between reader and historical or fictional truth—is also a linguistic artifice. The narrator's authority is also only a convention. Just as the "novel within the novel" is no more than illusion, since both stories are words on a page,[24] so Fernando Calpena is as fictional as "Churi," or the Espartero created in *Vergara*, and even as the hidden narrator of events. In the letter written to his mother, Fernando summarizes and corrects "Seda's" rendition of "Churi's" story, adding his own analysis and interpretation. These retellings and reinterpretations parallel the reader's own process of making sense of the text. Furthermore, there is the hidden organizer, editor, or narrator, who "arranges these letters." This narrator, though, is just as much a fiction as are Fernando and the pathetic "Churi." Chapter 11 begins:

Agotada la preciosa colección de cartas que un hado feliz
puso en manos del narrador de estas historias . . . su afán
de proseguirlas revistiendo de verdad la invención y enga-
lando lo verdadero, oblígale a lanzarse otra vez por valles y
montes. . . . Favorecido de otro hado benéfico, de los muchos que andan entre gente de pluma, tuvo la suerte de ad-
quirir en su primera salida conocimientos muy útiles.
(3:124)

In the above passage, so similar to chapter 9 of *Don Quijote I*,
the "segundo autor" is aided by two fairies. There is not even
the pretense of historical chronicle, frequent in Galdós, as the
long-awaited meeting of Fernando and his aristocratic mother
approaches. As if to emphasize his total control over the fiction
with ironic pretenses to history, Galdós does not allow his
reader to enjoy the reunion that has been deferred through five
episodios; it is simply passed over. In fact, the reader who
wishes to enjoy a romantic climax is made an object of ridicule:
"Y como el más lerdo puede imaginar, cual si las viera, las ter-
nuras, la hermosa efusión del encuentro de aquellas almas, se
omite la descripción prolija del suceso" (3:124). The choice of
the term "lerdo" marks the self-conscious irony of this anticlimax. And the absence of the scene, whose substance is left to
the creative imagination, is an ironic comment on the process of
imagination involved in creating meaning in the absence of historical presence.

The *Episodios* constantly address the dynamics involved in
the reading process. The reference to the helpful fairies forces
the reader to admit that this seemingly multitiered mediation
between the reader, invention, and truth, is an illusion. The in-
tervening second author is another fictional construction, not
the mediating "voice of truth." Even the presence of Espartero
and Maroto in this *episodio*, while it exemplifies Galdós's genius
for psychological portraiture, is no more constitutive of history
than any other literary device. Throughout *Vergara* and the
other *episodios*, there is a constant and continually redefined
awareness that the history per se can be as fictional as fiction can

be meaningful. They are both names for a reading, an interpretation, a mediation of events, that could never be reexperienced, even if they really occurred. This becomes particularly explicit in *Vergara*, which portrays the politics of the Carlist war and its termination, along with the conclusion to Fernando Calpena's romanticized involvement with Aurora.

Calpena is a mediator in many senses. He is, first, the novelistic protagonist who also serves as the primary vehicle for the presentation of history in the work. His journeys across Spain are the threads that weave the fictional tales here, particularly the denouement of his romance with Aurora. His travels also serve to unite what are conventionally considered two separate aspects: characters and events. Fernando is the medium of expression, through his actions and his observations, of what might be deemed universal literary themes. More than these commonplace and implicitly mediating functions, which are intrinsic to any protagonist, Fernando also fulfills the explicitly mediating function of the letter writer. More importantly, he serves as a living letter, who negotiates peace between Espartero and Maroto. He is, the reader is told, the unwritten letter, the secret—so well kept that history does not record it—of the intrigue which ultimately brings the war to an end.

When Espartero entrusts him with the delicate negotiations of his secret mission (which are only gradually revealed to the reader), Fernando ponders why he was chosen. He believes that he is given the mission "como hijo del secreto que soy . . . , el secreto mismo" (3:146). This statement is more than a union of the historical and the fictional plots of the Carlist war and Pilar's "pecado." The battle between religion and liberty in Spain parallels the struggle in Pilar's life between the social sanctions that prohibit her from recognizing her illegitimate son and her desire for the freedom to love him openly. Fernando is the axis around which these subplots in *Vergara* and in the major portion of the third series revolve. He is the invisible agent—at least to Aurora—who brings her husband, Zoilo, back to her from his imprisonment and idealized career as warrior. Fernando restores the peace and natural order of the classical family. He is the symbolic sacrifice of romantic idealism to realism. As Fernando restores health through words and food to Zoilo and his father, don Sabino, he almost becomes that sacrificial "cordero" that he feeds them.[25]

Fernando's representational function as word and sacramental function as flesh suggest two symbolic registers for his secret role as the agent who unites two fictional characters, just as he joins the seemingly historical characters of Espartero and Maroto, and through them, the warring factions of Spain. Fernando Calpena is that illusive/elusive enigma, that secret mediator who stands between a peaceful and realistic marriage and the exalted, almost insane, idealism of both Aurora's romantic love and Zoilo's romantic war. He is the mediating agent who fosters peace in place of senseless bloodshed for Spain, the mediator between chaos and order, or ultimately between the sense of words and the nonsense of mere noise. He is that invisible substance which vanishes when one tries to name it—the always immediate process of reading and understanding, of making real the ideas that only seem latent in words.

Calpena is a series of words on a page, a proper noun followed by a relatively stable set of adjectives, which becomes a "character" (in Greek, an imprinting)—the term which names the conventional attribution of personification to a linguistic structure.[26] He is, then, a living letter in more ways than one; as he says in chapter 18, he is Espartero's letter to Maroto, and vice versa: "el papel soy yo, mi buena memoria, y mi palabra, la escritura" (3:152). Fernando is hero, narrator, letter writer, letter, history, fiction, and word. His secret password for the mission is "Inquisivi." This is, coincidentally, the name of the town in Bolivia where Maroto and Espartero first met, and means "I inquired." The translation, "I inquired," describes both Fernando's mission and the process of reading. The word is the passkey to compromise; the hermeneutic impulse that it suggests is also the basis for the discourse of history or fiction. The word, language, is the secret that unlocks the door not to one, but to endless interpretations. The end of the *episodio* indicates that even the peace, so sought after, is only a word open to differing interpretations. Although Maroto might be viewed by the "cris-tinos" as a peacemaker, "en la opinión del carlismo quedó Ma-roto como el prototipo de la traición y perfidia" (3:213).

Just as words on paper, the Convenio de Vergara, ended the Carlist war, so did they begin it. Don Sabino, a pathetic Quijote figure, laments the bloodshed and the pitting of brother against brother in a senseless war, "todo por un papelito, la Pragmática Sanción" (3:182). Yet the Carlist war was not a paper battle, it was more than a war of words. The political power struggle be-tween María Cristina and don Carlos was a mediated one; their positions, their ideals, were debated by the real blood of Spain.

An official piece of paper can cause endless bloodshed, and so can forged documents. Words, whether considered true or false, original or translated, create reality, not the other way around, as the complicated events of *Vergara* reveal. The growing dis-sent manifested in the differing ideas and power struggles among the Carlists themselves (fomented by petty intriguers such as "el Epístola") becomes a bloody action when false papers alleging negotiations between Maroto and Espartero are found by Maroto's enemies in the Carlist camp (3:180). He learns of their plot to take him prisoner and turns their "burlas" into "veras" and the "festiva tramoya" into "trágico desenlace" by executing the conspirators. Ironically, although the documents were falsified, the negotiations were actually taking place in the person of the living letter, Fernando Calpena. The literary met-aphors common in *Vergara*, like those in all of the *Episodios*, symbolize the inevitable explanation of life through literature and the equivocation between history and fiction. Just as Maroto turns a comedy into a tragedy, so is the end of the tragic civil war in some ways comic. In a last-ditch effort to rally his now disaffected troops to his "santa causa," don Carlos appears be-fore his remaining men and asks them to shed more blood for him. When they do not respond to his "vivas" in the customary manner, one of his subordinates excuses it as their inability to understand Castilian. He appears to translate for them into Bas-que, but instead of don Carlos's exhortations, he shouts the Bas-que equivalent of "viva la Paz." Their enthusiastic response turns the scene, and consequently the "cause," into a "sainete" (3:208).

The prominent role of translation is again seen when Fernando, as secret negotiator between Espartero and Maroto, translates for the English intermediaries in the struggle for peace (3:196).[27] Mediation is again redoubled through translation. Yet whether literal translation, as in the case of Castilian to Basque or English, or the figurative translation of the words on the page into mental images and meanings, it is always a process of interpretation. Don Carlos's final mistake, the death blow to his cause, is a result, the reader is told, of his misinterpretation of Maroto's last letter to him, which contains another about-face and new pledge of allegiance to Carlism. Under bad advice, don Carlos reads the letter as treason (3:208) and his answer moves Maroto to sign the "Convenio" with Espartero. Don Carlos flees into France with his remaining "netos," whose last "holy" act is one of rape and pillage. There he continues his ineffectual "retóricas sermonarias" (3:212), the words he proffers as history.

Truth is ultimately indistinguishable from fiction because of their common reliance on language as a medium of interpretation. Whether in the service of history or novel, words on a page are always in between sense and nonsense. Even the so-called peace is only a "fórmula de cansancio o descanso," as Calpena and Santiago Ibero realize at the conclusion to *Vergara* (3:213). History, novel, or *episodio nacional* are also formulas for interpretations that rest in a language that mediates between constantly conflicting readings of illusions that are taken for truths.

THE CONFUSION OF LETTERS AND THE FUSION OF TEXTS

Calpena's activities in *Vergara* are an intensified extension of those he pursues in his first novel, *Mendizábal*. His function as scribe and translator for Mendizábal in Madrid and even "before" the novel begins, in France (2:901), establishes him from the outset as the vehicle connecting fictional and historical characters and plots through the written word. Again, too, his role as letter writer, either taking dictation from Mendizábal or composing letters for him to sign, emphasizes the merger of codes through language. Just as Calpena's path is directed by a series of letters from a mysterious protector, so the journey from fiction to history is one that relies solely on language for direction and interpretation. The movement, therefore, is in two directions at once, in an open-ended process of textuality.

Calpena becomes Mendizábal's literary alter ego when he is empowered with the minister's epistolary identity: "Tiene usted hermosa letra y buen criterio para contestar por sí mismo las cartas, con una simple indicación mía" (2:929). Such a merger of pens thwarts the impulse to identify an original or unique subject behind the letters. Fernando's implication in Mendizábal's correspondence, though different from his role with Espartero, is another example of how the multiple functions and connotations of the letter reinscribe the irreducible written process of these *episodios*. The confusion of the epistolary identities of Mendizábal and Calpena is another means by which the codes of fiction and history, the various characters and plots of the novel, become inextricable and interchangeable.

Mendizábal's office is the locus of this epistolary confluence of codes in several ways: two extensive passages of the novel are dedicated to the minister's activities there (chapters 13 and 30 to 31). In both sections he is alone, reading, writing, and interpreting letters that allude to the various characters and plots of the novel: the war, the election, the government's appropriation and sale of church lands and properties—the "desamortización," Aurora Negretti, Pilar, and so on. Mendizábal's writing style and his methods of reading and sorting correspondence are described in detail (2:931–32). Reading and writing are analyzed as processes in such passages, not just as products. At times Mendizábal's pen seems to write without direction, for example: "Aunque aplicar quiso toda su atención a la escritura no lo lograba: el pensamiento se dividía, fluctuaba, y dejando a la pluma formular con incorrecta sintaxis los conceptos epistolares, se escabullía por otros espacios" (2:932). Sentences like this appear to separate signifiers and signifieds, marking the autonomy of the written word. Just as Mendizábal's thoughts slide away from his pen and the pen seems to move randomly on its own, so does the narration slide back and forth from one code, character, or plot to another, here as throughout the series. Thus the illusion of a hierarchy among plots or characters, fiction or history, vanishes: "Era hombre don Juan que a lo mejor transportaba toda su atención de lo grave a lo menudo" (2:933). So he rereads and revises the first decree of the "desamortización" (2:997–98), scans a letter from a government spy (2:1000–1001), and contemplates bills from a shoemaker (2:993, 999). Like the *Episodios nacionales* that weave various fictional and historical elements, the letters in Mendizábal's office weave and confuse the diverse elements of this novel without apparent regard to their relative importance as fiction or history, plot or mere incident. Yet if the importance or meaning of any element is merely a matter of convention, since all elements depend equally for their value on their place in the system, such a confused array of letters only unveils convention, it does not break rules.

Mendizábal reads just parts of most letters, moving on rapidly to others: "echó a un lado la carta sin acabar de leerla" (2:1001). Just as the *episodio, Mendizábal*, like the series, begins in medias res and the textual processes of fictional and historical discourse are open-ended, these passages epitomize the open-ended—never finished, never absolutely begun—processes of reading and writing. He even reads one letter, from the duquesa de Berry, backwards: "A ver qué me cuenta. (*Lee por el final.*) Lo de siempre. . . . Y no le perdonarán, no. . . . (*Leyendo por el centro.*)" (2:1000). Her situation, coincidentally, is analogous to that of Pilar, another duchess, whose letter is also represented in the collection (2:1001–1002). However, the reader cannot identify the name Pilar with Calpena nor with the mysterious letters he receives; he cannot even make the analogy between the duchesses until later in the series. The reader must also read backwards, just as Mendizábal does here, and, like him, say, "A ver qué me cuenta."

Mendizábal frequently interrupts his reading to write abbreviated notes to himself, for example: " 'Asunto Negretti . . . *Din. jor.'* (Que quería decir: mandar dinero a la jorobada.)" (2:934). Thus the plot of Aurora's greedy, hunchbacked guardian to appropriate her fortune is also included in the convergence of codes in Mendizábal's office. This letter motivates him to arrange for a new guardian for Aurora; her plot, then, is transferred from Madrid and Calpena to Bilbao and Zoilo Arratia. The abbreviation *"Din. jor."* is a reflection of the way in which references to various plots and characters here are incomplete—abbreviations themselves. Aurora also writes to Mendizábal, but he only read the first line: "Soy la hija de Jenaro Negretti" (2:1002). He takes the letter home with him and thus "out of sight," much to the frustration of romantic readers of this novel.

The convergence and confusion of the codes of the various characters and plots of *Mendizábal* and the other volumes through letters calls attention to the function of words themselves. From Fago's glimpse of *"Mé"* on a torn and discarded letter, to Mendizábal's correspondence, to the epistolary novel, *La estafeta romántica,* the third series consistently confronts the process of the written word as such. Calpena's plot is determined first by mysterious letters, which become letters from his mother, by letters from Aurora and then from his future wife Demetria, and by letters to and from various historical figures throughout the series. Finally, in *Los Ayacuchos,* he receives letters from friends witnessing events in the palace. He will use these for his own documentation of a history he plans to write (2:313), an activity forecast by Beltrán in *La estafeta romántica* (3:80) and Espartero in *Vergara* (3:191). The letter, then, serves various functions. It is a reinscription of the *Episodios nacionales* as texts in which their historical and fictional discourses are rendered indistinguishable, since both are linguistic processes. It allows for an illusion of authenticity or documentation, much like the device of the historical chronicle. It also creates an illusion of an absence of narratorial mediation, as in *La estafeta romántica.* There the absence of narratorial comment allows the reader the illusion of being able to evaluate characters independently. But as Gilbert Smith has demonstrated, the narrator is still present in his titling and ordering of these letters.[28] The seeming lack of mediation between reader and letter in *La estafeta romántica* or on Mendizábal's desk masks on one level the preselective or constitutive process discussed by Lévi-Strauss. Yet, since even choosing facts—dates, letters, documents—is a process of fabulation, this illusion is merely one more aspect of the myth of documentation.[29] Like the "libros" or "lápidas desenterradas" in Julióbriga/Fuentes de Ebro, these written texts are part of a series that leads to no original subject, event, or thing.

An episode in the last novel in which Calpena appears, *Los Ayacuchos*, describes the theory and practice of letters as documentation in the series even more explicitly than in Calpena's first novel, *Mendizábal*. Chapters 10 and 11 of *Los Ayacuchos* consist of a letter from Valvanera de Urdaneta to Calpena's mother, Pilar, recording Valvanera's conversation with Demetria. Valvanera has been empowered to offer Fernando's love and hand in marriage to Demetria and to obtain the same from her. This yearned-for climax is thus unmistakably only an exchange of words, not the record of events. Valvanera speaks to Demetria and then writes of the conversation to Pilar, who in turn will show the letter to Fernando. Through these multiple forms of mediation, Fernando and Demetria are finally betrothed. Neither their joyful embrace nor their marriage are witnessed by the reader, since the events take place "after" the conclusion of the novel. The absence of such realistic/romantic events from the narration thwarts at least in part the reader's successful interpretation of these words as worlds and underlines the artifice of these worlds as words.

Valvanera's letter illustrates the inevitable distancing of the narrative process—in history or fiction—in another way. It is only through this letter that what transpired between Calpena and Demetria and between Demetria and her family since *Vergara* is revealed. Demetria recounts a series of exchanged and lost letters between herself and Fernando and her misinterpretations of his intentions during the last several years (3:331–

32). Valvanera also tells of the misinterpretations by herself, Pilar, and Fernando of Demetria, based on the verisimilar accounts of her engagement to her cousin Rodrigo or her desire to become a nun (3:332). These interpretive and temporal disjunctions, Valvanera and Demetria's resketching of times and interpretations, serve to describe the interpretive processes of the discourse. Moreover, the absence of these events from the series (they are present only as Demetria recounts them here; they were not written in earlier volumes) unmasks the illusion of the continuity in plots, times, and personalities conventional in realism.

This lengthy letter is highly self-conscious of its literary and historical functions, and practices a theory of discourse that encompasses both history and fiction, the text of the *Episodios nacionales*. Valvanera writes that she first put

> en forma narrativa los conceptos que Demetria y yo nos decíamos, mezclados con las observaciones que se me iban ocurriendo. Pero leído por Juan Antonio mi cartapacio, encontrólo pesado y obscuro, y no fue preciso más para que mi lastimado amor propio de historiadora me inspirara la idea de darle forma distinta. . . . He pensado que resultara mayor claridad para la lectora presentándole la copia de estas largas conferencias en disposición semejante a la de un Catecismo, con preguntas y respuestas. (3:331)

This passage—a commentary on narration and dialogue within the epistolary form of this chapter—is a sort of theory within theory at the same time that it is a story within a story.

Toward the end of the letter, Valvanera's husband, Juan Antonio de Maltrana, enters the dialogue and writes part of the letter: "No lo dijo mi marido tal como aquí lo lees, sino con mayor familiaridad y menos tiesura gramatical. Pero tómalo así, pues él me ha escrito el parrafillo, en que verás su pensamiento con toda claridad y precisión" (3:335). Juan Antonio alters in order to better express—he translates his own words. He makes different what can never be identical—the two versions whose original vanishes the moment it is uttered. Juan Antonio's alterations, his translation, then become the original since the verbal event has been erased. One reads at the conclusion of the letter that it has now become a document:

> Pues ahora, Juan Antonio, no contento con meterse a colaborar en mi carta, ha dado en retocarla toda, añadiendo parrafitos, borrando lo que no le parece bien, enmendando lo que cree obscuro. El cuento es que, por no enviártele llena de tachaduras y garabatos, tengo que ponerla en limpio, y al hacerlo veo que lleva un empaque gramatical que no entra en mis hábitos. Así se aprende. Dice mi marido que debe ir el *documento* muy bien apañadito, porque su indudable importancia lo destina ciertamente a la conservación; esta carta es de las que se guardan como oro en paño en las familias, y hallándose, por tanto, *amenazada* de pasar a la posteridad, debemos darle una pasadita de piedra pómez. (3:336)

The creation—writing, selecting, erasing, changing, and correcting—of the documents of history is a process of fabrication and refabrication where the original event is forever "lost in the translation." Moreover, it becomes impossible to identify the hand of the fabricator; as with the confusion of Calpena and Mendizábal, the reader cannot tell who wrote which words. All that remains is the cleanly transcribed version in Valvanera's hand with Juan Antonio's grammar. The hand of the historian disappears as the document seems to take on a style and an account of its own. The language of history—historical discourse itself—becomes the original, as it were, in its continual process of revision in which not even the first version, let alone the event, is visible. This is like a journey backwards; as we retrace the versions of Demetria and Fernando's relationship, and the tracing of its tracing, we are confronted with the eternal reinterpretation of those versions, in which the original cannot be witnessed, because it was not written—in *Vergara* or anywhere else.

DOCUMENTING THE ORIGIN

At another climactic moment in Calpena's life the problematic relationships of origin and history come to the forefront, again through a letter. Chapter 21 of *La estafeta romántica* recounts the drama "secondhand." Calpena writes to Hillo that Valvanera

> en presencia de Juan Antonio me descrifró el enigma de mi vida. Ya sabía yo que ella y mi madre son amigas íntimas, que desde la infancia se adoraban. Ahora sé el nombre que ignoraba, la condición social y otras particularidades de mi nacimiento y de mi niñez. . . . El desgarrón del velo que envolvía mi origen me hizo caer en un estupor parecido al idiotismo: he pasado un día sin darme cuenta de cosa alguna, mirando con embargada atención la fórmula resolutiva de mi problema. . . . Por la noche . . . lloré largo rato, sintiendo dentro de mí un desconsuelo inexplicable, no sé qué, sin duda reflejo de las aflicciones que por mí ha pasado la persona que me dió la vida. Pensaba que si yo hubiera muerto al nacer habría evitado sus acerbas penas, y luego las mías. Ya no puedo evitar nada; soy impotente para todo. (3:63)

A knowledge of his history is nearly a mortal blow to Calpena, not a life-giving force. This passage recalls Nietzsche's warning of how an excess of history can be an enemy to life (28). And rather than providing Calpena with new meaning, this knowledge paralyzes him so that he cannot imagine his own identity in his "idiotismo," "estupor," and "embargada atención." The missing links of his life story produce only impotence and regret, a frustrated desire to undo what was done at his birth. Valvanera's attempt to write Fernando's history, then, to fix his identity and to stabilize the chain of signifiers in an ultimately meaningful and transcendent sign, works instead to create a virtual absence of identity and meaning. The sense that would seem to be made of this sign called Fernando Calpena is not forthcoming. This passage illustrates the always elusive meaning of the sign and the never stable relationships of signification. An attempt to recapture an origin is not only futile, but destructive.

The elusive nature of the origin is inscribed here also by the mediation involved in Valvanera's revelation of Pilar's secret to Calpena, instead of allowing a direct conversation between mother and son. The letter form creates an increased linguistic and temporal distance, as has been observed in other passages. Just as Calpena is removed from original knowledge of his mother by being sent from her at birth, so this moment of revelation is a mediated one, as is all his contact with Pilar in the series. The series's refusal to allow the illusion of unmediated emotional contact between mother and son, between Fernando and Aurora, Fernando and Demetria, Zoilo and Aurora, or Santiago Ibero and Gracia, seems to be more than just a toying with the reader's sentimental expectations and thus a parody of romanticism. It is a statement about our inability to escape the confines of the written word.[30] This "prison house of language," if one will, is evident again in the final letter of *La estafeta romántica*. Here the processes of letters, documents, history, origin, and translation converge in a particularly striking way.

At the point in which Calpena writes to Hillo about his knowledge of his origin, it is still a partial mystery to the reader, since nothing has been revealed about his father. But at the end of *La estafeta romántica*, the enigma is resolved, though again in a manner that reveals as much about the processes of the text as about the identity of Fernando. Juana Teresa, Pilar's stepsister, writes to Valvanera with a threat for Pilar: "a ti, que es como confiarlas a ella, confío mis investigaciones" (3:101). She wants Fernando to stay away from Demetria, since she plans to have her own son, Rodrigo, marry her. Using words that recall Fernando's first wonderment about his mysterious course in Madrid—"Descíframe este acertijo" (3:100)—she facetiously proceeds to reveal her knowledge about his illegitimate birth. God or Providence, she says, placed "en mis manos el archivo

mundano del más glorioso perdido del siglo pasado y parte del presente, don Beltrán de Urdaneta" (3:101).[31] Juana Teresa has discovered several letters to Beltrán concerning Pilar's romance with the exiled Polish prince, "José Poniatowsky (pongo mucho cuidado en copiar este nombre diabólico letra por letra), general del Imperio, gran figura, caballero insigne, sobrino del rey de Polonia" (3:101). She also discovers information about Pilar's alleged illness and residence away from her husband, the duke, in Zaragoza during 1811 and 1812.

Juana Teresa's process of historical reconstruction here is to "atar cabitos," "hacer cuenta del tiempo," "ajustar meses, compaginando fechas con fechas" (3:101). Tying together dates, collocating pages, her chronicle produces the desired solution to the enigma of Pilar's protection of Fernando, a solution that Juana Teresa can use for her own ends. Her history, then, is interested, even if it is documented. But this process of historical reconstruction relies on other sources and interpretations in addition to these old letters to Beltrán. Rodrigo must translate them for her: "Traducida en su parte más interesante por Rodrigo, que, para que lo sepas, posee muy bien el francés" (3:101). The historian Juana Teresa's distance from the document to be interpreted is increased further through the necessary translation, a translation that is, moreover, selective. She completes her reconstruction, again with Rodrigo's aid:

hablando de esto con Rodrigo, que sabe muy bien historias de todos los países, agarró una Enciclopedia que le saca de todas sus dudas, y en ella vimos que el tal señor de Poniatowsky, el *Bayardo polonés*, como le llama, después de diversos hechos heróicos en las campañas de Rusia . . . murió el año 13, al pasar a caballo un río de nombre muy enrevesado. Y luego de leídas estas referencias, hojeó Rodrigo la *Historia de Napoleón*, con láminas, y me mostró una que representa al Príncipe luchando con la corriente del río en que se anegaron y perecieron tantas glorias. Si no miente

la estampa, era un guapo mozo y debía de ser hombre de gran coraje. (3:101)

Rodrigo's authority as linguist and historian notwithstanding, these passages tell as much about Juana Teresa as about the Polish prince. Moreover, her reliance on other texts for confirmation of the discovery increases the layers of texts between her interpretation—this letter—and the persons and events of the past. These referents—Calpena's origin—exist only as names and dates, the tools with which the historian creates his or her illusions of meaning and order.

The choice of an exiled Polish prince for Calpena's father has interesting connections to the various popular historical and philosophical concerns of the age. Polish Messianism, a development between Poland's two unsuccessful uprisings in 1830 and 1863, was a manifestation both within Poland and among her numerous exiles. It predicts "the coming of a new epoch and freedom and justice for all. Various points of contact existed between Messianism and contemporary philosophies such as those of Schelling, Hegel, Krause, and Lamennais."[32] Thus Calpena's origin evokes traces of several popular contemporary philosophies, including the distinctive Spanish Krausism. The implicit parody of these historical interpretations is obvious throughout the third series in Calpena's personal trajectory, which culminates in his deceitful dealings in Santiago Ibero's rescue, in his denouement as gentleman farmer and "apparently smug representative of the ruling class" (*Mature Thought*, 73), and in the coincidence of the death of his heroic father and his own birth with Spain's short-lived liberal constitution.

Just as *La estafeta romántica* concludes with Juana Teresa's discovery in Beltrán's archives, so does this episotolary novel begin there. In chapter 2, Juana Teresa, believing Beltrán to have been killed during his adventures in the Maestrazgo, sorts through his belongings after holding a lavish funeral for him. This was her first misinterpretation, for as the reader subsequently learns, "don Beltrán de Urdeneta, el gran aragonés, ha resucitado. . . . Si es el siglo, si es la época, si es un período histórico que no puede terminar hasta que la propia ley histórica lo dé por fenecido" (3:26). Beltrán outlives the series, like an epoch overstaying its welcome. Again aided by Rodrigo, Juana Teresa examines her father-in-law's collection of portraits of women, keeping those that "merecen" (3:13). Among the various letters that "no contienen nada de interés" (3:14), are love letters and letters from famous historical figures, "muchos de estos documentos históricos están en francés." The process of selection and rejection is thus determined by Juana Teresa's incapacity for French and her highly idiosyncratic and prudish definitions of worth and interest. She condemns many of the portraits because of the empire-line dress, for instance. And about Beltrán's books she writes that there are "algunos muy buenos, superiores, de Historia y letras profanas, otros endemoniados, novelas, . . . materia infernal" (3:14). Rodrigo wants to keep everything, however; "según dice, el libro que no es valioso por su contenido, lo es quizás por el lujo y la rareza de la edición" (3:14). His definition of value is purely monetary: "Propuse quemarlo todo, pero Rodrigo defendió la conservación del archivo. . . . Dice que entre aquellos papeles los hay de gran interés para los que coleccionan autógrafos . . . y . . . hay quien paga en buena moneda las cartas de celebridades" (3:14). Thus the moralist and the miser valorize and classify the documents that will become the stuff of history: "Consérvese, pues, todito, y archívese y catalóguese" (3:14).

Beltrán is not only a passive servant of history for having maintained these archives, but also the active transmitter of his experience, as seen in chapters 35 and 36 of the novel. He writes to Calpena, who now recreates "en los estudios históricos": "Yo voy a contarte sucesos recientes, presenciados por mí, y que mañana, si hoy mismo no, han de entrar en los dominios de Clío. . . . Tú, joven inteligente y lleno de vida, archivarás éste como otros sucesos que te he contado" (3:88). However, as seen in *La campaña del Maestrazgo* (2:1346), Beltrán is more than a truth teller, he is an excellent stylist and storyteller. He calls attention to his abilities frequently in *La estafeta romántica*, for example: "Trataré de poner método en mi relato" (3:89); "perdóname . . . que emplee un estilo que calificarás de zumbón, y formas de planear comedias, en este historico relato" (3:92); "Mi relato histórico pecará de burlesco" (3:96). Like Juan Antonio's correction of his own words, Beltrán will rewrite and reorganize his version of himself. His firsthand account to Calpena is really an account of events that, by their inexorable absence, gesture to the void behind words.

Beltrán cannot relate even his version of the whole story in question—don Carlos's march to Madrid and eleventh-hour retreat—alone. As with Valvanera and Juan Antonio or Juana Teresa and Rodrigo, Beltrán's history marks the confusion of subjects and interpretations. Seeking to explain the cause of Carlos's turnabout at the moment he seemed most likely to have taken Madrid, Beltrán writes, "No acertaba yo con la clave de este político enigma, ni pudo mi mente salir de confusión hasta que Pilar de Loaysa me refirió lo que te transmito, sintiendo que al pasar de sus labios a mi pluma no conserve el encanto y la gracia que ella sabe dar a cuanto dice" (3:95). This letter and this historical novel are a confused network of mediating voices, versions, pens, and styles. Events, origins, meanings, or truths are present only as they are rewritten and imagined. One of the final images evoked in Beltrán's narrative vividly and self-consciously illustrates this written and imagined process of historical discourse.

Unable to reconstruct the thoughts of María Cristina and her sister Carlota at their moment of triumph, Beltrán writes:

Se me ocurre presentarte aquí un lindo ejemplo de sombras chinescas. Imaginemos . . . un blanco muro, que es el fondo de la Historia patria. Sobre él aparecen dos lindos bustos negros. En las graciosas cabezas, de perfil, reconoces al punto a las dos napolitanas. . . . Ambas aplican el dedo pulgar a la punta de la nariz, extendiendo la mano y dando a los otros dedos un temblorcito gracioso. Vuélvense las caras y manos hacia la parte aquella del Abroñigal, donde se supone que está el Pretendiente recomendando a los su-

yos la confianza absoluta en la protección de la Santísima
Virgen de los Dolores. (3:96)

The white wall, or the blank page, serves as the forever absent
background, or past, upon which history sketches its shadowy
images, the interpretations—tragic or comic, romantic or burlesque—that it offers as truth. Beltrán's account is like the pages
of Calpena's own history; his origin is representation—letters,
encyclopedias, pictures. Beltrán writes to him that "la Historia
eres tú, el hombre del porvenir" (3:90); Calpena is history, historian, novel, word. The two directions that trace his path—the
movement toward knowledge of his past and his adventures forward through the series beginning in *Mendizábal*—describe the
seemingly different but ultimately indistinguishable movements of history and novel.

As history and novel, Fernando Calpena is the process of the
written word. His journeys across Spain describe these functions. *Vergara* relates, for instance, that Calpena and his friend
Echaide "llevaban, en sentido contrario el mismo camino que
había recorrido con las niñas en el éxodo de Oñate. . . . La vieja
historia se le presentaba página por página, como un libro repa-
sado al revés (3:159). *Vergara*'s relation to *De Oñate a la
Granja*, Calpena's past to his present, novel to history, invoke a
constant recursive movement that is intrinsic to the signifying
process. Only by looking back can the present volume be understood, and an earlier one is incomplete without its sequel. This
is the network, the confusion, and the process of textuality that
has been observed throughout the third series in letters, translations, journeys, documents, and *episodios*. Manfred Frank defines the term textuality in a way that relates directly to the
concerns of these ten volumes:

Textuality is a general term and characterizes all signifying
formations as texts. By text (*textum*: that which is woven)
I understand a fabric of sense-expression-unities, of which
each acquires its "local value" (as Schleiermacher calls it)
through its differential relationship to all others. An
expression does not carry its meaning out in the open (*auf*

die Stirn geschrieben: literally, "written on its fore-
head"—Tr.). This can be ascertained only through recourse to all other expressions. The sense of the poetic (indeed, of any) composition is not revealed directly in the
positivity of the "mark" [Derrida's "semiologically neutral
term"], but rather through a retracing of the relations it
entertains to all other "marks." The metaphor "text" refers thus to the *gaps* proper to every fabric which in the
final analysis endow its "full and positive terms" with
sense and significance. To understand the "complete sense"
of a text means, then, to retrace its weaving and to reflect
upon it as a generative process. (73)

The third series traces and retraces the constant weave of journeys, letters, translations, and the passions of love and war that
in their relations to each other constitute, while they simultaneously illuminate and demythify, the creative processes of the
ten volumes themselves. The self-consciousness of the characters, the styles, and every aspect of these *episodios* ceaselessly
makes of them the theory of their own practice of novel and/or
history, of the ever-engendering process of their only apparently hybrid genre.

GENERATIVE DEGENERATION IN *BODAS REALES*

Such self-consciousness of the generative processes of historical
and fictional discourse is evident, finally, in *Bodas reales*. This
last volume of the third series serves in part as a retracing and
reinterpretation of the period addressed by the entire series, and
implicitly by the first two as well. At the same time that it retraces the generation of these texts, however, it inscribes the
degeneration of their historical and fictional components. Such
a simultaneously constitutive and deconstitutive process is observable in the political, historical, geographical, emotional, and
temporal movements of *Bodas reales*, an *Episodio* that again
challenges the conventions of history, origin, and interpretation. The style of the novel incorporates a back-and-forth move-

ment, too, since it is intensely ironical. Each element of this volume, from its historical and fictional codes, political and temporal plots, to the very style of narration itself, is a retracing of the weave of its language.

The novel begins with a disassociation of time and history:

> Si la Historia, menos desmemoriada que el Tiempo, no se cuidase de retener y fijar toda humana ocurrencia, ya de las públicas y resonantes, ya de las domésticas y silenciosas, hoy no sabría nadie que los Carrasco, en su tercer domicilio, fueron a parar a un holgado principal de la Cava Baja. (3:409)

There are several implications here: that time, ceaseless movement, has no memory; that memory comes into being only when the historical text designates a temporal moment for reconstruction; that recorded history is filled with events as unworthy of being remembered as this third move of the Manchegan Carrasco family, the protagonists of the novel. History, at least in this case, is not a source of instruction, but rather an assortment of insignificant details.

The novel's opening passage also invokes the journey motif once again, although on a much more reduced scale than in any of the previous nine *Episodios*. The move to a Manchegan neighborhood in Madrid comforts the uprooted Leandra Carrasco, who "dominó, sin brújula la topografía, y navegaba con fácil rumbo en el confuso espacio comprendido entre Cuchilleros y la fuentecilla" (3:409). The reduction of movement here is underlined by the diminutive "fuentecilla" and particularly through the use of navigation metaphors. There are numerous instances throughout the *Episodios nacionales* in which the course of Spain is likened to that of a ship. In this series, for instance, the narrator remarks in *De Oñate a la Granja* after the fall of Mendizábal:

> Así hemos venido todo el siglo, navegando con sinnúmero de patrones, y así ha corrido el barco por un mar siempre proceloso, a punto de estrellarse más de una vez; anegado

siempre, rara vez con bonanzas, y corriendo iguales peligros con tiempo duro y en las calmas chichas. Es una nave esta que por su mala construcción no va nunca a donde debe ir; . . . pues el defecto capital está en la quilla, y mientras no se emprenda la reforma por lo hondo . . . no hay esperanzas de próspera navegación (2:1050).

By comparing Leandra's successful navigation among the streets of her neighborhood to a passage like this, one can establish a series of substitutions between Leandra and Spain. Spain's leaders are incapable of successfully steering her course, no matter what the political conditions; the quixotic Leandra, however, who knows exactly where she wants to go, can successfully chart her course within the confines of the Madrid neighborhood, although not to her home in La Mancha, the novel will reveal. Successful navigation in Spain is only possible, it appears, on a minute scale and by the slightly unstable; the only journeys that reach their objective are the mundane jaunts like Leandra's. Through the comparison of these two passages from the third series, the parodic relationship between the earlier and later volumes becomes obvious. Moreover, a comparison of either of these passages or similar ones to other series illustrates how "far" the ship of Spain has come since *Trafalgar*, for instance.[33]

Such repeated metaphors and motifs as those of navigation and travel demonstrate a progressive process of irony and parody at work in these volumes. While they reach their most intense expression in *Bodas reales*, the ironic style and the specific references to the persistent and degenerating repetition of Spain's same errors occur elsewhere in the series. *Montes de Oca*, for example, relates how Spaniards seek a new cause for revolution as soon as the last one is over. After the signing of the Convenio de Vergara, the new cause for contention is the disagreement among the successive regents María Cristina and Espartero. With a sardonic style prefiguring that of *Bodas reales*, the narrator exclaims:

¡Qué delicioso país, y qué Historia tan divertida la que aquella edad a las plumas de las venideras ofrecía! Toda ella podría escribirse con el mismo cuajarón de sangre por tinta, y con la misma astilla de rotas lanzas. El drama comenzaba a perder su interés por la repetición de los mismos lances y escenas. Las tiradas de prosa poética y el amaneramiento trágico ya no hacían temblar a nadie; el abuso de las aventuras heróicas llevaba rápidamente al país a una degeneración epiléptica, y lo que antes creíamos sacrificio por los ideales, no era más que instinto de suicidio y monomanía de la muerte. (3:284)

Montes de Oca still retains a sense of adventure, however, in its plots and a certain quixotic grandeur in its fictional and historical protagonists, Santiago Ibero and Montes de Oca. In *Bodas reales*, though, all pretense of effective action and lofty idealism has finally vanished. The characters, metaphors, and styles— the codes—of this novel write the plots of its history and fiction as degeneration. History is like Leandra, who "en estas idas y venidas de mosca prisionera que busca la luz y el aire" (3:409), looks for a breadth of vision that cannot be found, despite the retracing, remembering, and recording of public and private events. The details of the period—such as Espartero's fall, Narváez's ministry, and Isabel II's marriage—are to be chronicled only reluctantly, as the beginning of chapter 2 reveals:

Aunque todo lo dicho puede referirse a cualquier mes de aquel año 43, tan turbulento como los demás del siglo en nuestro venturoso país, hágase constar que corría el mes de las flores, famoso en tales tiempos porque en él nació y murió con sólo diez días de existencia, el Ministerio López, fugaz rosa de la política. (3:412)

The birth and death of ministries, the comings and goings of the Carrascos, are absurdly insignificant, adjectives like "venturoso" ironically suggest. Moreover, the insipid maneuvers of men and ministries weave the history of the entire century. Complaining of the self-interest of Spain's governors, the narrator laments: "Por esto da pena leer las reseñas históricas del sinfín de revoluciones, motines, alzamientos que componen los fastos españoles del presente siglo; ellas son como un tejido de vanidades ordinarias que carecen de todo interés" (3:417). Such senseless and repetitive movements comprise the texture of vain history, the endlessly insignificant journey of Spain.

What is true of the ups and downs of politics is true of the politicians:

> la historia de todo grande hombre político en aquel tiempo y en el reinado de Isabel no es más que una serie de enmiendas de sí mismos, y un sistemático arrepentirse hoy de cuanto ayer dijeron. Se pasan la vida entre acusaciones frenéticas y actos de contrición, flaqueza natural en donde las obras son nulas y las palabras excesivas, en donde se disimula la esterilidad de los hechos con el escribir sin tasa y el hablar a chorros. (3:421)

Passages like these call attention to the vacuity of the words of historic men, who must constantly repent and emend their versions of themselves and history. Dendle writes of *Bodas reales* that "the gravest defect in the national character is, for Galdós, infatuation with words. Empty rhetoric ('palabrería') is the substitute in Spain for willpower and rectitude" (76). The words of politicians, history books, or *episodios nacionales* have no meaningful or stable relation to events or people. When Espartero is removed from the regency, for example, Prim "llamó a Espartero *soldado de fortuna, aventurero, egoísta,* y a Mendizábal *intrigante, embaucador* y *dilapidador de los intereses públicos.* Andando el tiempo fue de los que creyeron que la memoria de uno y otro debía perpetuarse con estatuas" (3:417). Espartero and Mendizábal's identities are a function of the political language of the moment. The combination of signifiers that describe them are a product of the interpreter's prejudice, not fixed signs. And even the statues that will later be raised to their memories offer no more perpetual an interpretation of their significance than the "lápidas desenterradas" that mark the glory/bloodshed of Julióbriga's heritage or the capitals of the Cistercian monastery that seem to portray past versions of Nelet and Beltrán. The words used to eulogize or discredit, the stones that commemorate or fall into ruin, are equally subject to the fluctuating interpretations of time and history.

Even terms that conventionally connote transcendental, absolute values are unstable in *Bodas reales*. When the provinces and the military protest the restrictions imposed by the new government, for instance, it "tuvo que desmentir su programa de reconciliaciones, concordias y abrazos, metiendo en la cárcel a infinidad de españoles que días antes fueron proclamados *buenos*, y ya se habían vuelto *malos* sólo por querer armar su revolucioncita correspondiente" (3:425). Good and bad are only more signifiers in a ceaseless sliding of words without meaning or reality. The ups and downs of men and events of 1843 to 1844 are rapidly catalogued in chapter 12, which concludes, "y, en fin, mil sucesos y menudencias que, tejidos con estrecha urdimbre, forman la historia del vivir colectivo en aquellos tiempos, la Historia grande, integral" (3:442). The weave of this narration is itself a back-and-forth process, since irony makes the reader move from one interpretation to another. The history described is not literally "grande" or "integral." One must constantly "enmendar," "desmentir," or "arrepentirnos" of the meanings and interpretations that one affixes to such signifiers, just as with "bueno" and "malo."

The intensely ironic mode of the narration is a movement that questions any relationship of identity or difference. Hayden White writes in *Tropics of Discourse* that

> irony sanctions the ambiguous, and possibly even the ambivalent, statement. It is a kind of metaphor, but one that surreptitiously signals a denial of the assertion of similitude or difference contained in the literal sense of the proposition. . . . What is involved here is a kind of attitude towards knowledge itself which is implicitly critical of all forms of metaphorical identification, reduction, or integration of phenomena. In short, irony is the linguistic strategy underlying and sanctioning skepticism as an explanatory tactic, satire as a mode of emplotment, and either agnosticism or cynicism as a moral posture. (73–74)

Metaphor, translation, the representations of history and fiction: these are processes of identity and difference that the *Episodios* consistently undermine. While, on the one hand, these processes can allow for the illusion of a better understanding, expression, or interpretation of one phenomenon in terms of another, irony, on the other, forcefully exposes the impossibility of any ultimate meaning. Frank discusses the creation of the open-ended text through irony and observes that

> the text owes this open-endedness to that deficiency of an authentic representation of "absolute meaning"; to the temporalization of the subject, the phantasm of the aimless journey and the structure of the endless text.
>
> The endless deferral of the goal which our texts relate thus corresponds to an endless deferral of sense within the structure of the texts themselves. (77–78)

After the journeys and the romanticism of all of the third series, the pervasive, biting, and sardonical irony of *Bodas reales* undoes all that has been done to the plots of history and fiction that precede it.

Bodas reales ceaselessly rejects the idea that history is meaningful by self-consciously calling attention to the equivocation of language. Like the continual emendations in their rhetoric that the politicians must make and the ironic adjustments in the narrative itself, Isabel II has been taught from earliest childhood "el código de las *equivocaciones*" (3:430). Her first official acts upon being declared of age at thirteen are to sign a decree first dissolving the Cortes and then to immediately reconstitute them (chapters 9 and 10, 3:428–34). The versions of the causes of her "error" range from Olózaga threatening her at knife-point to childish ignorance. When she is made to say that she was forced to sign the first decree, some doubt the truth of her statement. Yet, "no podemos poner en duda la palabra de la Reina, quien, como tal Reina y señora de los españoles, no puede haber dicho cosa contraria a la verdad. . . . La verdad no se pondrá en claro, y cada cual seguirá creyendo lo que quiera" (3:433–34). The various interpretations offered of this event are all unable to reconstruct its truth because the truth depends on the interpreter, not the event. The characters who offer their versions and claim to know the truth, instead reveal the multiple distancing effects of mediation observed in other novels in the series. The "pajarero *Sacris*" gives one version (3:428–29), while a "zapatero y miliciano nacional" give another (3:429). Milagro repeats his version until 1846, "asimismo recordaba Centurión, con admirable retentiva, la perorata que soltó Fermín Caballero . . . cuando ya la escandalosa discusión estaba en el quinto o sexto día" (3:432). These different voices and conflicting versions reflect the shifting, recursive, and equivocating movements of this novel's historical, fictional, and ironical discourses.

Not only the interpretation of historical events like Isabel II's first acts of majority, but history as process, is the subject of irony, as, for example, in chapter 13: "Vemos luego como dicha Historia, mansamente, por el suave nacer de los efectos del vientre de las causas, siendo a su vez dichos efectos causas que nuevos hijos engendran, va corriendo y produciendo vida" (3:442). By placing the conventional notion of history as cause and effect in the context of these ironic metaphors, the notion itself is called into question.[34] In contrast to terms like "mansamente" and "suave" and metaphors of the birth process, the details that follow these lines are a sarcastic chronicle of the petty causes and effects of the Carrasco existence and the minutiae of numerous political uprisings. The most poignant irony consists of the "bárbaro, torpe y extremado castigo, que había de ser semillero de odios intensísimos, irreconciliables" that culminate in the execution of twenty-four Alicantine revolutionaries. Gentle History gives birth to hatred and death. In the same vein is the narrative of the not "totalmente estéril" five-month ministry of González Bravo, "el gran cínico . . . el que en vez de moral tenía la prontitud imaginativa para fingirla" (3:443). His fall is accompanied by Bruno Carrasco's "cesantía" and Narváez's rise to power, "continuando con pasmosa fecundidad el desarrollo de la Historia, grande, como un hilo de vida sin solución (3:443). The terms "pasmosa fecundidad," like "no totalmente estéril" and the reproductive analogies, form an intensely ironic association between the terms life and history. When not death itself through revolution and execution, history is an endlessly unresolved thread of life without meaning or resolution, much like Beltrán, who outlives his epoch but will not die. Nietzsche writes of the dangers of such an excess of history: "Lastly an age reaches a dangerous condition of irony with regard to itself, and the still more dangerous state of cynicism, when a cunning egotistic theory of action is matured that maims and at last destroys the vital strength" (28). This irony, cynicism, egotism, deformity, and weakness are evident in every aspect of *Bodas reales*, its characters, style, history, and fiction.

The simile of history as an unending thread of life incorporates the weave of the character Leandra Carrasco and her endless journey. The prematurely aged Leandra wants to go back to her life in La Mancha. But the materialist aspirations of her daughters—dress, theater, marriage—and the political ones of her husband Bruno have "cerrado el camino de sus ilusiones de patria manchega," the same chapter 13 (3:444) relates. Leandra can find solace only "en los viajes imaginarios al país de sus amores," traveling there on Clavileño or a witch's broom (3:445; 486). Her only journeys, then, are the mundane ones through the streets of her neighborhood, those of her imagination, and finally that to the cemetery in her funeral procession. In earlier volumes Fago and Nelet, and witchlike messengers such as Malaena, traveled through fantasy at times, too, but they also traced, like Calpena, Ibero, Beltrán, Arratia, Aurora, and Demetria, wide geographical movements. Yet for Leandra and *Bodas reales*, all journeys, like historical events, are reduced to ironically trivial proportions or vanish into the spaces of the imagination, the blanks between words.

Leandra's imaginary journeys through space and time to her provincial home are presented in great detail. Dendle writes of her that "foreshadowing, however, the unhappy marriage of Isabel, her healthy instincts are thwarted by outside pressures. Out of place in the Madrid she hates, far from La Mancha, which she adores, she degenerates, like a Spain diverted from healthful goals, into paralysis and madness" (77).[35] As the novel progresses, Leandra becomes physically paralyzed; while unable to undertake even routine geographical journeys, her travels are limited now only by her mind. Her madness, in a way, is a solution to her yearning for a return to a meaningful (i.e., stable) existence; through madness or death alone can a journey come to an end. Leandra's madness and death seem to be the only escape from the endless and vain webs of *Bodas reales*. Unlike politicians who repeat the same mistakes, Leandra seeks and finds a way out of her meaninglessness, her endless mentally and physically degenerative identity.

Leandra's imaginary travels reread the journey motif of the third series in another way. She loses all notion of time and place: "Del tiempo hacía mangas y capirotes" (3:486); "Os pregunto si estamos en hoy o en ayer, si ayer os vi y hoy vuelvo a veros" (3:487). The confusion of both time and place in Leandra's mind confuses the codes of geographical and temporal journeys, that is, those plots that the third series has traced in history, novel, love, and war. Yet all of these more conventional paths were also written texts, as elusive and illusory, as much products of the imagination, as are Leandra's mad flights.

The relegation of virtually all movement in this last *Episodio* to the spaces of the imagination corresponds to that thread of history whose greatness is now merely an ironic gloss on the errors of vain and ignorant men and sovereigns. Narváez is the most striking example of this degeneration of a historical personality, as can be observed particularly through his juxtaposition to Leandra. The confluence of the codes of history and fiction through the characters of Narváez and Leandra occurs frequently, as when she is awakened from a reverie and the next paragraph begins, "También a Narváez le llevaba su demencia del orden a estados imaginativos muy parecidos al éxtasis" (3:446). Yet as with any analogy, the differences in the relationship subvert the similarities. Thus at the end of 1844, while Leandra dreams, Narváez occupies himself "fusilando españoles, tarea fácil y eficaz a que se consagró desde el primer día de mando" (3:445). This is what he means by *"hacer país"*; this term has become

> como una formulilla en los amanerados entendimientos; siempre que entraban en el Poder estos o aquellos hombres se encontraban el país deshecho, y unos gobernando detestablemente, otros conspirando a maravilla, lo deshacían más de lo que estaba. Narváez vio quizás más claro que sus sucesores y hacía país por eliminación, no creando lo bueno, sino destruyendo lo malo y corrupto. (3:445)

To create is to destroy, to do is to undo; Narváez sees this paradox quite clearly. He is both similar to and different from the most brutal of Carlist commanders depicted in *La campaña del Maestrazgo*:

> el hombre iba quitando de en medio gente dañosa; y tanta fue su diligencia, que a fines del 44 ya iban despachados 414 individuos. Esto era una delicia, y así nos íbamos purificando, así continuábamos la magna obra de Cabrera y de otros cabecillas de la guerra civil, que tiraban a la extinción de la raza. (3:445)

Purification is extinction; Narváez believes that "sacrificando una porción de la Humanidad aseguraba la dicha de la Humanidad restante. Su falta de cultura, su desconocimiento de la Historia, su ignorancia infantil de las artes de gobierno lleváronle a tan descomunal sinrazón" (3:446).[36] This is the "sinrazón" of "purificación/extinción," "hacer país/eliminar," "crear/destruir," "bueno/malo," or any other equivalence between different terms. In a world woven of vain words, all correspondences are as nonsensical as sensible, as reasonable as demented, since the relationships among them are ironic.

Narváez's extremes result not in creating life or progress—not in generation—but in degeneration: "Llevaba, como se ve, al Gobierno la maña de la caballería morisca degenerada; era, como muchas de sus predecesores, poeta político, un sentimental del cuño militar, como otros lo eran del retórico" (3:446). In Narváez's character converges the degeneration of other novelistic codes traced through the series: poetic, military, sentimental, rhetorical, political. The dominant literary code of the series, romanticism, has degenerated as well:

> Tras esta grandiosa procesión romántica que iba pasando y en el ocaso se desvanecía, vino otra procesión cuyas figuras traían menos poder literario, arreos no tan vistosos, vestiduras poco brillantes y armas enteramente flojas, afeminadas y deslucidas. Vino un sentimentalismo baboso que en los años siguientes hubo de dar frutos de notoria insipidez, un suspirar, un quejarse continuos, como expresión única del amor. La suprema fórmula estética fue la languidez; púsose de moda el estar lánguido; languidecían los poetas, languidecían las niñas casaderas y las jamonas que ya habían corrido el ciclo romántico en toda su extensión. . . . Los novios, en sus inflamadas cartas, no hablaban ya de tomar fósforos . . . se entretenían en dar cuenta de *suspiros que ahogaban el alma*, o de *quejidos exánimes inspirados por un deseo*. . . . Hasta la Prensa se veía tocada de esta demencia ñoña. (3:450)

Just as the romantic degenerates to the languid, all of the codes and characters of the third series are rewritten here. Eufrasia and Lea Carrasco, the Manchegan bumpkins turned "cursi," marriage-minded, Madrid materialists, replace the romantic Aurora and the classic Demetria. The long-suffering Leandra or the gossip Cristeta Socobio replace Pilar, Valvanera, Marcela Luco, or even Juana Teresa. These earlier women characters, despite their diversity as romantic or classic, sympathetic or antipathetic, have in common a strength of will pitifully unrepresented in the final volume of the series. The male characters have degenerated tremendously, too, as has been seen already with the portrayal of historic figures. These men are denied even the ambivalent grandeur accorded them in *Zumalacárregui, Mendizábal, Vergara,* or *Montes de Oca.* The fictional Bruno Carrasco is a father and husband too weak to resist Madrid's temptations or preserve the family honor and fortune. His daughters' boyfriends are either "cursi" or adulterous.

They and others like them categorized in the above passage are clearly pale images of Fernando Calpena, who was imprisoned to prevent his suicide over Aurora, of José Fago, who willed himself to death, or of Nelet, who literally killed himself. Even the styles of dress, hair, love letters, and theater have become insipid, languid, the above passage goes on to relate. These elements invoke the historical, social, and literary codes of the series that merge here in their manifestation of degeneration and foolishness.

The characters, plots, and words of *Bodas reales*, then, are an ironically degenerate version of the characters, plots, and modes of the nine previous volumes. The journeys of characters throughout Spain are paralyzed within the confines of Madrid. The ups and downs of the war are now one-sided butcheries. Love plots are depicted only in the trivial marriage games of Rafaela Milagro, Eufrasia, and Lea Carrasco, in the adultery of Eufrasia, and most poignantly in the disastrous negotiations for Isabel II's hand. This royal marriage will send Spain on an even more socially, economically, and morally degenerate course, the fourth series will reveal. Adventure and heroism, even if rather hyperbolic as with Calpena's "herculean" efforts, quixotic as with Santiago Ibero, Zoilo Arratia, and Don Beltrán, or driven by uncontrollable passion as with Fago and Nelet, leave their trace in one fictional character alone, Leandra, who only travels to La Mancha in her demented nostalgia. Her husband Bruno is not even able to go home to look after his interests: "deber de don Bruno era dar una vuelta por allá; mas cuando lo pensaba, le invadía la pereza, la terrible parálisis de su voluntad" (2:452). *Bodas reales* is a rewriting of the earlier *Episodios* in every way. Its characters and plots stand in the same relation of identity and difference—of reflecting and rejecting or doing and undoing— to the rest of the series as Fago or Beltrán stand to their past. The novel has the same relationship to the rest of the series as the translated text has to the translation, or as the copy has to the original.

REWRITING HISTORY THROUGH
THE NARRATION OF ISABEL II'S MARRIAGE

The temporal, historical, and interpretive retracing in *Bodas reales* is most conspicuously manifested in the reconstruction of events leading up to Isabel II's marriage to her cousin, Francisco de Asís. The narrative returns to 1833 (2:462), backtracking to a moment before the opening of the series in 1834 with *Zumalacárregui*. This journey back in time in order to establish a chain of causes leading up to Isabel's marriage and its consequences for Spain again places in the foreground the problematics of cause and effect, of historical discourse, of mediation, and of an origin, in self-consciously ironic ways.

The narrator of this revisionist journey in *Bodas reales* is Cristeta del Socobio, aunt of another mediator of history, Serafín del Socobio, one of Calpena's palace correspondents in *Los Ayacuchos*. Cristeta herself merits "los honores de la Historia," having entered palace service in 1818. Now a favored "camarista" of Isabel II, she receives a salary but does no work (3:457–59). All of chapter 18 is dedicated to a description of Cristeta and of how she and Leandra come to be friends. Like the history she will recount, their contact with each other takes place by means of a lengthy series of mediating people and events (3:457). And just as Cristeta claims to know the original cause of a series of events leading to Isabel's marriage, so Leandra values Cristeta for her Manchegan origin: "bastaba el origen para que doña Leandra le tuviese en gran estimación" (3:457). However, Cristeta is not herself from La Mancha, but rather "viuda de un manchego . . . [que] salió de su pueblo a los cinco años" and never returned (3:457). This origin, then, is shifted from one character to another, an exchange that establishes a functional, although not a true identity. Cristeta's mythic Manchegan origin is also the cause of her influential effect on and credibility with Leandra. This identity and this effect well illustrate the infinite regress and ultimate emptiness of origin and causality themselves.

Cristeta traces the events leading up to Isabel II's alliance with the son of María Cristina's sister Carlota, for whom Cristeta claims to have been "la persona de su mayor confianza" (3:461). This marriage is an effect of a truce between the two families, following a lengthy alienation that resulted from Carlota's disapproval of Cristina's morganatic marriage to Fernando Muñoz in 1833. The cause of that marriage was Cristeta herself, she claims:

> Lo peor del caso, amiga querida—prosiguió Cristeta tomado aliento y limpiado el gaznate—, es que yo, con la mayor inocencia, fui la primera persona que supo del devaneo de Cristina, y no sólo fui quien primero lo supo, sino algo más, Leandra, pues a mí me escogió la Providencia . . . para que abriese la puerta por donde entró la flecha de Cupido. . . . Yo llevé a Palacio a la modista Teresa Valcárcel, fundamento de todo ese enredo; tras de la modista fue el guardia don Nicolás Franco, que la cortejaba, y con Franco se coló su amigote Muñoz. . . . De modo que aquí me tiene usted oficiando de *causa histórica*, porque si yo no hubiera llevado a la modista . . . a estas horas la Historia de España llevaría en sus hojas cosas diferentes de las que lleva. (3:462)

The mediation that facilitates the meeting of María Cristina and Muñoz, however, is as attributable to Cristeta bringing the "modista," or "fundamento," as it is to Teresa bringing her guard, as it is to Franco bringing Muñoz. The original cause is as undecidable here as are the reasons for the friendship between the two guards or Teresa's flirtation. Cristeta has her own ordering of cause and effect; she privileges, classifies, and chronicles according to her desired interpretation. The chain of relationships among the signifiers Cristeta, Teresa, Franco, Muñoz, Cristina, Carlota, Francisco de Asís, and Isabel II is open-ended. It derives its momentary meaning, coherence or causality from Cristeta's fixing a sequence that makes her its origin and self-present truth.

Cristeta's role as historian is further compromised when she describes María Cristina's announcement of her engagement:

> pues quien primero tuvo en Palacio noticia de tal escena fui yo, por un guardia que vio pasear solos a la Reina y a don Fernando, y lo refirió a mi marido . . . y, naturalmente, Nicolás me trajo el cuento. . . . Yo, que siempre he mirado a la conciencia antes que a nada, me guardé muy bien guardado el secreto, hasta que empezaron a correr por Madrid y por Palacio rumores graves, malignos de toda malignidad, como que Muñoz paseaba en una berlina muy elegante y tenía casa puesta, lujosísima; que llevaba en la pechera y en la corbata alhajas pertenecientes al difunto Rey. . . . Lo de las alhajas lo dudo . . . yo no las vi, ni he conocido a nadie que las viera. . . . Pero ¡ay, es tan malo el público!. . . ¡Qué perro es el público, ¿verdad? . . .! (3:462–63)

Her primal knowledge is based on accounts of a guard who tells her husband who tells Cristeta. Moreover, although she will not carry tales about evidence she does not see—"las alhajas,"—, the reader might assume that indeed she passes along the "rumores, malignos de toda malignidad" of the coach and mansion, just like the "malo," "perro," "público." Her additional remark that she knows of no one who has seen the jewels also implies that she attempted to search out information to complete her story. Even her role as palace favorite does not exempt her from the same malicious gossip, the same biased and interested interpretations for which she condemns others.

Cristeta explains the "causa" of the "muerte prematura" of Carlota as grief over her angered rupture with Cristina (3:464). According to this version, Cristeta's authority extends to reprimanding Carlota:

> "Pero señora—le decía yo no menos desconsolada que ella—, ¿por qué no hizo Vuestra Alteza caso de mí, que mil veces tuve el honor de advertirle que previera este matrimonio?" Y ella bajaba la cabeza, humillada, y decía:

"Tienes razón: he sido una bestia, sí, Cristeta, una bestia."
(3:464; see also Cristeta's narration on pp. 461–62)

The conversations she selects to document her history corroborate the authority of her interpretation and thus her role as interpreter. But just as with Juana Teresa's analysis of Beltrán's archives for her own purposes or Nelet's reading of his history in the capitals, these passages reveal more of Cristeta's subjectivity than anything else. Descriptions like "tomado aliento y limpiado el gaznate" portray her overzealous, unconscious participation in the story. And Carlota seems to speak in Cristeta's voice, not the other way around, when she repeats herself— "una bestia . . . una bestia"—as does Cristeta in phrases like "malignos de toda malignidad" or the reiteration of the "malo," "perro público." Cristeta's true objective history of the original causes of events everywhere reveals the prejudices, idiosyncracies, and short-sightedness of its narrator. This is nowhere more evident than in her prediction of Spain's glorious future.

Cristeta's interpretation of the royal marriage is hyperbolically rosy. This is also due to the authoritative role she accords herself in the chain of causes and effects, specifically her part in the formation of the infante Francisco's character. She says of the future king consort that "puedo dar informes como no los dará nadie, pues estos brazos le han zarandeado de niño. . . . ¿Y quién, sino yo, le puso los primeros calzones?" (3:461). It is only consistent with her interested roles as participant and observer that she predict a happy outcome to the history she claims to have witnessed from the start:

> ¡Vivan Isabel y Francisco!, y dennos una cálifa de príncipes robustos, guapos, listos, buenos españoles y buenos cristianos. El Trono, el Orden y la Religión están de enhorabuena, que para mirar por todo le sobran virtudes al niño.
> . . . Así le llamo porque su infancia graciosa no se aparta de mis recuerdos. (3:466)

Her optimism is increased further after the wedding; the end of *Bodas reales* relates her pleasure over el casamiento de Isabel con un Príncipe español que ha de colmarla de ventura, de lo que resultará nueva hornada de reyes católicos, y una era como dicen los periódicos, una era de prosperidades y grandezas que devolverán a este reino su preponderancia entre los reinos de la Europa. Ello es claro como la luz. (3:508)

What is as clear as day, however, is the irony of her imagined denouement in relation to the texts of Isabel's reign not yet written for Cristeta. As one reads 1833 and 1868 into Cristeta's narrations as well as into other histories, including the fourth series, Cristeta's words can only be translated with irony. Moreover this narrative's apparent apology for Isabel II, whether through Cristeta's voice or that of an omniscient narrator, must also be read with caution. In a volume as bitingly ironic as *Bodas reales*, a literal interpretation of any passage is subject to undoing. To attribute fault, origin, or cause to Cristeta, Cristina, Carlota, or Isabel is equally a product of the narrator/interpreter's desires, not unbiased knowledge or possession of original truth. The juxtaposition of Cristeta's discourse to the narration of the royal wedding itself and the final scenes of the third series illustrate this clearly.

THE PROCESSION OF HISTORY THROUGH MARRIAGE, ADULTERY, AND DEATH IN CONCLUSION TO THE THIRD SERIES

The happy future that Cristeta predicts for Spain becomes an unhappy slide into moral, social, and political degeneration for the monarchs, the fictional characters, and the Spain of the fourth and fifth series. This degeneration is clearly foretold by the death of Leandra Carrasco at the conclusion to *Bodas reales*. Her death marks a transition, just as did that of Ulibarri at the outset of the third series. Leandra's death comes at a point of transition between series, between the regency and Isabel II's married reign, between a moment of optimism at the royal wedding and the steady degeneration toward 1868 and beyond.

Moreover, she is the series's last Quijote, the death of whom in Cervantes's work, as well as over and over again in other texts, marks dramatic change. For Lukács, *Don Quixote,*

> the first great novel of world literature stands at the beginning of the time when the Christian God began to forsake the world; when man became lonely and could find meaning and substance only in his soul, whose home was nowhere; when the world, released from its paradoxical anchorage in a beyond that is truly present, was abandoned to its immanent meaninglessness.[37]

The passage suggests Fago, Nelet, or Leandra; their battles are doomed from the outset, their gods—transcendental meaning—have utterly forsaken this world of the third series. The only way to attain meaning, wholeness, a complete sign, or to return home is through death, they discover. There is no happiness in their pursuits and no fulfillment, as there was perhaps for don Quijote. Lukács writes that

> *Don Quixote* is the first great battle of interiority against the prosaic vulgarity of outward life, and the only battle in which interiority succeeded, not only to emerge unblemished from the fray, but even to transmit some of the radiance of its triumphant, though admittedly self-ironising, poetry to its victorious opponent. (*Theory of the Novel,* 104)

There is no radiance or poetry imparted to the world that Leandra leaves behind, only her absolute refusal to participate in its prosaic degeneration.

One of Leandra's last lucid visions is of her family's and Madrid's moral decline:

> Mirándolo bien, sus hijas no eran honradas, pues no había honradez con tanto manoseo de novios. . . . Y en cuanto a Bruno, también estaba *horriblemente echado a perder.* . . . No, no; no era aquélla su familia. ¡Mentira, engaño! Las personas que veía no eran sino una infernal *adulteración* de

sus queridos hijos y esposo. La verdad radicaba en otra
parte, allá donde vivía despierta, que en Madrid no era la
vida más que una soñación. Y esto se probaba observando
que en Madrid estaba baldadita y sin movimiento, mientras
que en su pueblo iba de un lado para otro con los remos
muy despabilados, sin cansarse. (3:490)

Leandra rejects the distorted, adulterated, and paralyzed reality
she sees. She seeks instead truth, identity, and movement in her
imagination. The world she rejects as dream and lie is literally
accurate, however, since both Bruno and Eufrasia are or are soon
to be adulterers. She sees Isabel II and Francisco clearly, too,
unlike the historian Cristeta:

"¡Vivan Isabel y Francisco!" ¡A mí con esas! . . . ¿Cómo
he de gritar yo tal cosa si lo que me sale de dentro . . . y lo
que me manda el corazón es lo otro . . . que no vivan, sino
que mueran . . . pues ellos y su casamiento son la causa de
que yo esté como me veo? (3:504)

If Leandra is history searching for fresh air, if she is the last don
Quijote, then her death is the death of the illusion of meaning,
the ultimate refusal of sense in the novel histories of the third
series. She attributes her paralysis and death to Isabel and Francisco, the emblems of Spain's ever more meaningless journey.
The adultery that will characterize both Isabel and Eufrasia's
trajectories in the fourth series, the prostitution of Spain, continues the degenerating but endless weave of their texts; they
are distorted images of illusory ideals. Leandra's vision and her
death, Eufrasia's dishonor, and the marriage of Isabel and Francisco converge and become interchangeable in their historical,
social, and moral codes at the end of *Bodas reales*. Marriage,
death, and adultery coincide in one moment; the substitution of
the terms enabled by their coincidence is the final irony, the
final identity within difference of the third series.

Leandra's vision and the final scenes of *Bodas reales* well illustrate the ironic processes of the series: what seems meaningful is not, what seems good is bad, life is death, since all is illu-

sion. Madrid's adornments for the royal wedding are nothing more than the illusion of grandeur. The decorations that hide the "raquítica y casi asquerosa fachada" of the Buen Suceso church, for example, are "una figuración arquitectónica y académica, pues la berroqueña, el mármol rojo y la caliza de Colmenar eran de tela pintada, al modo de teatro, y el adorno escultórico era yeso, cartón o pasta imitando mármol con admirable ilusión de verdad" (3:503). This forgery, theatricality, and imitation is characteristic of Leandra's Madrid, of the illusions of characters and narrators. These imitations know themselves to be such, thus emphasizing once again in these final scenes the image-making processes of the novel. All this effort has the result that "semejase fantástica creación de un cerebro delirante" (3:503). However, it is not the delirious creation of Leandra, but rather the orchestration of the government that creates such fantastical shams. The ramshackle "Inspección de Milicias" is transformed

en el más espléndido palacio gótico que podía soñar la fantasía. Lo más extraordinario de tal fábrica era que todo debía iluminarse al transparente, con lo que resultaría un efecto de ensueño, romántico poema arquitectónico, según la feliz expresión de un cronista de aquellas soberanas fiestas (3:504).[38]

In a movement of apposition to the romantic impulse to unearth and restore the past seen in previous volumes, here the prosaic present is masked for a moment with papier-mâché.

These illusions, however, are no longer the stuff of enduring art, but shoddy, "languid." Such passages not only inscribe their own signifying processes, but reveal the almost hyperbolic vacuity of those signifying images. Art and architecture, marriage and politics converge to parody their own efforts at representation, just as "los bien dispuestos palitroques representaban soles, lunas, estrellas, constelaciones, como una parodia del sistema planetario transportado del cielo a la tierra" (3:504). While these decorations parody universal or transcendental meaning, in like fashion Isabel II and Francisco will parody the "Reyes Católicos," not repeat them as Cristeta predicts. Their reign will be anything but a return to past glory. Parody is degenerate imitation, a deliberately false translation, just like the "sistema planetario transportado del cielo a la tierra." The chain of images, imitations, translations, and parodies is endless, too, as with Leandra's parody or the parodic knight. In passages like these, the third series rewrites its own interpretations, parodies itself and all other interpretations as well.

Cristeta recounts the details of the wedding ceremony, during Leandra's wake, claiming that

> son datos precisos, de una exactitud matemática, como deben ser en estos casos los datos históricos. Si alguno de los que han de escribir de tan gran suceso quiere esta noticia y otras, véngase a mí, y cosas le contaré que no me agradecerá poco la posteridad. . . . Vamos, la Reina más pareciá divina que humana . . . dijo el "sí quiero" con voz muy apagada, don Francisco con voz entera. . . . Aumale muy gallardo, su hermano siempre tan asustadico. . . . En la comitiva de estos viene un mulato, con el pelo como un escobillón: le llaman Alejandro Dumas. (3:507)

Like her divine interpretation of the mundane Isabel or the virile picture of the insipid Francisco, Cristeta's exact history parodies a romantic novel and thus constitutes a parody within the series's parody of romanticism.

Cristeta is a degenerated historian like Beltrán in many ways, but different, too. Glorious in her time, she believes, now even on the most stately occasions she no longer has even the appearance of elegance she presumes. After the wedding, for example, she loosens the bodice of her "traje de corte," "del cual se escapaban los mal aprisionados pellejos que un día fueron lucidas carnes" (3:507). The kind of ridiculing description seen in this passage and on most occasions when Cristeta assumes a knowledge of history is not characteristic of the portrayal of Beltrán. Beltrán may be morally corrupt and cowardly in *La campaña del Maestrazgo*, but he is not such a subject of ridicule as Cristeta. And the historical information that he provides Cal-

pena, while clearly only his often idiosyncratic versions, is not usually itself an object of parody.

Cristeta is an anachronistic Beltrán, just as Beltrán, the antiquarian, is himself an anachronistic historian. By the conclusion of *Bodas reales* only the faded and senile versions, like Cristeta, of these already, always anachronistic texts remain. Romanticism, the monarchy, Spain's social rites, are plodding gestures toward the past, the marriage procession illustrates:

> No es bien que la Monarquía se eternice en este barroquismo, negándose a la feliz asimilación de las formas de la industria moderna, y persistiendo en las lentitudes, en la insufrible pesadez de aquel paso de procesión, llevando a las Reales personas en urnas, como si fueran reliquias. (3:509)

The translation of Spain's "glory" is a tedious and useless endeavor; it is a journey with no functional value. These royal relics do not look to the future, but cling to the meaningless routines of the past:

> Fue a parar toda esta máquina de barroquismo elegante a la más ruin y destartalada iglesia que han visto los siglos cristianos, Atocha, inexplicable fealdad en el país de las nobles arquitecturas, borrón del Estado y de la Monarquía, pues uno y otra no supieron dar aposento menos miserable a las cenizas de los héroes y a los trofeos de tantas victorias. (3:509)

Spain's glory is dead and buried, its passing marked by the ink blot of Atocha. The choice of the term "borrón" to describe the shrine of Spain's historic grandeur again evokes history as a process of writing. The smear of ink signifies nothing other than error, so Spain's past holds no meaning, makes no sense, or charts no course for her future. Yet even an intelligible stroke of the pen or a beautiful monument signifies only as illusion, whether it be a written document or a plaster facade.

The above passage finds a parallel in the last lines of the novel, where Madrid, after the wedding,

estaba obscuro, solitario; sólo vieron el triste desarme de los palitroques y aparejos de madera, lienzos desgarrados y sucios por el suelo, y las paredes de todos los edificios nacionales señaladas por feísimos y repugnantes manchurrones de aceite. Parecían manchas que no habían de quitarse nunca. (3:511)

The "manchurrones" now pay tribute to the seemingly transcendental event of Isabel II's marriage. The wedding is over, however, and so is the glory, if it existed as anything but sham and pretense. All that remains are the ceremony's undoing—the de-articulation of the process of its composition—and the perhaps indelible "manchas" and "borrones" of its forever absent and unintelligible moment of meaning.

The above two passages are extremely negative statements; the ugly tribute to Spain's past that is Atocha and the repugnant, sad, and dirty after-effects of the celebration do not offer an inspiration to the readers and interpreters of these historical events. This is rather an almost degrading discourse that would be most happily forgotten. A degrading tribute describes Leandra's funeral, too. Her final journey, delayed and rerouted by the royal parade—"Hasta el caminito del cementerio hubo de ser contrariada en sus direcciones y deseos la pobre doña Leandra"—is characterized by a "precipitación irreverente" (3:510). Her pallbearers place her abruptly "en el nicho donde sus pobres cenizas debían labrarse, con ayuda del tiempo, la petrificación del olvido" (3:510). Cristeta but briefly renders "a sus amiga difunta el tributo de sus lágrimas," until "no pudo contener . . . su ardoroso afán de echar de sus labios un par de renglones de página histórica" (3:507). History continues its ever degenerating dis-course, learning nothing from the past that is now ashes, forgotten, smudged, and rendered meaningless as soon as it is written.

Just as Cristeta mixes her tears and prayers with her narration of the wedding, on the way back from the cemetery two other inveterate historians of the series, Centurión and Milagro, "hablaron de política y del duelo de los Carrasco, entremez-

Chapter One

clando ambos asuntos por exigencias ineludibles del discurso'' (3:510). Their discourse, this text, demands the interchange and indeterminacy among history and fiction, Eufrasia and Isabel II, marriage and adultery, life and death. Just as these discourses are interchangeable, so the wedding and funeral processions— the respective journeys of the historical and fictional plots— converge once again in the final scenes of the series. The third series ends as it begins, in the deaths of Leandra and Ulibarri. It begins in a temporal disjunction—in medias res—of the Carlist War and Fago's fatal pursuit of himself and his past. These are destructively romantic impulses as illusory as Cristeta's final romanticized projection into the future of the monarchs' reign. And just as the first volume begins in a journey that will never reach an end, so the last closes with Milagro and Centurión suspended in their return home from the cemetery, and with Isabel and Francisco embarking on a new course in the ship of Spain. In its characters, journeys, translations—of Leandra's body to its soon-to-be-forgotten grave or of the monarchical relics to the ''borrón'' of Atocha in these last cases, and in the narratives offered as truths by characters like Cristeta, *Bodas reales* comprises a gloss on the entire series. Through irony and caustic parody, this *Episodio* retraces, reinterprets, and rewrites those characters, translations, and journeys which precede it.

The revised interpretations that *Bodas reales* offers of the third series also encompass, though more obliquely, the journeys, heroes, heroines, narrators, and metaphors of the first two series. It is impossible to avoid reading one character in another, to avoid the journey from one *Episodio* to the ones that are already read and to those yet to be explored. The reader is caught in the inextricable weave of these texts, just as are Leandra or Cristeta. In the third series the ship of Spain, the Quijote figures like Nelet or Leandra, the texts of history or novel, are condemned to pursue their ceaseless, often aimless, always endless, course of writing. This is the inescapable condition of language itself. Frank writes of

an old metaphoric tradition which conceives of literature in terms of navigation—as the casting off and venturing forth

98

of an *ingenii barca* into the unexplored regions of interi-
ority. As Derrida has shown for the navigation metaphor—
which is often held to be the embodiment of poetic language—the figure of carrying over . . . of translation . . .
from one expression to another takes recourse in the linguistic play of navigation: "The figure of the vessel or of
the boat . . . was so often the exemplary vehicle of rhetorical pedagogy." As soon as the play of metaphor becomes
autonomous—but was it not always so, as the processes of
linguistic transformation evidence?—there is no longer
any possibility of controlling the transfer. . . . The aim-
lessly drifting ship begins its passage upon the tide of
speech itself, and poetic speech makes conscious this process as such. . . . The endlessness of the trip clearly becomes a problem in the interminability of writing itself.
Literature reflects its own condition when it de-limits . . .
the metaphor of the journey of life.[39]

All of the symbolic and temporal projections of the third series
demonstrate such an awareness of the unlimited and endless
writing process.

The journeys of these ten *Episodios Nacionales* constitute
both symbolic and temporal expressions of the path of writing.
But at the same time, these projections are illusions. The structure of the series, which begins in the middle and ends with
Cristeta's retracing of an elusive and absent origin, the disasso-
ciative effect of the epistolary novel, or the chain of "episodes"
themselves, describe their own constituting and structuring processes. Temporal organizations are only another interpretation,
one more type of narration, not a group of definitively traceable
causes and effects. The documents in Beltrán's archives that
translate into Fernando Calpena's origin reveal the ultimately
irreducible textuality of Calpena himself, as word, character, fiction, and history. In the journey from letter to letter, syllable to
syllable, word to word, symbol to symbol, in the third series,
the weave of textual relations constantly does and undoes itself,
through the play of identity and difference, metaphor and irony,
parallel and parody, presence and absence. Fago's search for and

flight from "Mé," Beltrán's pots of gold, Nelet's ruins of history, Cristeta's original testimony, and many other elements in the third series continually illustrate how the pursuit of meaning, whether in another, in the past, or in oneself are idealized historical or artistic explanations. They offer no ultimate truth, no return home, and no complete sign.

Women and Writing
in the Fourth Series

Almost every critic who has written about the fourth series of Galdós's *Episodios nacionales* notes the differences in novelistic procedure that appear to set it apart from the preceding series. The fourth series, written between 1902 and 1907, seems to lack the cohesive artistic unity of plot development that characterizes, for the most part, the first three series. These ten novels display a marked decrease in the number of historical references, and a distinct change of tone.[1] Most notably, the series lacks a protagonist whose activities serve as the focus of the plot extended through most of the novels, in the manner of Gabriel Araceli, Salvador Monsalud, and, although not as extensively, Fernando Calpena. The major male characters who could be designated as protagonists of the fourth series—Pepe Fajardo, Santiuste, Diego Ansúrez, and Santiago Ibero—exhaust their leading roles in one, or at most two, novels. Yet even more than through their relatively brief participation in the series, these characters differ from their episodic predecessors through their lack of "heroic" properties. While there surely is ambiguity in the heroism of Araceli, Monsalud, Calpena, and the others, there is still a conventional and more or less persistent reference to the heroic stock type. In the fourth series, only Santiago Ibero manages to achieve something of a typically heroic stature at the last, but this is hardly of the consistency of previous protagonists, including his father in the third series. The absence of a sustaining and heroic protagonist in the fourth series has several important ramifications. The period of history to which these historical novels correspond—the adult reign of Isabel II, 1848–1868—is one of decadence, immorality, and spiritual anticlimax. So if the protagonists are to continue to characterize the spirit of the age as they have in the previous *Episodios*, they must represent "abulia," as Pepe Fajardo does, or decadent "quijotismo" and ineffective "donjuanismo," as Santiuste does.

There is another—and apparently overlooked—consideration suggested by the absence of the heroic and of the hero. A host of female figures comes to fill the protagonistic void, with roles just as prominent as, if not more prominent than, those of the male characters of the fourth series.[2] There are monarchs like Isabel II or María Cristina, nuns like Sor Catalina or Dominiciana Paredes, upper and middle class women of more or less virtuous comportment like María Ignacia, Eufrasia, Virginia, or Valeria, courtesans and prostitutes of diverse categories like Teresa Villaescusa, Manolita Pez, or the Hermosilla sisters, and any number of other women from different ranks, vocations, and religions, such as Lucila, Antoñita, Donata, Yohar, Mara, or Mazaltob. But whatever their stations, their activities are the axis around which most of the novelistic and historical interest in the fourth series revolves. The focus on women is appropriate to the fourth series because it deals with Isabel II's reign. Its portrayals of her and the other women characters illustrate the social, political, and moral contradictions associated with this period of Spanish history. These characters serve as the focal point for the multiple levels of historical and artistic meaning that distinguish Galdós's novels. This chapter will treat primarily Lucila Ausúrez and Teresa Villaescusa, respectively, and their relationships to Isabel II and various other characters in the series. The processes by which these fictional and historical protagonists are associated display inevitably the narrative mechanisms and strategies of the discourse, in its fictional and historical guises.

THE SOVEREIGN CONTRADICTION OF ISABEL II

The interplay of identity and difference inherent in the associations of fictional and historical plots and characters is nowhere more evident in the fourth series than in the figure of Isabel II. Isabel II represents many things: the monarchy, Spanish society and politics of her reign, the religious and moral conventions of her time. The individual women characters that revolve around her represent one or another of these aspects, too. Both they and

Isabel II usually represent certain features and their opposites at the same time. Pepe Fajardo labels Isabel II "síntesis del espa-ñolismo" (3:707); even more, she is a "synthesis of the contra-dictions" found in the Spain of which she is protagonist.

Such a synthesis of contradictions appears in all the feminine characters that populate the fourth series. One of the most il-luminating comparisons of another character with Isabel II is found in Lucila Ansúrez, "la celtíbera." Read together, Isabel and Lucila present a broad commentary on each other and on Spain. Most important, the interpenetration of these two char-acters describes the process of the historical novel. Throughout the fourth series, Lucila and Isabel are juxtaposed in the con-sciousness of the historian Pepe Fajardo. At important points in the narrative they even become indistinguishable to him. These points frequently coincide with momentous historical events such as Merino's attempt on the queen's life, the birth of Prince Alfonso, the July Revolution, or Isabel's departure from Spain in 1868. The narrative passages that offer the most extended and nearly simultaneous focus on Isabel and Lucila have historical reference to the "Ministerio relámpago" of 1849. It is during these moments in the novel *Narváez* that Fajardo sees them as most alike, and that the private and public history depicted through these two characters approach each other most closely in his mind. Because of this merger, and because of Fajardo's roles as historian and novelist, such passages serve as commen-taries on the art of writing historical novels and on the nature of history.[3] These passages reveal many of Galdós's most so-phisticated narrative techniques and contain numerous explic-itly stated theoretical concerns regarding the writing of novels and of history, and the way in which they are or can be read. What results from the merger of Lucila and Isabel is a theory of narrative, of the role of point of view in history and in fiction, and of the individual's ability to penetrate the truth of life or art. Fajardo's account of private and public history, of Lucila and Isabel II, and of his own problems in seeing their truths and in writing about them, is a lesson in history telling and history reading.

Narváez, the second *Episodio* in the fourth series, contains Fajardo's first encounters with Lucila and Isabel II. Lucila, the feminine representative of the Ansúrez clan, is, as those who have written about this character have noted, a symbol of Spain. According to Ventura Miedes, the "sabiotonto" historian (3:631), she belongs to "esta soberana raza, la más bella, . . . la mejor construida en estéticas proporciones, . . . la que mejor personifica la dignidad humana, la indómita raza que no consiente yugo de tiranos" (3:634). The symbolism here is poignant and ironic. Spain, the Ansúrez family, does indeed rebel against tyranny and eventually ousts Isabel II. Yet this is only in order to replace one tyrant with another in an endless repetition of the same mistakes, as was observed in *Bodas reales*. When there is no monarch to play the role of tyrant, the Spanish people become their own, as the events following the revolution of 1868 will reveal.

Despite the overt or covert subjugation of the Spaniards by their own follies, there are still to be found remnants of the innate dignity of the race, such as the Ansúrez family, and especially Lucila.[4] The above passage subtly initiates an identification between Lucila, Isabel, and the "pueblo español," which intensifies as the narrative progresses.[5] Lucila, "un tanto desdeñosa" (3:634), and Isabel II are both nineteen years old when Fajardo first sees them. The Ansúrez family is a "soberana raza;" it is the "original" "pueblo español" (3:634). Lucila, as Spain, "pueblo," and "la celtíbera," is "soberana," just like Isabel. This term is applied numerous times to both Lucila and Isabel throughout the fourth series, as well as to many other women characters who thus participate in this system of repetition and difference. For example, Fajardo tells how his wife, María Ignacia, has a "soberana filosofía" (3:693) that maintains separate rules of conjugal behavior for the husband and the wife. In the next paragraph, Fajardo describes the "soberana hipocresía" of his sophisticated, highly immoral mistress Eufrasia's behavior in hiding their affair from the public eye. The application of the word "soberana" therefore varies within a few sentences; it associates two characters at opposite ends of the moral spectrum, Eufrasia and Ignacia, who come together, nevertheless, in society. They are also associated sexually through Fajardo, just as are Isabel and Lucila in his imagination. The behaviors deemed sovereign entail their contradictions too: maintaining separate norms of marital behavior, like hypocrisy, is inherently contradictory. In passages like these a single term serves as the axis around which several women characters—Isabel, Lucila, Eufrasia, and María Ignacia—and the divergent material, social, and moral codes that they incorporate come together and are "synthesized." The conflict latent in such a synthesis, however, is also demonstrated by the term "soberana," as it is by many other terms to be discussed in this chapter.

After Fajardo's first vision of Lucila in a ruined castle there is a disastrous storm, beginning with "un relámpago" (3:638) that destroys the crops of the village of Atienza. When Fajardo mentally bids farewell to "la más bella representación del alma hispana," he addresses the "imagen de la errante Lucila, mentira de la realidad y verdad casi desnuda que pasaste como un relámpago de hermosura entre el polvo de los deshechos terrones" (3:654). Both Lucila's "relámpago de hermosura"—which instigates Fajardo's mental "trastornos"—and the physical "relámpago"—which announces nature's destruction—foreshadow the "Ministerio relámpago." That name designates the short-lived ministry of 19 October 1849 that becomes an emblem of the spiritually, morally, and materially destructive aspects of Isabel II's reign. Thus another term, "relámpago," associates Isabel with Lucila, and both characters, interchangeably, with the fictional and the historical plots of the series.

Ventura Miedes and Fajardo both see Lucila as the representation of the Spanish people and of history: "Y como la Historia es la figura y trazas del pueblo, ved a *Illipulicia* en la forma de pueblo más gallardo. Sabed que todo pueblo es descalzo, y que la Historia es más bella cuanto más desnuda" (3:647).[6] Lucila is unclothed history, unshod pueblo, nearly naked truth. These ambiguous and suggestive metaphors have various meanings for Isabel and Spain, its people, and its history. They also comment on the nature of truth, "mentira de la realidad." Reality belies truth, or, as María Ignacia and Fajardo discuss at the end of *Narváez*, truth is never present in reality (3:730). The sexual implications in these descriptions of Miedes's and Fajardo's imagined goddess—which become most explicit when Fajardo jokes about undressing and washing Lucila (3:640–41)—continue throughout the fourth series. As a result, Isabel II and Lucila, history and fiction, become metaphorically interchangeable through sexual terminology.[7] This interchange is observable in virtually all of the female characters of the series—Dominiciana Paredes, Mazoltob, Donata, Valeria, Eufrasia, etc., and particularly Teresa Villaescusa, as will be seen. It is not only characters, but the political, military, economic, fictional, and historical plots of the series that are described, at least in part, in sexual terms. Such pervasive sexual innuendo underscores what is a major concern of the fourth series, the morality of Isabel II and of society at all levels. Only María Ignacia, Fajardo's ugly, yet clearheaded wife, among all the major female characters in the series, escapes without the stigma of adultery, prostitution, or celestinism.

Religion does not elude the series's extensive sexual associations either. The figure of Lucila also suggests the integration of sexual and religious codes. Miedes's delirium pictures Lucila as a "virginal sacerdotisa, la diosa casta, en quien está representada el alma ibera, el alma española" (3:647). This sentence has ironic applications to Isabel, too, and even more to the nuns who play such an important role in the historical and fictional events. For example, Sor Catalina de los Desposorios masterminds the wealthy marriage of her brother Fajardo. Dominiciana Paredes is an ex-nun, who appropriates Lucila's lover, Bartolomé Gracián, in *Los duendes de la camarilla* and also serves as a courier between palace and convent. Both of these nuns function as counterparts to Sor Patrocinio, the infamous stigmatic who had such a disastrous influence over the throne. The concealed corruption of the convents, their influence on political events, and the social acceptability of pious promiscuity practiced by individuals from all social classes are objects of criticism throughout the series, where nuns and other religious figures often take on

Celestina-like or even diabolical characteristics and appear as primary sources of society's ills.[8]

The terms that connect Isabel, Lucila, and Spain comment on Spanish politics, society, and history in general. If Spain's true history resides in its "pueblo," then the official politics that presume to write the history of Spain are false. Eufrasia says that Spain's politics are a "masquerada" (3:677). This term recalls her role at the masked ball where she impersonated Fajardo's Italian lover, Berberina, in the first *episodio* of the series, *Las tormentas del 48*. Fajardo likens entering politics to putting on "un vestido elegante o un lucido uniforme social" (3:677). In other words, official politics is a role, uniform, or mask, which contrasts with authentic Spain, the "pueblo," symbolized by Lucila's scanty dress in Atienza. When in Madrid Fajardo first glimpses the "soberana imagen" of Lucila (3:685), he sees that she "vestía como las hijas del pueblo más elegantes, entre manola y señorita" (3:685). He then compares this vision of her to the women of his class, with the result that "hasta las señoras se me hacen odiosas y soberanamente grotescas con sus modas de París y el artificio vano de su exótica finura" (4:688). In this passage the terms "soberanamente grotescas" associate very diverse connotations regarding the sovereignty of the grotesque and the grotesqueness of the sovereign. They suggest the contradiction in high society between exterior grandeur and interior degradation and, above all, the contradiction in a sovereign who is at once noble and ignoble, pious and immoral, naive and tyrannical. Isabel II synthesizes Spain's history, but she is also its antithesis or anticlimax. Ultimately Isabel II is no more than a reflection of majesty, not majesty herself. She is a mere shadow of a queen—a "soberana imagen"—and like the fictional Lucila, the Isabel II of the *Episodios nacionales* is a verbal image—simply words. Likewise, the history of her reign is nothing but images on paper, traces of events that have forever disappeared. The fourth series is a statement about Isabel II through the fictional characters who seek to describe her and about the relationship between words and events, fiction, and reality. The merger of Lucila and Isabel reveals the "mentira de la realidad" in general: everything that seems real—clothing, conventions, majesty, history—is only the appearance of truth; reality and truth are not the same. Casalduero acutely observes that "movido por su nueva orientación estética, al escribir la cuarta serie de *Episodios* ya no se propone la interpretación de los hechos históricos que narra, lo que quiere es adentrarse en el alma española. Una cosa es lo que se propone y otra lo que consigue" (155). Fajardo seeks out Lucila, who seems to symbolize Spain's soul, just as others seek the causes of the "Ministerio relámpago." But just as he cannot find her, and just as no one can identify Isabel's true motives or the causes of such events, so the desire to know true history is doomed to frustration. Fajardo seeks, in sexual terms, to "penetrar" the truth, "posesionar" and "dominar" Lucila. His failure is like that of both historians and readers; it is like the failure of the written word to capture, to be, or to beget the truth. The vision of Spain's history here in *Narváez* and in the fourth series as a whole, through Isabel, Lucila, and many other characters, is that it is perhaps only "la mentira de la realidad." "La verdad desnuda" is beyond the grasp of the novelist, the historian, and the reader alike.

Fajardo's first glimpse of Isabel II, the first textual reference to her, links her to Lucila in beauty, a certain "pueblo" attitude, and, of course, her "aire soberano":

> No he visto mujer más atractiva que Isabel II, ni que posea más finas redes para cautivar los ánimos. Pienso que una gran parte de sus encantos los debe a la conciencia de su posición, al libre uso de la palabra para anticipar un pensamiento al de los demás, lo que ayuda ciertamente a la adquisición de majestad o aire soberano. . . . Es la síntesis del españolismo y el producto de las más brillantes épocas históricas. (3:706–707)

At this moment in *Narváez*, she is a product of Spain's brilliant history, a synthesis. But her degeneration, like that of Spain, calls into question both the nature of such a synthesis and the brilliance of the past.[9] In this instance, too, Isabel's facile use of words, which lends her an "aire soberano," questions the stability of the definition of the term "soberano." She speaks with "soberana modestia de gran persona" (3:709) while explaining to Fajardo why she mistook him for someone else. The collocation of the terms "soberana" and "modestia" in this context is satirically incongruous, given the other possible applications of these terms to the queen. Isabel's own discourse is unconsciously self-satirizing. She claims that she was merely "víctima de un error" (3:708); however, she was clearly a victim of her own mistake. Here, as with the events of the "Relámpago," the first act of her majority in *Bodas reales*, and all the other disasters of her reign, Isabel II is perhaps only a victim of herself.[10] She tells Fajardo that "lo único que como Reina me han enseñado es el conocimiento de las personas. . . . En este arte he sido siempre muy segura" (3:709). She remarks on her faulty education in two ways here: first, that this was the only thing that she was taught; and second, inadvertently, that she is obviously not very sure even of this "art." After the tumultuous change of ministry, Isabel's apologizers attribute the fiasco to Sor Patrocinio and her cohorts, who must have employed an "encantamiento que imprisionaba su soberano albedrío" (3:719). This phrase functions in the same incongruous way as does "soberana modestia."

The identities and differences that traverse Isabel, Lucila, and Spain are manifested in many ways: in structural proximities of characters, parallels in plot developments and character descriptions, and above all in narrative style, such as the repetition of key words and phrases. The often ironic, usually incriminating effect that these strategies have on the creation of Isabel II's character suggests that the critical view of Galdós's depiction of the queen in the *Episodios* as being highly favorable is rather simplistic.[11] Isabel II's characterization is as contradictory as her reign and as any history of Spain. The picture that emerges of her, although not devoid of sympathy, is too replete with irony to be deemed favorable. While Fajardo's first description of her is as "brilliant synthesis," their encounters belie this interpretation. Isabel's supercilious conversation—in which she skips from subject to subject like a "pájaro" (3:711) or a "mariposa" (3:712)—reveal her fickleness and frivolity. It is clear from Fa-

jardo's interviews with her that she is, indeed, in large part a
victim of her birth and education. Nonetheless, she manipulates
the conversation, just as she manipulates the people surrounding her in the palace: "El movimiento de las figuras que com-
ponían la reunión era determinado por la Reina" (3:712). And
so, it is implied, might she manipulate the government. This
early characterization of Isabel II foreshadows the change of
government that lasted only one day, as well as the frequency
of such changes (though generally of slightly longer duration)
that typified her reign.[12]

   The fourth series portrays Isabel II's self-conception as both
apparently modest and cognizant of shortcomings, yet also supremely self-deceptive (or merely unconcerned). At one point
she says that it is more comfortable simply not to think about
anything (3:713). This remark follows her conversation with
Fajardo about choosing advisors and following the impulses of
her heart. Although she admits that "no es fácil percibir la verdad en medio de esta grillería" of the palace, she trusts in God
and believes that "Dios no abandona a Isabel II, Dios quiere a
Isabel II" (3:713). This is ironic in light of the denouement of
her reign, and also in view of her description of the nature of
God's favor:

> La verdad es que Dios me ha traído al mundo con bendición,
> pues bendición es el sinnúmero de personas honradas que
> me han defendido, me defienden y me defenderán en lo que
> me quede de reinado. He sido muy dichosa. . . . Tú calcula
> los miles de hombres que se han dejado matar por mí, y los
> que aún harán lo mismo cuando llegue el caso, que ojalá no
> llegue. . . . Por eso quiero yo tanto al pueblo español, y
> créelo, estoy siempre pensando en él. . . . ¡Qué pueblo tan
> bueno!, ¿verdad? El me adora y yo le adora a él. (3:712–13)

Her superficial and egotistical view of the bloodshed of Spain
during the First Carlist War indicates the self-interested moti-
vation of her professed love for the "pueblo." It also satirizes
conventional notions that God mandates or directs this bloodshed, and those who defend such beliefs. Isabel II's love for
Spain, like her belief in God, reveals above all her vanity. An

ironic and humorous identification of the terms Isabel II, Lucila, Spain, and God is achieved when Isabel remarks that God is "soberanamente bondadoso" (3:713).

One of Fajardo's last encounters with Isabel before she leaves for exile in France, at the end of the fourth series in *La de los tristes destinos*, displays once again, at best, the ambiguous treatment of the queen. He sees that her eyes reveal her "absoluto desengaño, los ojos de un alma que ha venido a parar en el conocimiento enciclopédico de cuantos estímulos están vedados a la inocencia" (4:127). This recalls Fajardo's description of Eufrasia's eyes in the first novel of the series, *Las tormentas del 48*: "vi que en mí clavaba sus negros ojos, y en ellos se me reveló su soberano talento, su apasionado corazón . . . y su profunda inmoralidad. . . . Eran sus ojos el signo de los tiempos" (3:616). Eyes are another one of the many terms of association between the women characters and the plots of the fourth series (see also, for example, 3:716 and 733). The moral ambiguity that accompanies these references to "ojos" or "ojos del alma" functions as an ironic application of traditional associations of the eyes as the surest instrument of knowledge, or of the eyes of the soul as a metaphor for insight or spiritual knowledge.

Repeated terms such as "soberano," relámpago" and "ojos" are linguistic indicators that mark connections between apparently diverse elements. A relationship of one to many is achieved through these common terms. One term applied in many contexts necessarily associates all those contexts, those texts. The repetition of the term allows a reinterpretation of each text according to the other. The consequences of this linguistic play are not simply literary, but historiographical, epistemological, and moral.

THE INTERPENETRATION OF HISTORY AND FICTION
THROUGH THE MYSTERIOUS
TRUTHS OF *NARVÁEZ*

Many words create identifications between Lucila, Isabel II, other women characters, and the diverse meanings that they suggest for such labels as history and novel. The terms "misterio," "enigma," and "secreto" are used repeatedly by various characters in *Narváez* with reference to Lucila's disappearance, the events surrounding the "Ministerio relámpago," and to the general existence or nature of truth, history, Spain, and the ideal. "Misterio," "secreto," and "enigma" at times also substitute for "historia," "verdad," and "alma." These mysteries are the objects of endless pursuit by Fajardo and others. Repeated verbs like "penetrar," "descubrir," "posesionar," "apoderarse," and "dominar" describe his pursuit. These verbs join the political and philosophical concerns in the narrative with the sexual connotations of Fajardo's search for Lucila, a search that constitutes an allegory of the possession or apprehension of beauty, truth, and the ideal. Such verbs are frequently interchangeable with "escribir" and "traducir," for example: "¡El vivir del pueblo, el vivir de los reyes! ¿Quién la ha podido penetrar y menos escribir?" (3:730). In numerous passages like these, the plots of the search for the truth of the "Ministerio relámpago" and of Lucila's whereabouts are inextricable from the emplotment of Fajardo as would-be historian of himself, Isabel II, and Lucila. Moreover, these plots enter into the confluence of values, roles and functions that constitute the history writer in general. But where terms like the above mark the unattainability of truth, the text is also filled with repeated terms, traditionally applied to literary creation, that seem to imply its successful apprehension. "Inspiración," "imaginación," "representación," "representar," "imaginar," "vislumbrar," "cerrar ojos y representar," and the impulses of the "corazón" often appear to approximate truth more closely than the processes of active investigation. Yet these insights and approximations can also be misleading.

Isabel II tells Fajardo that "no hay guía como nuestro corazón" to find "la verdad" and that "no queda más que la inspiración, y pedir a Dios que me dirija" (3:713). This scene parallels the subsequent confrontation between Eufrasia and Fajardo after the events of the "Relámpago." There, Eufrasia, "actuando de ideal dictadora," assures Fajardo that Isabel only signed the decree because of "el misterio más impenetrable"

(3:726). She alludes to a secret liaison: "Voy a decírtelo, y per-
dóneme Dios esta sospecha, esta . . . inspiración. Para mí, se
apoderaron de un secreto de la Reina, y con ese secreto, . . . la
han amenazado" (3:726). Fajardo responds: "la captación in-
fame del secreto, ¿a quién la atribuyes? Tu lógica infernal . . .
seguimos en el melodrama . . . tu lógica, como aguja imantada
por los demonios, ¿señala un punto fijo? ¿Es Fulgencio, es la
monja?" (3:726). The text never reveals whether these inspira-
tions or visions of Isabel, Eufrasia, Patrocinio, and others are to
be read as divine or diabolical, "inspiración celestial" or "lógica
infernal," true or false, historical or melodramatic. No one
interpretation, inspiration, historical account, or verisimilar
representation remains fixed in the text. Rather, there is a constant alternation among contradictory accounts. Truth, or its
approximation, is a synthesis of contradictions, a mixture of lie
and fact, of the marvelous and the mundane. The eyes of the
soul—Eufrasia's, Isabel's, Patrocinio's, Lucila's—may reflect
either the sovereign or the grotesque.

The passage quoted above suggests how historical events take
on the appearance of a fictional account—here a "melodrama,"
in other places a "folletín" or a "comedia." If Spain's official
history is a lie—"la Historia oficial, académica y mentirosa"
(3:714)—then perhaps the penny-novel or fantastic versions of
historical events may be more accurate. Terms denoting truth,
history, and so on, conventionally stand as antonyms of those
denoting fiction, lies, etc. Yet in *Narváez* and the entire fourth
series, these polarities are not so easily fixed. María Cristina's
label of "folletín" for Spanish history (3:714), like María Ignacia's of "comedia" (3:730), suggest not that they see history as
false, but rather absurd. When the marqués de Molíns recounts
his inside view of the events immediately surrounding the "Relámpago," he does so "con elegancia narrativa" (3:719). Fajardo
remarks that the vulgar political event (hyperbolically or sarcas-
tically labeled "crisis," 3:720ff, and "contracrisis," 3:724) "habría carecido totalmente de interés si el cuentadante no hubiera
marcado muy bien en el relato la nota patética, que acrecía su
valor histórico" (3:720). The effect on the audience is an in-

creasing appreciation of an otherwise absurd and trivial occur-
rence: "Maravillados escucharon todos esta relación, y la crítica
del suceso adquirió un tinte compasivo. No quedaba duda de que
las circunstancias y resortes misteriosos, que los de fuera no po-
dían penetrar, constreñían a Isabel II a cambiar de Gobierno"
(3:720). Such remarks evaluate historical accounts by their literary style. Turning history into literature is the process, of
course, of the *Episodios nacionales;* remarks like these reinscribe the work in which they appear. They also serve to parody
the history that cannot resist investing historical events with
melodrama. And this parody constitutes a criticism of the
whitewashing of Isabel II's reign by official history and of that
historiography which appeals to sentiment or uses other rhetorical tactics in order to increase interest.[13]

Idealizing, making literary, or aggrandizing the trivial and
vulgar in historical discourse is precisely what Fajardo does with
Lucila, what Miedes does with his etymologies, and what historiography does when it selects and defines which documents
are important and which are not. When the level-headed María
Ignacia recounts her version of the events of the "Relámpago"
to Fajardo, she insists that there is no mystery: "No hay nada
más que lo que se ve." Fajardo responds: "Si lo sucedido fuese
tan vulgar, no valdría la pena de contarlo. Hay algo más"
(3:730). He wants novelistic, fictional interest in a vulgar, historical affair. His desire is what leads him to idealize Isabel II, in
spite of her perceived shortcomings. He sees her as more real
than the hypocrites who surround her, including himself: "las
conversaciones con personas reales le llevan a uno a las mayores
hipocresías del pensamiento y a las más chabacanas formas del
lenguaje. Sólo la Reina, con su libre iniciativa y su arte deliciosa
para revestir de gracia la etiqueta, rompía la entonada vulgaridad
de hablar palatino" (3:712). Isabel, too, sees the hypocritical
world that surrounds her. She closes her eyes to this truth in
order to represent a better one: "muchas veces, cuando estoy
solita, cierro los ojos y procuro borrar de mi memoria las caras
que comúnmente veo. . . . Pues lo hago para representarme el
pueblo, de quien sale todo, los pobrecitos españoles" (3:713).

Her husband Francisco asks Fajardo to write "una *Historia de España* verdad" and "una Historia imparcial" (3:714). He describes a plan which coincides, except for its beginning in 1814, with that of the *Episodios nacionales*. And Isabel declares: "Yo aspiro a que de mi reinado se cuenten maravillas" (3:714). She does not define "maravillas" as falsehoods, because for her this term does not oppose the impartial or the true. The interplay of identity and difference among the qualifications impartial, true, and marvelous illustrate the equivocal definition and function of history itself.

Isabel II's request for a marvelous history prefigures the *Historia lógico-natural de los españoles de ambos mundos en el siglo XIX* that Juan Santiuste (or *Confusio*) will begin to write in *Prim* and *La de los tristes destinos*, the last two volumes of the fourth series. Santiuste's *Historia* attempts to correct the factors that contributed to Isabel's disastrous reign and the revolution that Prim led to overthrow it. It is thus an ironic counterpoint to the depiction of Isabel II in those *Episodios*, just as those last two volumes of the series are a counterpoint to the first ones; they describe the very characteristics of her story that the Isabel II of *Narváez* did not foresee. Santiuste's *Historia* also forms an ironic commentary on the *Episodios* overall in several ways.

Fajardo describes Santiuste's project:

> escribir la Historia de España, no como es, sino como debiera ser, singular manía que demuestra el brote de un cerebro brutalmente paradójico y humorístico. . . . En su estilo no se advierte ninguna extravagancia; en la narración de los hechos está lo verdaderamente anormal y graciosamente vesánico, porque *Confusio* no escribe la Historia, sino que la inventa, la compone con arreglo a lógica, dentro del principio de que los sucesos son como deben ser. (4:29)

Geoffrey Ribbans's incisive 1982 discussion of Santiuste's history, "La historia como debiera ser," sees it as "a further critical dimension of the *episodios*." He writes:

115

the presence of an idealistic dreamer like Santiuste or of an ultra-conscious critic from within the system like Fajardo does not add to the realism of the presentation. Their value is not primarily documental, mimetic, symbolic or psychological but contrasting and universalizing. . . . *Confusio's* history, then, has the function of establishing a distance from the *faits-divers* of history by encompassing them within a more universal, specifically Aristotelian, framework.[14]

Although Ribbans's use of the Aristotelian distinction between poetry and history assumes that there is a true history, his insights into Santiuste's narrative reveal how it encourages the reader to look critically at that history, even if he does not reject its truth. He writes that Santiuste's "counter-history casts unexpected light on the true history and enables readers to readjust their sights about historical events" (272). He believes that Santiuste "was confounding a rigorous deterministic concept of Spanish history while it was actually evolving" (272).

It seems clear that Santiuste's narrative is not just a counter-history within the *Episodios nacionales*. It is a reinscription of the process of the *Episodios*, which are themselves always counter to conventional history, even as they seem to narrate it. Fajardo's comment that it is not Santiuste's style that is exaggerated, but the events that are abnormal, certainly suggests many of the events of the third and fourth series already discussed here and prefigures the wild stretches of imagination that the fifth series portray. Moreover, Fajardo's description of the intensive humoristical and paradoxical mind of the narrator of *La historia lógico-natural* could be easily applied to the narrator of any of the *Episodios*. The *Episodios nacionales* constantly question the events and perceptions called history. They are thus always poetic, in Aristotelian terms, and always counter-histories as well. Santiuste's history epitomizes the entire project of the *Episodios* because it demythifies history by exposing itself as another myth.

The interchangeability of the terms history, truth, fiction, and lie, as employed by Isabel II, María Cristina, Francisco, Fajardo, or *Confusio*, confuses their conventional connotations and values. This economy of indeterminate definitions of history and fiction also includes the codes that traverse and thus constitute that historical novel as text. Just as sex and religion are interpenetrating codes in the series, so are religion and storytelling and sex and storytelling interwoven and interchangeable. When Isabel is outlining her plan for Fajardo's history of Spain, she says that after he writes his "relación verídica, escrita con talento" it will be "revisada por personas peritas y autorizada por la Iglesia. . . . Y la publicación de esa obra no faltará quien la patrocine" (3:714). The connection between historical discourse, truth, and the Church— especially Sor Patrocinio— is clear. Through the fourth series, the Church, divine inspiration, and even God are depicted as purveyors of a truth that is at best ambiguous. The last scene of *Narváez* succinctly identifies the conflicts between religion, truth, history, fiction, Spain, Lucila, and Isabel II.

Fajardo goes to the convent in search of Lucila, since his informer, Gambito, led him to believe that she was there. Because of a speech impediment, Gambito's syntax is twisted, his ideas come out "al revés." After listening to him, Fajardo determines to "traducir que Lucila está en el convento de Jesús" (3:732). He hopes that "de esta horrible jerga sale una verdad, la presencia de *Illipulicia*," but his search for his ideal is again fruitless. What he does witness in the convent is a ceremony in which Sor Catalina and Sor Patrocinio participate, before they are to be interrogated about their roles in the "Relámpago." He describes "la famosa Patrocinio, cuyo semblante iluminaban los cirios próximos. . . . En verdad que la monja de las llagas me pareció hermosa, y su grave continente, su mirar penetrante . . . eran el exterior emblema de un soberano poder político y social" (3:733). She utters "alguna frase mística" that Fajardo cannot understand, "tanta unción y misterio quiso poner en ella" (3:733). Fajardo pursues the truth that is Lucila, but instead he finds Patrocinio, the imposter who "inspires" Isabel II. The conjunction of the terms "mirar," "penetrar," "soberano," and "misterio" in this passage determines their respective values. Fajardo remarks that he did not find truth, only the surface of things: "si había yo visto un hermoso cuadro de la vida española, faltábame ver el corazón y la interna fibra de aquel extraño asunto" (3:733). But he still maintains the hope that he will: "la verdad estaba próxima: Yo la descubriría pronto; yo encontraría la representación viva del alma española. Lucila se acercaba" (3:734). But as the denouement of the fourth series reveals, he never does possess Lucila, nor does the reader learn "esa verdad que se nos oculta" (3:734) regarding the "Relámpago." Fajardo's search is not unlike Fago's in the third series for the elusive "Mé," the text of history whose trace is always beyond reach. The last word of *Narváez* is "Amanecía," but this dawn never sheds enough light to illuminate the truth of Lucila, Isabel II, the Spanish soul, or history.[15]

TRACING LUCILA IN THE ORIGINAL WORDS OF HISTORY

At various times, Fajardo, María Ignacia, Eufrasia, Isabel II, and Francisco de Asís discuss how history should be written, and if it can be. Isabel believes that it should be written as it occurs (3:714), the king believes that it is better written after the fact (3:714), and Fajardo believes that it is impossible to write, even while he is in the act of doing so (3:730). When the writing of history is discussed, Fajardo imagines truth represented by Lucila, for example: "veo la historia interna de los pueblos, la historia verdad, representada en una mujer vestida de ninfa, de diosa" (3:727; see also 654, 687, 714–15, 716–17). Eufrasia is an "historiadora" (3:726) who creates an origin for the "Ministerio relámpago" simply by naming it, when she says "Bien se le puede llamar *el Ministerio relámpago*." Fajardo notes: Ved aquí el origen de una denominación" (3:725). The function of the historian here is more to assign names than to record events. As in the third series, there is no origin, only the arbitrary designation of what begins with the designation itself. But if these designations, these words, are incapable of penetrating or possessing the truth, then the language of fiction or history is incapable of it also. Eufrasia's act of coining the term "Ministerio relámpago" has special relevance to the writing of novels, of histories, and to writing as process. The act of naming that marks the central historical event of *Narváez* serves to inscribe the discursive process of the *Episodios nacionales*.

From the beginning of *Narváez* the problematics of historical fiction is marked by the term "origen." Ventura Miedes seeks the origins of the Spanish race through etymologies, and he argues one theory at the expense of others. Modern philology, he avers, rejects the Latin origin of Castilian surnames, and hence he declares: "Búsquese el origen de nuestros apellidos en los troncos góticos o germanicales y sarracenos" (3:628). When searching for the origin of the Ansúrez clan, he rejects his first hypothesis of Arabic ancestry for that of a more remote and pure Celtiberian one:

> Dando vueltas en el magín a esta pícara idea, he venido a rectificar mi primera opinión, y, cayendo del burro de mis preocupaciones arábigas, opino y sustento que estos Ansúrez no tienen nada que ver con el caballero *Ab Assur* . . . y que su abolengo es celtíbero, pura y castizamente celtíbero, . . . tronco y fundador de los afamados vascones. (3:633)[16]

This is more than a parody of self-important pronouncements in philological polemics at the turn of the century; it is a comment on the historian who seeks to define the truth or the origin, and who believes that to specify an origin is to find historical truth. Any truth or origin, and consequently any historical objectivity, is a confluence of often contradictory events, just as Isabel II symbolizes a synthesis of historical epochs.

Miedes's search for the origin of the Ansúrez name and of the Spanish language foreshadows both Fajardo's pursuit of an idealized, elusive Lucila and of an illusory truth, and Eufrasia's act of naming the "Ministerio relámpago," in other words, the pursuit and the writing of history. Moreover Miedes's endeavors reflect on the historical accounts of Isabel II's reign; Miedes, Fajardo, and later Santiuste are the fictional counterparts to the flesh and blood historians who seek to find the origin of the problems of this period and of Spain's nature in general. The ambiguous treatment of origins continues throughout the fourth series. Lucila, in her own novel, *Los duendes de la camarilla*, often acts as a storyteller and frequently confuses the sequence of events. When her lover Gracián inquires about the beginning of her story, she replies "Cualquiera sabe dónde está el principio de las cosas" (3:738). The statement is applicable not only to Lucila's tale of palace and convent intrigue, but also to Isabel's reign and to the process of the *Episodios nacionales* as well. In the fourth series, as in the third, the events of one volume are often intelligible only retrospectively, from the vantage point of events recounted in a later novel. The process of rereading and reinterpreting mirrors that of writing and translating, as discussed in chapter 1; it is applicable, of course, to all forty-six volumes together. The *Episodios nacionales*, taken as a whole, appear as an enormous and complex puzzle, which Galdós skillfully works from novel to novel; its intricacy only begins to become apparent after rereading all of them. The various interpretations of the events of the "Ministerio relámpago" and Isabel II's role in them in *Narváez* range from the rumors of the populace (3:717ff), to Narváez's comment (3:720), to a conversation that Fajardo imagines between María Cristina and Isabel (3:728) that is reminiscent of the one imagined by Beltrán between María Cristina and Carlota in the third series. These attempts to decipher the mystery behind events, their origin or cause, like the efforts of Eufrasia and Fajardo or Fajardo and María Ignacia described above, always result in conflicting versions of Isabel and Sor Patrocinio. No one version, of course, is sufficient for Fajardo, or for the reader, nor does any one version dominate the others. Eufrasia's opinion that Isabel had a hidden sexual affair, María Ignacia's that she acted from mere inexperience, or Fajardo's that it is an enigma, a puzzle yet to be solved, are equally convincing or unconvincing, depending on the perspective. Neither *Narváez* nor the fourth series ever provides an unambiguous interpretation or resolution to the problem. The series refuses to lend either the historian or the novelist the privileged possession of truth, since neither the seemingly historical nor the clearly imaginary version is more valid than the other. Not even the historical novelist—Fajardo or Eufrasia, Galdós seems to write, perceives the unknown clearly. The incapacity of either fictional or historical discourse to uncover truth, and the paradoxes inherent in the endeavor, are underscored by Fajardo's own contradictions. A would-be historian who must resort to imagination, he searches for the hidden truth, but at other times states that it does not exist. After denying the truth of official history he says: "la que merece ser escrita es la del ser español, la del alma española, en la cual van confundidos Pueblo y Corona" (3:714). But he later exclaims: "¡El vivir del pueblo, el vivir de los reyes! ¿Quién lo ha podido penetrar y menos escribir?" (3:730). His futile pursuit of his ideal of Lucila-Isabel II-Spain-Truth causes his illness, "la efusión de lo ideal, de lo desconocido, de lo que, debiendo existir, no existe" (3:715).

Miedes acts out the other side of the historian's dilemma. He seeks the ideal origin of Spanish history and thinks he finds it in Lucila, while Fajardo sees Lucila and begins his pursuit of her, or of the ideal. For the two historians who cannot escape fiction, Lucila represents either the origin or the ideal end of history, yet she is neither. Both their pursuits of Lucila, like their pursuits of history—in the past or in the future—are in vain. Miedes is a "trastornado investigador de la Historia" (3:633), just like Fajardo and Santiuste become. Miedes's persistent search into the past for the origin and purity of the Spanish language and race is obviously a quixotic task. He is ruined both materially and mentally by his "pasión de los libros" (3:63). His crazed insistence on the single truth that the Celtiberians are the progenitors of Greek gods, the Hebrew race, and so on (3:634), foreshadows his total mental collapse and death. Unlike don Quijote, Miedes dies in the throes of his insanity, with his Dulcinea intact: Lucila has become his princess "Illipulicia" whom he seeks to protect from vanquishers. This unredeemed "quijotismo" is repeated later in the fourth series, in Santiuste. If it is not unredeemed "quijotismo," it is at least unrewarded, as with

121

Fajardo and later Santiago Ibero. The four principal Quijote figures in the fourth series become deranged either through reading history, as do Miedes and Ibero, or through attempting to
write it, as do Fajardo and Santiuste.

The mental "trastornos" of Miedes, Fajardo, and Santiuste
underline further the futility of the historian's task. Fajardo's
idealization of both Lucila and Isabel II is no less quixotic than
Miedes's idealization of Lucila and the origins of the Spanish
race, the idealized history written by Santiuste, or the aggran-
dized—yet official—accounts of the Spanish conquests that
cause Ibero to leave home in search of a warrior's glory. Fajardo
cites the inopportunity of Miedes's history lessons (3:627): in
spite of the fact that, after thirty years of study, Miedes has
managed to "dominar todas las ciencias históricas" (3:631), his
lessons are worthless because the knowledge that he has mas-
tered is already obsolete or prejudiced. Likewise, Fajardo never
masters Lucila or history. In *La de los tristes destinos*, after
twenty years of observing Isabel II's reign, he sees only disen-
chantment, in Isabel's eyes as well as in his own. He says at the
beginning of *Narváez* that his memoirs will probably not teach
posterity anything; the same mistakes will continue to be made.
Fajardo sees his own defects as "abolengo" of those of his future
readers (3:619).[17] Yet in spite of the futility of hoping that history might teach lessons, Fajardo writes for his own satisfaction
as "historiador y crítico anatómico de mí mismo" (3:619).
Statements like these describe the historian's—or at least this
historical novelist's—self-analysis of his task and of the nature
of his narrative.

The frequent instances in the fourth series of this type of
metahistorical discourse again imply, as in the third series, the
novelist's self-conscious stance and an awareness of the limitations of any narrative to represent truth or real events. Fajardo
laments to María Ignacia:

> Esa historia no puedo escribirla. . . . Para conocer sus ele-
> mentos necesito vivirla, ¿entiendes? Vivirla en el pueblo y
> junto al Trono mismo. ¿Y cómo he de estudiar yo la palpi-

tación nacional en esos dos extremos que abarcan todo la vida de una raza? . . . ¿No ves que es imposible? El ideal de esa historia me fascina, me atrae . . . pero ¿cómo apoderarme de él? Por eso estoy enfermo: mi mal es la perfecta conciencia de una misión, llámala aptitud, que no puedo cumplir. (3:730).

Fajardo is not unlike the protagonists of the third series, for this is romantic irony, the dilemma that Lukács considers intrinsic to the novel; the life of the spirit, perfect consciousness of the ideal can never be realized in practice. Because it is an ideal, the pursuit of history shares in this dilemma and reveals its converse: the truth of the practical, of events as lived, always escapes mastery by the ideal. Isabel II attempts to assert this mastery when she asks Fajardo to write her history as it occurs, and so does Fajardo when he writes his memoirs almost simultaneously with the events of his life. But by making history as written simultaneous with history as lived, Fajardo simply assimilates the former to the latter. The dilemma of the historian ultimately becomes his inability to write the history of his own writing of history, unless he treats as practice, as a lived event with its own autonomous truth, the pursuit of history that is his ideal. History written as events one lives is no closer to the truth of those events than history written at any other time. The fourth series of Galdós's *Episodios nacionales* suggests that the truth of events, in order to be written, must be created.

NAMES FOR THINGS IN *O'DONNELL*

The association of the names Lucila and Isabel II in *Narváez* and throughout the fourth series enables the interpenetration and the interchange of all the political, sexual, moral, and social plots that these characters traverse. As protagonists of fiction and history and as objects of scrutiny by Fajardo and other would-be historians *cum* novelists of the series, they and the terms that seek to define them also weave together fictional and historical discourse, so that the one is inseparable and indistinguishable from the other. The third series illustrated this process as well, but without the numerous "feminine" aspects that the fourth series incorporates into its various relationships among the characters, the plots, and the fictional and historical narrations. The fifth novel of the series, *O'Donnell*, introduces another protagonist, Teresa Villaescusa. She is also associated with Isabel II, but to a much different effect than Lucila. In *O'Donnell* the discourse of the novel's fictional and historical terms again reveals the interdependence of those terms through their inability to maintain inalterably the separate identities of the political, moral, economic, and even gastronomic categories that the novel offers. This interdependence offers several suggestions for what the general consequences of a critical reading of the *Episodios nacionales* might be.

To begin with, an examination of the distinction between history and fiction in *O'Donnell* clearly illustrates the novel's representational self-consciousness, which becomes evident in the opening paragraph. Consideration of these introductory lines is a useful prologue to understanding other distinctions among political, economic, sexual, and gastronomic terms in the novel. The relationships that Galdós questions between historical phenomena and historical discourse in these opening lines effectively include the linguistic and real status of those distinctions. The opening lines thus establish the whole range of the problem at the outset of the novel.

El nombre de *O'Donnell* al frente de este libro significa el coto de tiempo que corresponde a los hechos y personas aquí representados. Solemos designar las cosas históricas, o con el mote de su propia síntesis psicológica o con la divisa de su abolengo; esto es, el nombre de quien trajo el estado social y político que a tales personas y cosas dio fisonomía y color. Fue O'Donnell una época, como lo fueron antes y después Espartero y Prim, y como éstos, sus ideas crearon diversos hechos públicos y sus actos engendraron infinidad de manifestaciones particulares que, amasadas y conglomeradas, adquieren en la sucessión de los días carácter de unidad histórica. . . . *O'Donnell* es el rótulo de uno de los libros más extensos en que escribió sus apuntes del pasado siglo la esclarecida *jamona* Doña Clío de Apolo, señora de circunstancias que se pasa la vida escudriñando las ajenas, para sacar de entre el montón de verdades que no pueden decirse las poquitas que resisten el aire libre, y con ellas, conjeturas razonables y mentiras de adobado rostro. Lleva Clío consigo, en un gran puchero, el colorete de la verosimilitud, y con pincel o brocha va dando sus toques allí donde son necesarios. (3:947)

At first glance this is an extended statement about the relationships of words to things, of this book to historical people, events, times, etc. Yet this seemingly straightforward statement about the nature of representation, about the meaning of history, hinges on a fictive, mythical character, Doña Clío, the muse of history. Such a history is the work of a purely literary being who writes "conjeturas razonables y mentiras de adobado rostro" where few "verdades" are apparent. In other words, historical events are not wholly knowable through the words of this narrative as though it were transparently representative. The "nombres," "rótulos," "motes," etc., have no truthful and therefore no ultimately stable relationships to the "hechos," "cosas históricas," "personas," "épocas," that are "aquí representados." The passage therefore questions the role of representation and the reality of historical truth. Yet whether the label be representation or truth, novel or history, it is the same medium in every case and so displays, as White observes, the *"aporia* or sense of contradiction residing in the very heart of language"* (*Tropics*, 130). In order to come to terms with any text, including the historical novel, the reader must incorporate the paradox, *aporia*, and contradiction of those "nombres," "motes," and "rótulos" themselves. Only through them can one conjecture the "coto de tiempo," "los hechos y personas," "las cosas históricas;" only through words can one conjecture meaning. The history or the meaning that seems to be created is thus always conjecture.

It is easy to see how the attempt to maintain opposed categories of fiction and history becomes untenable in *O'Donnell*, and therefore how the *Episodios nacionales* undermine their own representational pretentions. The same kind of subversion occurs among apparently more tangible categories of the novel as well. One can identify, for example, three primary activities in *O'Donnell*—politics, sex, and eating. These activities appear in the text as codes of signifying terms that represent those activities, but that also mutually define each other in non-representational and often contradictory ways.[18] Moreover, when taking one of these activities as a primary representation or literal meaning in a particular context, its code also inevitably admits some influence from the roles of other activities, which thus appear as connotations in that context. The remainder of this chapter separates examples according to their literal meanings or represented activities in order to facilitate discussion, while acknowledging in advance that each example incurs the ambivalent distinction between primary and secondary meanings and the mutual influence of each code.

POLITICS AND SIGNIFICATION

In *O'Donnell*, as in other *Episodios*, the hermeneutic activity of the reader and critic has an analogue within the events of the very story that is being read. For example, the characters of *O'Donnell* are engaged in a constant effort to find an intelligible relationship between politics and their daily lives. Specifically they seek in revolution, changes of government, shifts from liberalism to conservatism, and finally in the ideal of "Unión Liberal" an improvement in their real living conditions—the jobs they have, the clothes they wear, the food they eat. In semiotic terms, they seek a meaningful connection and exchange between one type of discourse and activity (viewed as a signifier) and another (viewed as a signified). Each of these activities exists as a code in the text, of course, and, more important, in the represented world itself. Hence the relationship between political discourse or activity and economic conditions is certainly not an

126

univocally significant one, as the course of events narrated in *O'Donnell* reveals.

The novel traces the events of the period between 1854 and 1859: the aftermath of Vicálvaro and the Espartero-O'Donnell government, the suppression of the "Milicia Nacional" and Espartero's departure, the successive ministries of O'Donnell and Narváez, and the return to power of O'Donnell and the "Unión Liberal."[19] It also introduces Teresa Villaescusa, heroine of this and two subsequent *Episodios—Prim* and *La de los tristes destinos*. During Serrano's shelling of the "Milicia," her father, Colonel Villaescusa, suffers excruciating pain from a stomach cancer and finally commits suicide. This leaves his wife and daughter virtually penniless. In a rebellion against social pretense and a desire for material comfort, Teresa takes for herself a series of wealthy lovers, whose substitutions more or less coincide with the changes in ministries. The climax to the novel comes when she must decide between "pobreza honrada," symbolized in a union with Santiuste, also introduced in this novel, or "deshonra brillante" (3:1054), symbolized in a liaison with an even richer lover than before.[20] Her dilemma is that she must choose between categories that are labeled as irreconcilable in the novel—the moral and the material. Teresa's dilemma is parallel to the one that political parties perceive in Spain with regard to the "desamortización." Yet this parallelism itself is clearly paradoxical, as will be demonstrated. Rather than establishing a stable connection between broad political events and specific individual situations, the problematic parallelism between them reaffirms the inherent difficulty of attempting that connection.

One of the most evident consequences of this difficulty involves the events and situations that the novel offers as its plot. It is often said with reference to the *Episodios* in particular and the novel in general that multiple plots are alternative workings of a larger meaning that becomes clear through relationships among those plots. Now, the actions of Teresa Villaescusa can be seen as a commentary on her society as depicted in the novel, and on O'Donnell and Isabel II as portrayed in the fourth series.

At the same time the fluctuations in ministries, political alliances, political rhetoric, and economic policies (such as the "desamortización") also create Teresa's character. Dendle writes: "The contradictions of Spanish society—unsure of herself, caught in a web of corruption, but nonetheless with generous impulses—are expressed in the character of Teresa Villaescusa" (*Mature Thought*, 121). However, it is not just that society and Teresa are filled with contradictions, but that the relationships between and among the various plots themselves continually fluctuate. An attempt to induce a fixed significative relationship among any of these plots, characters, or themes—that is, to make one of them a signifier and the other a signified—results in a sign that is scarcely univocal. Every sign depends upon the pursuit of meaning through other signs constructed in the text. Any larger meaning attained through these signs remains provisional, unstable, and compromised. The relationships between the various plots in *O'Donnell* and the character of Teresa Villaescusa also become structural analogues for the relationships between social structures and the individual. Neither the novelistic character nor the individual in society is a wholly fixed and stable construct. Their instability can be demonstrated through an analysis of the constitutive elements in the codes that intersect and create characters in the novel. These codes identify characters in multiple and often contradictory ways. Their mutual influences create relationships that in turn make fixed meanings necessarily untenable.

An obvious example of this mutual influence involves ways in which the sexual categories invade and eventually subvert the political categories of the novel. The several changes of ministry described in *O'Donnell* and the corresponding alternations between liberal and conservative politics are portrayed in large part as hinging on Isabel II's willingness or refusal to allow the "desamortización." Her shifting back and forth on this issue is emblematic of the fluctuating policies of her reign. The amorous plot of the novel revolves around Teresa's career as a self-launched high courtesan. In spite of her sexual promiscuity, she is presented as morally superior to socially acceptable adulteresses like the hypocritical Valeria Socobio. Thus Teresa's moral depiction is equivocal and ambivalent, since she is at once more and less "moral" than the society that pretends to define this term. The combination of Teresa's love of material comfort and her overwhelming generosity also makes her character a paradoxical reflection on the political figures and their rhetoric. In many instances Teresa seems to embody O'Donnell and to oppose Isabel. Yet there are numerous ways in which she is like the queen and distinct from O'Donnell; neither the similarities nor the differences between these characters, plots, or the codes that constitute them remain fixed. The term "soberano" here, as with the characters and plots discussed before, is one of many elements that promote this ambivalence. It appears in an initial description of Teresa, just as with Lucila and Isabel, and thus lends its political value to her characterization. The difficulties that this ambivalence creates in stabilizing either the likenesses or distinctions between sexual and political characters and plots, and therefore in fixing the relationships between them, are also obvious in numerous juxtaposed passages. For example, Teresa's sexual promiscuity makes her like Isabel II, although she is, of course, without social or political status while Isabel enjoys the highest. Or, where the queen should conform to rules and dance at the palace with whom diplomatic protocol dictates (3:995), Teresa is "reina" at least in her own house (3:990). Broadly, Teresa must function on the fringes of society while Isabel II is a symbol of society itself.[21]

Such juxtapositions of related terms frequently occur concerning the "desamortización." For example, chapter 15 ends with Isabel II telling O'Donnell that she will not allow the "desamortización," while chapter 16 begins with Teresa stating that she wants it (3:996). A juxtaposition of this sort can occur within the same sentence, for example: "al tiempo que Isabel de Borbón decía con desgarrada voz de maja: 'Yo no desamortizo,' la otra maja, Teresa Villaescusa, gritaba: 'Juro por las Tres Gracias que a mí nadie me gana en el desamortizar' " (3:999). The passage simultaneously establishes identities through "maja" and differences through "desamortizar"/"no desamortizar." By extension Teresa and Isabel, along with the political connotations attached to their characters, are both alike and not alike. In an earlier instance, before Teresa's "fall," her mother, Manolita Pez, advises her to choose a husband "que sea resueltamente del partido de O'Donnell" (3:967); Teresa listens to the "sabios consejos . . . fingiendo admitirlos, como palabra divina; mas en su interior se propuso hacer su gusto" (3:967). This scene precedes by only two sentences the announcement that "en el Consejo con Su Majestad aquella mañana, O'Donnell y Espartero habían rifado. . . . La Reina se decidía por O'Donnell" (3:968). The relationships are complex here. Teresa and Isabel both do as they please; Isabel, in this instance chooses O'Donnell over Espartero, "el hombre que personificaba la Libertad" (3:976), while Teresa is on the verge of choosing complete liberty. However if the ideal of O'Donnell "no es más que comer, comer, comer" (3:976), then Teresa is choosing food and only by extension O'Donnell, since the suicide of the Colonel leaves wife and daughter in a state in which "apenas tenían para comer, y obligadas vivían a una representación pública incompatible con su menguado haber, eran, en realidad, más infelices y más pobres que las últimas vendedoras de hortalizas en medio de la calle" (3:985). Teresa's activities parallel those of Isabel II, O'Donnell, and Espartero at the same time, uniting in complex and paradoxical ways the codes of political and sexual behavior that include these characters. In the process, whatever distinctions between those activities that exist in these codes disappear within the complex play of shared relationships.

THE PRESENCE AND ABSENCE OF FOOD

The previous example further illustrates how the code of elements involving the consumption of food also affects those involving politics and sex. Their mutual influence appears throughout the novel. An outstanding example occurs at the moment when Isabel, after the "bienio liberal," ousts O'Donnell in favor of Narváez, and says, "al revés te lo digo, para que lo entiendas" (3:998). Government jobs are taken from the progressives and the moderates "entraron a comer" (3:998). The jobs, clothes, and food produced from these changes in ministry can be reduced to "¡Comer, comer! De eso se trataba, y toda nuestra política no era más que la conjugación de ese substancial verbo" (3:998). The implicit contradiction in the phrase "substancial verbo" is an emblem of the contradiction between political ideals and food, between words and things, and between signifiers and signifieds. In the attempt to fix a connection—a complete sign—that joins political activities (as signifiers) and economic satisfaction in jobs and food (as signifieds), the inherent instability of that connection or sign becomes obvious. The signified—food—slips from one signifier (progressive) to another (moderate), thus compromising the identity of the meaning suggested.

The above passages are juxtaposed to the description of Teresa's change in lovers, thus implicating the value of her sexual activity within the play of these political and gastronomic values. After the "breve reinado" of her first lover, Aransis, comes to an end ("la abdicación de Guillermo"), she ponders who will succeed him:

> Base de su criterio en estos graves asuntos era el principio de que la peor cosa del mundo es la pobreza; de que el vivir no es más que una lucha sistemática contra el hambre, la desnudez . . . y partiendo de esto, eligió entre los tres o cuatro individuos que la solicitaron aquel que ofrecía más templadas armas para luchar contra el mal humano. (3:999)

Teresa relates her sexual activities, life's problems and all politics to distinctions in the loss or acquisition of food. She attempts to fix the same kind of a relationship between her sexual partners and food that others seek between political parties and food. Her precarious situation and identity is a consequence of the shifting, rather than the stable, nature of the sign, just as occurs with political identities.

The extensive scene in which Teresa accepts her new lover, the French capitalist Isaac Brizard, after he gives a lavish ban-

quet in her honor (chapters 17 and 18), displays in detail how
the three major codes of activities in the novel—politics, sex,
and eating—are interconnected. The ostensible focus of these
chapters is Brizard's conquest of Teresa, and her coquettish performance for her "nuevo contratista de amor" (3:999). Naturally the "signing" of the agreement—its resolution—cannot be
witnessed, as the narrator says: "pues el hecho de arreglarse y
cerrar trato aquella misma noche Teresita y Brizard es de esos
que, por descontados y claramente previstos, no piden más que
una mención . . . menos aún, una raya de cualquier color tra-
zada en la página sin letras de esa historia que llamamos *Chis-
mografía*" (3:1005). The remark recalls the first paragraph of
the novel; a history without words is no history at all, since
history is only words.

The chief topic of conversation at the banquet is food and the
art of eating. Present is the gourmand don José de la Riva Guisando "que parecía simbolizar la posesión de cuantos bienes existen en la Tierra" (3:1001). The reader learns in a scene immediately following the banquet, however, that his ostentatious
appearance and eating habits incur the label of "milagroso vivir"; they bear no meaningful connection to his only income, a
small government job. He is "un artista genial del buen porte,
de la buena vida, del buen comer" (3:1008). In other words, he
is external opulence and luxury, with no substance underneath.
Even his name, "Guisando," is a literal contradiction in terms.
It connotes an activity—the cooking, the mixing, of foods—that
he has no means to pursue. His name is a signifier without signified value. His mixture or synthesis is indeed superficial, and
as with Isabel II, it is contradictory. The metaphors used to describe Riva Guisando—"artista" and "imagen sintética"—emblemize his very nature. The artist deals in representation, not
reality, and an image is still an image, no matter how synthetic
it may be.

Yet for all his lack of "substance," Riva Guisando functions
easily within his society. He appears wealthy and so eats well,
even though he has no material reality (a sufficient income) to
support that identity. However, in a society that values the

sheer appearance of luxury, substance is unnecessary. Just as a signified can shift between signifier and signifier—as in the case of political parties or Teresa's lovers—here even the presence of the signified (a good job) is unnecessary to the function of the signifier and to the effectiveness of the sign. It is the signifier that marks out identities and differences in this system, not the signified. It is never a question of who has the food or not that spells a success here, but rather the political designation or—in the case of Riva Guisando, the appearance of success—that activates a character's function or position within the novel. This is why Riva Guisando is able to weather any political change, while Centurión and other "cesantes" like him are not. Riva Guisando knows that his identity rests on his appearance, the signifier alone, while others continually seek a fixed connection between signifier and signified. Their attempts to stabilize their identities, as with any attempt to fix meaning, are futile in a system of constantly shifting values and terms.

Riva Guisando wishes to "enseñar a los españoles a comer . . . comer bien, dando al cuerpo todo lo que pedía" (3:1002). He complains that "uno de los mayores atrasos de este país consiste en que aquí no saben comer" (3:1002). In this scene relationships between food, the banquet, sexual conquest, and the political and economic health of Spain are established through "el tema de si saben o no comer los españoles" (3:1003). Riva Guisando enumerates the progress Spaniards have made in "civilización" (i.e., clothes, theater, etc.), but "sólo en el comer estamos atrasados." Such backwardness exists because the Spanish "no han llegado a penetrar la filosofía del condimento," to "distinguir los innumerables acentos que forman el lenguaje de los vinos" (3:1003). Food terms become signifiers interchangeable with the signified categories of civilization, philosophy, and even language itself. Brizard reminds the guests of this semiotic function of food when he declares that he will begin "por el principio, enseñándoles a buscar lo que han de comer" (3:1003). Teresa disagrees with him, noting that Riva Guisando wants to teach "la filosofía de la buena mesa . . . a un pueblo que no tiene sobre qué caerse muerto. ¿Cómo quiere usted que sepa comer el que no come?" (3:1003). Teresa unveils the lack of correlation between their systems of words and Spain's economic system. The differential values that structure each system are simply incompatible.

The chapter following this banquet scene begins with a description of political activity during the new Narváez-Nocedal ministry: "Los moderados . . . estaban otra vez en campaña, comiéndo los niños crudos y los buenos platos guisados del presupuesto" (3:1009). One of Narváez's first acts is to suppress brutally and execute the rebels at Arahal, just as the previous ministry had put down another rebellion. Centurión, Teresa's uncle and former "gentilhombre" to the child Isabel II, notes that the rebels did not ask for "libertad," "la Constitución," or "la Desamortización," only "pan": "y este pan lo pedían llamando al pan democracia, y a su hambre reacción. . . . Quiere decirse que para matar el hambre, o sea la reacción, necesitaban democracia, o llámese pan para mayor claridad" (3:1012). Political designations here, like civilization, philosophy, and language in the previous scene, are interchangeable with food or the lack of it. As before, the political and the gastronomic merge, here in an incongruity as ironically grotesque as the fusion of reproductive metaphors with the narration of Narváez's executions in *Bodas reales*. Whereas one would conventionally connect political terms with various political events and parties, and food terms with distinctions in foodstuffs, here the terms change places. "Democracia" and "reacción" signify "pan" and "hambre." In other words, the terms of one code designate the terms of another code; the illusion of meaning as it is usually conceived dissolves here in a system of differences among signifiers alone. The soldiers who put down the revolt "apuntan a los estómagos, que son las entrañas culpables. . . . No van los tiros a matar las ideas, que no existen; no van a matar los sentimientos, que tampoco existen; van a matar el hambre." What is "present" is "absence." The food that the revolutionaries do receive is death: "pues escogidos 100 democráticos, o dígase 100 estómagos vacíos, . . . les sirvieron la comida, quiero decir, que los fusilaron" (3:1012).

The scenes in which terms for food become interchangeable with those for politics, philosophy, culture, and even human life and death, reveal the unstable relationships among these various codes or plots and between words and meanings. If the terms comprising a code slide among several categories or values with ease, their doing so questions the distinctions among those categories and values. Following his comments on Arahal, Centurión, now "cesante" under Narváez, describes himself and other "buenos liberales" as analogous to the revolutionaries; their pain results not from an "empacho de libertad," but from a "vacío de alimentos." He asks, "¿no sería más sencillo que al decretar las cesantías en un cambio de Gobierno nos reunieran en un patio . . . a todos los cesantes con sus familias respectivas?" Then the officer in charge of the firing squad would yell: "¡Preparen! ¡Apunten! ¡Cesen! . . . y pataplum . . . cesábamos" (3:1012). To be labeled a liberal now is to be out of a job, to starve, to cease to exist, just as to be labeled a conservative under the previous ministry was to suffer the same consequences. Changes in government continually undo with one hand what they do with the other, because "cesantes" like Centurión seek to fix a connection between two continually shifting systems—politics and food. When two different signifying terms (two ministries or two political parties) depend upon the same signified element (jobs or food) to establish their identities as signs, either the difference between the terms breaks down or one identity must dissolve in order to permit the (momentary) existence of the other. So the system is both binary—have/have not—and unitary—one element can substitute for the other.

The play on the terms "cesante" and "cesar" gestures to the void behind political rhetoric by placing its commonplaces out of context. This strategy reveals that such terms are commonplaces as well as the vacuity of their context. Moreover, Centurión's comparison of the revolutionaries to the liberals subverts the distinctions between the two political groups. This is similar to what occurs with Colonel Villaescusa's suffering and suicide. This "crónico mal del estómago" is exacerbated to such an extent during the shelling of the Milicia (the suppression of liberty) that he must kill himself, which, Rodríguez writes, "exemplifies the nature of military solutions." The colonel's role is reversed as it were; he attacks himself as well as his enemy. Thus there is no "solution," only a dissolution of the distinctions between friend and foe, self and other. Opposing categories such as revolutionary and peace keeper are again rendered indistinct.[22] The colonel finds it impossible to eat: "Comer, comer. . . . ¿Y sé yo acaso cómo se come, con este infierno que llevo aquí?" (3:983). His inability to eat identifies him, ironically while he is putting down a revolt, with those hungry revolutionaries who fight for democracy. Like the relationships between Teresa and Isabel II, Teresa and O'Donnell, or liberal and conservative, that between revolution and repression fluctuates between identity and difference.

Terms for food or its absence correspond to both political revolutions and their suppression, to different ministries and political parties, and to Teresa's various lovers. Yet even these relationships are paradoxical; the identifications sought between food and politics, food and sexuality, or sexuality and politics, are never stable. The meaning of Narváez or O'Donnell, conservative or liberal politics, revolution or reaction is not fixed, as Teresa tells Santiuste in a dream: "No pienses en destinos del gobierno, que no son más que pan para hoy y hambre para mañana" (3:1037). What is done today will be undone tomorrow; the relationships that seem established between codes, characters, or plots become problematical as the terms that create them take on opposing connotations, or simply become indistinguishable among themselves.

The colonel bequeathes his pain to his wife and daughter, "mujeres de Madrid" (3:985), whom he "veía como dos pobres pulgas que andaban brincando de cuerpo en cuerpo, en busca de un poco de sangre con que nutrirse" (3:983). These women who turn to illicit sexuality in order to survive are like the latest batch of "cesantes"; their political and sexual machinations coincide in their dependence on food. In this respect, their activities are signifiers that establish a functional exchange with certain signifieds and create the identities of their characters as well. Sexuality gives the women meanings, just as political in-trigue does to the "cesantes." Where the sexual and political activities coincide, so do the identities of Teresa, Manolita, the ministers, and the bureaucrats. Yet there remains a distinction between these political and sexual activities, and between Teresa and the bureaucrats. Their characters or their activities are ul-timately distinguished as signifiers by the fundamental differ-ences between the two signifieds of food and hunger. Teresa is eventually able to transcend this binary opposition between food and hunger in a way that the bureaucrats never achieve. In part this occurs because her sexuality produces food not only for herself, but for others as well; that is, she is a sign whose sig-nificance overcomes its difference from other signs. Where Riva Guisando tends to become a free signifier, Teresa tends to be-come a free signified, so that the moral and political distinctions that appear in the discourse of the novel never delimit the func-tional value of her character, as the following pages will attempt to explain.

THEORY AND PRACTICE OF THE "DESAMORTIZACIÓN"

The difference in the relationships between Teresa and food and between O'Donnell and food becomes clear when O'Donnell and his followers theorize about, and Teresa practices, the "des-amortización" of which they all speak. O'Donnell and other pol-iticians use various food terms in their political discourse. In some cases, food is a metaphor for political ideas, as when he calls the "Unión Liberal" "mi pan nuevo" (3:993). In this case, the forced coincidence of signifiers ("Unión Liberal," "pan nuevo") suggests a corresponding coincidence in their signified ideas. This metaphorical shift of signifiers is not unidirectional, however, and hence the coincidence of signified ideas blurs their distinction, with a consequent loss of significance for both sig-nifiers. Because O'Donnell proposes to unite the "useful, best, and most intelligent" in his government, Riva Guisando (appro-priately) can explain at another banquet described in lengthy detail (chapters 28 and 29) the mixture of various national cui-

sines as "tomando lo bueno de uno y otro para formar lo exce-
lente y superior; vamos, una verdadera *Unión Liberal* del
comer" (3:1041). Eufrasia asks "¿Qué es la Unión Liberal más
que una mixtura gastronómica?" (3:1041). According to Manolo Tarfe, who is O'Donnell's favorite and bears the nickname
"O'Donnell el chico," "Don Leopoldo es el primer revolucionario, porque al par de los derechos políticos para todos los españoles, trae los derechos alimenticios. . . . Su política es la regeneración de los estómagos, de donde vendrá la regeneración de
la raza. Sin buenos estómagos no hay buenas voluntades ni ce-
rebros firmes" (3:1042). The values that Manolo creates here
are perfectly clear: it is obvious how he correlates the differentiated elements of food and hunger with democracy and reaction. What is not clear is the significance of these correlations:
which of the elements are signifiers and which signifieds? In
pragmatic terms, this significance *is* the effectiveness of O'Donnell's political discourse and of his own character. Because of the
uncertain realization of this exchange or significance in O'Donnell's discourse, his ministry is unable to satisfy Spain's hunger
or create good will and clear-sightedness. The political system
of O'Donnell, and of Spain, has no meaningful connection to
the nation's social or economic system; hence there is no stability, and nothing is produced. Teresa, on the other hand, transcends the distinctions between these systems; her discourse
thereby becomes meaningful.

O'Donnell demonstrates how various apparently opposing
codes, such as politics, sexuality, and food, define one another
and how their individual terms, such as "pan," "democracia,"
"hambre," "reacción," "cesante," Unión Liberal," etc., do so as
well. The necessary interdependence of these terms is nowhere
more obvious than in the character of Teresa. No one of the
social, moral, or representational codes alone in the novel can
contain her. She transcends each novelistic system and its antithesis, revealing that even antithesis, like extreme difference
itself, is unstable. She, unlike any other character, acquires real
value, yet without attempting to fix a correspondence between
codes and meanings. Like *Misericordia*'s Benina, and unlike the

politicians, she overcomes the critical opposition of food to hunger.[23]

Teresa's role as an embodiment of generosity is unsurpassed in the *Episodios*, just as Benina has no equal in this respect in the *Novelas contemporáneas*, Teresa's revulsion at the prospect of Aransis's poverty does not belie her true generosity when she relinquishes him at Fajardo's request. When she finds Santiuste and the family that he protects starving to death in a filthy garret, she is confronted with what she thought existed only in words: "¡Morirse de hambre! Esto se dice; pero rara vez existe en la realidad" (3:1024). She encounters a distinction that has shifted, for her, from being meaningful or functional only in language to being meaningful or functional among persons as well. Her response is to ignore other distinctions applicable to these persons and thereby render those distinctions meaningless in the language of moral or social standards that expresses them. Just as she refuses to judge others or qualify her behavior toward them according to social, moral, or economic codes, neither can she be adequately defined or encompassed within the limits of such categories. She gives abundant aid to the family and to Santiuste, of whom she soon becomes enamored. She also finds jobs with her "mano liberal" for "tres cesantes infelices," and disregards their ingratitude and hypocrisy (3:1046). In accepting the job from Teresa, Centurión must himself abandon the correlation between certain words and deeds: he sacrifices his principles to put food on the table, as he says to himself: "Hombre menguado, aceptas tu felicidad del hombre público más funesto . . . y por mediación de tu pública sobrina. . . . Lo que no lograron los principios de un varón recto lo consigue la hermosura de una mujer torcida. . . . ¡En qué manos está el Poder!" (3:1048).[24] As so frequently happens, the subversion of a meaningful connection between words and deeds leads to their loss of differential value with respect to other words and deeds. While the terms "torcida" and "recto" seek to distinguish between Teresa and O'Donnell, "público," "principio," and "mano" link the characters, politics, sexuality, and food. The functional oppositions between Teresa and O'Donnell or sex and politics disappear as the differential values become less distinct for other terms constituting their characters.

The terms which seem to establish differences between the codes of moral stances, political persuasions, characters, or plots do not retain fixed definitions for long. Hence the codes that depend on these unstable relationships must be constantly reevaluated. If Isabel II and Teresa are both "majas," yet one wants the "desamortización" and the other does not; if one infuses it with sexual connotations and the other with political, then the term cannot hold exclusive value for either character's identity in the novel. Likewise, if Teresa is a "mujer pública," and Tarfe or "O'Donnell el chico" is "el primero de los hombres públicos" (3:1052), and if even O'Donnell himself is "el hombre público más funesto" (3:1048), and all politicians and soldiers are "mujeres públicas" (3:979), then the moral, social, or sexual identities of these characters cannot remain fixed in the text. If "principio," "pan," "comer," "cesante," "democracia," etc., signify any number of things, then these alternating expressions call into question the effective differences between those things. The relationships between words and things depend on those between words and words. Thus *O'Donnell* first assumes connections between sexual and political events and words, but then subverts those connections by blurring the distinctions between those events and words.

Finally, even the love plot in this novel is undermined and loses its primary or literal meaning and function, becoming one more element governed by the terms of its discourse. It is Santiuste's language that attracts Teresa: "Siempre que *Tuste* hablaba este lenguaje de vaporosa espiritualidad, Teresa se conmovía y se le aguaban los ojos" (3:1038). She asks how he came to express himself so eloquently, and he answers: "este lenguaje mío es el reflejo del espíritu de la elocuencia sobre mi pobre espíritu." That spirit of eloquence is Castelar, "el verbo del siglo XIX": "¡Castelar! Este nombre llenaba mi espíritu" (3:1028).

However it is not the signified "spirit" or the ideas that Santiuste has appropriated, but the signifying "verbo" and
"nombre." Santiuste has learned to use the same system of signifiers that Castelar manipulates so effectively. While Santiuste
believes he is voicing pure ideas (signifieds), he is really only
mouthing the words, juggling the signifiers.

Teresa tells Santiuste: "todas las faramallas bonitas que has
aprendido de Castelar . . . En la vida real, eso no sirve para nada.
Yo no soy señora, aunque como las señoras me visto; yo . . .
soy una mujer mala, una . . . que se ha dejado poner en la frente
el letrero de mujer mala. . . . Llevo ese letrero, que leen todos
los que me conocen" (3:1032). Teresa contradicts herself here.
In the first place, the "faramallas" that Santiuste has learned do
serve a function: they move her emotionally, just as Castelar
and other politicians' rhetoric creates change in the political, but
not the economic, system. Nonetheless, society also defines her
through one code—the moral system that includes the "letrero
de mujer mala"—because the coherence of this code would collapse if it had to include distinctions in her actions. Her moral
designation is her functional identity for society. But Santiuste,
again with Castelarian eloquence, rejects these labels, or so he
believes: "Para mí, las denominaciones de señora y caballero son
motes que éste y el otro gustan de ponerse en un juego social.
. . . Yo no pongo motes; no clavo tampoco letreros. . . . Yo
miro al alma, no miro a la ropa" (3:1037–38). Santiuste refuses
the differential values created by "motes" and "letreros," while
using them himself. As a consequence of his refusal to join the
"juego social," he is a social outcast now and eventually goes
insane.[25] Because he refuses to make distinctions, however arbitrary they may be, he cannot function in society. No signified
can be identified exclusive of its signifiers, so the "liberated"
Teresa that Santiuste seeks to create out of her soul does not
exist. He chooses to see only one signifier for Teresa—her
"goodness"—and refuses the others that affect her identity.
Hence she does not join him at the end of the novel, because she
would cease to exist in the process. Likewise she does not go all
the way back to Madrid, which designates a different side of her

character. The ambivalence of Teresa, her compromised identity, is marked in the very moment of hesitation between her different facets.

The description that immediately follows Santiuste's remarks is of Teresa staring at a "fea pared que como a 20 pasos se extendía, triste superficie con letreros pintados anunciando alguna industria, y otros escritos debajo con carbón por mano inexperta. . . . Sobre aquellas letras y garabatos dejaba correr sus ojos Teresa sin ver nada, sin darse cuenta de lo que allí estaba escrito" (3:1038). Teresa at this point cannot see anything either, which is why she is suspended in a moral and even a physical limbo: she is between lovers, between moral and social values, between idealism and materialism. Her momentary inability to function within the signifying chain is signaled physically by the location of this scene: she sits morosely upon a rock on the outskirts of Madrid (3:1037–38). Since she does not see the distinctions in "letreros," "motes," or "denominaciones," she cannot see the functional identities of the labels in this system. They are what separate Eufrasia, Valeria Socobio, or Isabel II from Teresa, since the women's sexual activities are largely the same. They are what determine her own character in the plot of *O'Donnell*. Just as Santiuste's rhetoric sways Teresa in one sexual, economic, and social direction, so Tarfe's eloquence in the final scene moves her in the opposite. Her choices between and the identification of her character with poverty and riches, honor and dishonor, conservatism and liberalism, and even love and materialism, shift with words.

INCONCLUSIONS

The ambivalence in Teresa's identity and in her relationship to the sexual and political distinctions in the novel remains unresolved at the conclusion of *O'Donnell*, which is a statement about conclusions and meanings as well as about sexuality and politics. This final irresolution illustrates that, in the novel, meaning can be nothing other than a process of continual contradiction. Teresa's steps toward the country picnic with Santiuste, and her subsequent retracing of those steps back toward Madrid and a brilliant liaison, emblemize the irresolutions of this *Episodio* and its major characters. Teresa's doubts and her literal retracing mark a mental and physical hesitation between two seemingly exclusive alternatives. She stops halfway back to Madrid, between her two choices; nothing is ultimately resolved. As happens to many of the characters in the third series, her novel ends before her journey is over.

Teresa's hesitation and halfway movement illustrate the continual shifting of signs within the text: one can apprehend at most the fluctuating correlations of their signifieds and signifiers. This is the effect of the novel: there are no clear-cut distinctions between moral and immoral, liberal and conservative, sexual and political, historical and fictional, or signifying and signified elements that can be maintained. Teresa is both immoral and moral; the solution proposed by O'Donnell's "Unión Liberal" is neither truly liberal nor wholly conservative, neither unified nor separate. Just as an "infinidad de manifestaciones particulares" becomes "unidad histórica" in the opening paragraph of this *Episodio, O'Donnell* is an example of how language continually creates identities in differences.

The last two chapters follow Teresa's steps toward Santiuste and her retracing of those steps. Tarfe stops her by saying:

> Tú eres . . . el numen de la Unión Liberal; eres la expresión humana de los tiempos. . . . Los millones de la Mano Muerta pasarán por tu mano, que es la Mano Viva. . . . Eres tú la fatalidad histórica y el cumplimiento de las profecías. . . . Tú serás la ejecutora de lo que decimos y predicamos yo y . . . los que evangelizamos el verbo de O'Donnell, que es el verbo de Mendizábal. (3:1054)

This passage is quite similar to the opening paragraph of the novel, but here it is Teresa who is the emblem of the times, not O'Donnell. She is at once "numen," "expresión humana," "fatalidad histórica," and "cumplimiento de las profecías." In these self-reflexive functions Teresa is like the Clío who is both a creator and a creation of the narrative. Like Clío, and prefiguring

Mariclío of the fifth series, Teresa is a novel and a history; she is a series of implicit shifts or substitutions among terms. She brings together conflicting terms of inspiration, humanity, history, or prophecy, just as did the opening of *O'Donnell*. The interweaving of the terms of the codes of characters and plots is both general, as it encompasses the novel as a whole, and specific, as when a single scene illustrates the convergence of particular terms. Here, Teresa's political and sexual representations inspire Tarfe. He is "llevado ya por el hervor de sus ideas y de sus apetitos al punto de la inspiración, de la sugestiva elocuencia" (3:1054). He tells her that her eyes speak the words of his party: "Yo desamortizo. . . . Yo soy la niveladora, yo soy la revolucionaria. . . . yo quitaré el plato de la mesa de los ahitos, para ponerlo en la mesa de los hambrientos" (3:1054). Politics, sexuality, and food are once again all associated in this final scene.

The eloquence of "O'Donnell el chico" turns Teresa in the opposite physical, emotional, moral, and economic direction from that of Santiuste. After he leaves her, Teresa thinks that his words were "tan bien dichas y con tan hondo sentido" (3:1055). She decides that she must dedicate herself to "las funciones de intérprete del verbo de O'Donnell, que era el verbo de Mendizábal" (3:1056). Just as Santiuste's words were taken from Castelar, even O'Donnell's words are not original with him, but interpret those of his predecessors; they have no origin within the system to which they belong. In like fashion, the fourth series rereads the third, and the fifth rereads them all, as will be seen in the next chapter. Teresa's relationship to O'Donnell is one of a successive series of interpretations, substitutions, or shifts in terms, just as is the reader's understanding of her, the novel, the fourth series, and the forty-six *Episodios* as a whole. However, Teresa does momentarily interrupt this succession and establish an effective origin for these terms by translating or interpreting them into another system. Here lies the difference between Teresa and the other characters, like Lucila or Eufrasia. By contradicting the very novelistic system that functions as contradiction, Teresa is the exception that proves the rule. Teresa exemplifies the system that creates her, the very constitutive process of *O'Donnell*: contradiction. Her character practices what the others, even Isabel II, only theorize; she puts into food what they put into words. Thus the contradiction that underlies words and food is again contradicted through the practice of Teresa.

Teresa's "interpretation" takes the form of providing food, for Santuiste and for others. The final scene of the novel describes her as she feeds the poor children:

> De la cesta de la vendedora pasaban las rosquillas a la falda de Teresa, que las repartía graciosamente y con perfecta equidad entre aquella mísera chusma infantil. Y cuanto más daba, mayor número de criaturas . . . acudían. . . .
> Sin dar paz a su mano generosa, Teresa iba consolando a toda la chiquillería. (3:1057)

In the last sentence of the novel, as she commends herself physically to another illicit sexual liaison and mentally to O'Donnell, she thinks: "Maestro, Dios te guarde. . . . Toquemos a desamortizar. . . . Ya está aquí al *Mano Viva*" (3:1058). The *Episodio* is consistent even to the end in its shifting relationships between Teresa and O'Donnell, sexuality and politics, life and death, or fiction and history. The relationships among the historical, fictional, political, sexual, or alimentary codes in *O'Donnell* depend on words that blur the distinctions among them. The resolution of the novel brings these various codes together, not to resolve, but rather to dissolve the relationships that structure the entire text. Such an endless series of substitutions of words for words reveals the unstable and indeterminate nature of interpretation, of the knowledge of history, of the concept of origin, of the relationships of history to fiction, of Teresa to O'Donnell, and of the various plots to each other. All these relationships depend on a discourse whose production of meaning relies on a continuous process of contradiction. The meaning attributed to any element in that discourse—such as a character—is defined as that process itself.

Just as the last paragraph of *O'Donnell* tells how Teresa views

Madrid's personages as they pass her in their coaches "entre una ligera neblina polvorosa" (3:1058), so must one view meaning itself in the historical novel. The ambiguous values of "Teresa," the "desamortización," or the moral and social labels of the novel, create the narrative. Any meaning created in the *Episodios nacionales* is paradoxical, never unambiguously identifiable, because it cannot fix or hold an inherently ambiguous, non-identifiable, unstable medium: language. Teresa's momentary hesitation, her struggle, between different moral, social, and economic codes at the conclusion to *O'Donnell* is the moment of meaning itself.

THREE

Strategies of Reading
in the Fifth Series

The fifth and last series of *Episodios nacionales*, addressing the period of 1869 to 1882, has always presented problems to readers of Galdós. This is partly because most scholars consider the series to be unfinished; there are only six volumes instead of the usual ten. Also, many critics see a rather dramatic change in tone from the first four series, since these last *Episodios* are more fantastic than the generally realistic modes of the earlier volumes. There are formal distinctions within the fifth series as well: the last four volumes, *Amadeo I, La primera República, De Cartago a Sagunto*, and *Cánovas*, are often viewed as separable from the first two, *España sin rey* and *España trágica*.[1] Moreover, the series contains unusually ludicrous characters and plots, in contrast to the more or less conventional characters and plots seen before. In these and other ways, the last *Episodios* resist facile interpretation, either as lessons or statements about history. They also make the analysis of narrative strategies in general extremely problematic: the symbolism of characters, the plot sequences, the themes, and so on, are particularly difficult to identify in the first place, even if that identification is subsequently undermined. All this, of course, makes the question of the relationship between fictional and historical discourses even more complicated than in the works discussed thus far.

Evidence of these novels' difficulty are scholars' radically different assessments of the value, meaning, and intent of the works. A few critics do laud the stylistic innovation and virtuosity of the fifth series, such as Richard Gullón in "La historia como material novelable" and Stephen Gilman in "The Fifth Series of *Episodios nacionales*: Memories of Remembering." Gilman calls the author of the fifth series "the veteran, neither mellowed in spirit nor diminished in memory, who is capable of transforming his desolation into the bleakest of humour and of

147

chortling at the wild excesses of his own imagination."[2] Similarly, Joaquín Casalduero praises Galdós's benevolent attitude to Spain in the works; he sees him taking a supremely ironic stance from which to view his country with compassion (165–72). On the other hand, José Montesinos cites these *Episodios* as being noteworthy for their unaccustomed "acritud" and "violencia," and he questions their overall literary worth.[3] Miguel Enguídanos believes that "Galdós ama y rechaza" the Spain that such highly creative works depict, and that their intent is not at all didactic: "Lo que Galdós escribe es *historia de verdad.*"[4] This is in direct contradiction to Brian Dendle, who focuses chiefly on the didactic import of the fifth series, even if its "final teaching" was extremely bitter (180–81). Regalado García takes a middle position as to Galdós's intent and to the truth of the Spain he describes, saying that "resulta difícil saber qué cree o qué no cree el novelista, qué es mera objetividad en ellos y qué es ficción, cuáles son sus opiniones personales" (495). But he rejects Berkowitz's assessment that the novels show the beginnings of senility in Galdós, written as they were near the end of his life, between 1909 and 1912.[5] Like Regalado, Rodríguez cites the difficulty in reading the works and summarizes: "The effectiveness of the last four *Episodios Nacionales* is questionable. The degree of disfiguration achieved encumbers the reading and occasionally impedes comprehension" (196). According to Geoffrey Ribbans's 1986 study of the fifth series, Galdós "succumbs to a new technique in which the narrative structure itself is undermined."[6] These radically different interpretations of the fifth series call attention above all to the nature of interpretation itself, which continually tries to make sense out of a medium that often resists, even undermines, such an impulse. This chapter seeks to illustrate how the numerous interpretive difficulties presented in the fifth series serve to focus the reader's attention on the act of interpretation itself.

Literary criticism often assumes that it makes novels more meaningful by a provocative rewriting that illuminates key relationships between words and ideas or things; in other words, it makes novels more representative—either literally or figuratively—of something else.[7] The critical process usually involves, especially with respect to the novel, making the literary world conform to common perceptions of psychological and/or material worlds. This process is frustrated by the novels of the fifth series, as the efforts cited above to make sense of them as stories or histories, or as illustrations of Galdós's intentions, politics, state of health, or mind, reveal. Such questions, and the larger ones posed by all of the *Episodios* about the relationship between history and fiction, cannot be answered without also questioning the role of the reader who attempts to relate history to fiction, to make sense of the world of the fifth series, and to affirm the validity of the sense that has been made. The strategies employed here are no less questionable, naturally, than any others. After offering another sense of these volumes, however, this chapter will also attempt to show how the interpretations provided here become merely an extension of the ungrounded process of reading, interpreting, and writing already inscribed in historical fiction.

The fifth series subverts all the interpretations it seems to invite: those concerning historical epoch and fictional content, and those concerning efforts to form relationships between their codes, characters, symbols, themes, and plots. In fact any attempt to form connections and relationships becomes one more aspect of the series's network of reversals. By viewing the narrator as maintaining an ultimately ironic stance, or by assessing meaning as ironic, the reader becomes subject to irony when one explanation gives way to a conflicting one. I have elsewhere indicated that the complexities of irony might help explain the difficulty that critics have in finding meaning in the *Episodios*, particularly in the fifth series (*Galdós and the Irony*, 127). In these volumes any meaning or interpretation always gives way to another. Irony can sometimes be a strategy that leads to closure, if only that of irony for its own sake. Yet in the fifth series there is no end to the play of meaning; there is no synthesis of the diverse elements of these novels that remains stable, even as irony. Another explanatory tactic, such as viewing these volumes as parodies of the historical epoch, becomes virtually a parodic effort itself. The fifth series comprises a direct self-parody when the roles of writer, novelist, historian, and interpreter are personified in Tito, "Galdós's friend," the semiconscious helper of Mariclío, the muse of Spanish history. His futile efforts at making sense of Spain and himself parody those of any interpreter of novel or world. Another interpretive strategy for making sense of the series's diverse elements is to reduce, subdue, or literally write off some of them. Thus the symbolic and mythic elements of the works, like Tito's magical journeys or changing sizes, may be labeled allegorical, for instance. Rereading and rewriting in this way is only partially satisfactory, however, since the label "allegory" must bridge the gap between two still largely unreconciled texts—that of Tito and his often absurd fantasies and that of a historical Spain as it is conventionally perceived. If the literal and the figurative elements of these *Episodios* resist stable relationships between signifier and signified, then the series becomes an allegory of the facetiousness of interpretation itself.[8] The following pages will examine how allegory, parody, and irony function in these six novels in their relation to previous *Episodios*, to programs of historization proposed in the fifth series and earlier, to the relationships among historical and fictional discourses in general, and to those between text and reader in the act of interpretation overall.

One of the most illuminating insights of modern critical methodology concerns the analysis of how the reader's desire to know the truth is a force in narrative.[9] A desire to solve enigmas, to see what happens, to understand how certain elements mean, and how symbols relate to events, and so on, encourages the reader to finish the story. In the fifth series, as in previous *Episodios*, a prevailing enigma is once more how fiction relates to history. The readers of Galdós's historical novels are conditioned to solve this enigma and to make connections in more than just the usual ways one finds in narrative. The general title, *Episodios nacionales*, and the individual titles of each volume, the narrator's stated intentions of historical explanation and veracity, the repeated references to "public and private," and in general the conventions of nineteenth-century fiction and historiography as naively understood, all suggest seemingly obvious relationships between Galdós's words and a historical Spain. The forty volumes that precede the fifth series do lend themselves, although not always simply, to a relatively conventional interpretation, even if that interpretation is only one of many, and perhaps the most naive. But the six volumes of the last series frequently seem to resist actively all conventional interpretations and actually often prohibit the reader's making any connections between words and worlds. [10]

In the fifth series, the effort to form conventional representational relationships is complicated, first, by three largely unrelated stories. The first of these revolves around Fernanda Ibero's disappointed love for the superficial and deceptive politician, don Juan de Urríes, in *España sin rey*. The second sequence depicts several exercises in frustrated idealism. Vicente Halconero's exalted love for Fernanda is thwarted by her sudden death. His "heroic" attempt to defend his mother's honor also fails miserably, coinciding with the assassination of Prim in *España trágica*. Third, Tito Liviano's erratic and often imaginary travels across Spain occupy the last four volumes, which trace the constitutional monarchy of Amadeo, the brief republic, the expiration of both the republic and the Canton of Cartagena, and the Bourbon restoration, in *Amadeo I, La primera República, De Cartago a Sagunto*, and *Cánovas*, respectively. The differences in plots, in narrative styles, and many other aspects to be explored in this chapter, are ways in which these six *Episodios* disorient a reader striving to make meaningful connections.

Understanding how the series thwarts the reader's usual approaches to the *Episodios* unmasks conventions and prejudices involved in the attempt to define their meaning or historical content in the first place. However, such an unveiling of literary convention is not an end in itself either. As Culler writes in his critique of reader-oriented criticisms, "The outcome of reading, it seems, is always knowledge. Readers may be manipulated and misled, but when they finish the book their experience turns to knowledge—perhaps an understanding of the limitations imposed by familiar interpretive conventions—as though finishing the book took them outside the experience of reading and gave them mastery of it" (*On Deconstruction*, 79). The fifth series questions both the reader's desire and ability to make sense of the world, of Spain, through language. It also seems to suggest that one can never get outside of the reading experience, outside of language, let alone master it.

There is another way in which the structure of the fifth series subverts the acquisition of knowledge and thus prevents closure and mastery: its problematical conclusion. Victor Shklovsky observed how, through strategies such as parallelism, oppositions, realized predictions, etc., a text enables the reader to feel that it has satisfactorily come to an end. Because of the diversity that characterizes the episodic novel, a differentiated epilogue is usually necessary in order to tell the reader, finally, how to look back and interpret the series of episodes that constitute the text.[11] The fifth series, considered incomplete by most critics, does seem to lack an epilogue; this may account for a small part of its difficulty. Yet to use this "incompleteness" as a primary excuse for the problems in reading that it presents only leads to more problems.

Berkowitz claims that there were to be four more titles in the series—*Sagasta, Las colonias perdidas, La reina regente,* and *Alfonso XIII*—and suggests that, for reasons of age and progressive blindness, Galdós could not finish the series (344). Regalado disagrees with this and sees the reasons for its incompleteness as political (441 n.18). Enguídanos writes that the last paragraph of *Cánovas* "could" serve as a splendid epilogue, if "only" it was not known that there were to be four more volumes (434 n.11). Ribbans cites an interesting document, *El Liberal* (16 January 1908), that states that "Galdós had originally intended to conclude the *Episodios*" after *España trágica* and hesitated to continue because of "the physical problems caused by his increasing loss of sight" ("Literary Presentations," 10 and n.39). In such a scenario the series contains supplementary volumes rather than lacks them. These differences of opinion about how many volumes constitute a complete series, what the apparently missing ones were to be about, and why they were not written, are examples of the way that preconceived structures and the desire for closure condition the reading experience. The fifth series seems open-ended, but critics usually believe that this was unintentional; since closure is the conventional mode of the novel, its absence must be an accident. Yet since each *Episodio* lacks a typical epilogue, it could be just as easily said that there is consistency in the series' resistence to closure and that it was intentional. An intentional closure is, in fact, what Gilman sees:

> One wonders what would have emerged from his pen, had Galdós had the heart, the energy, and the eyesight to compose the *Episodios* of "la Semana Trágica" and "la Guerra de '98". Perhaps the hidden reason for the failure to complete the promised ten volumes was the same as that given for concluding the Second Series; even with the madcap assistance of Tito Livio the pain would have been far too great to bear. ("Memories," 50)

Either type of supposition assumes a truth and an intention that cannot be demonstrated conclusively enough to direct critical analysis. The six volumes can only be read now as they are written. Seeking a phantom epilogue is as fruitless as seeking a phantom origin, a hidden reason, or an objective reality behind words. This chapter will examine such open-endedness and the ways in which these *Episodios*, individually and collectively, refuse to function conventionally. Ultimately, perhaps, the fifth series cannot be understood or interpreted except to say that it shows how the relationships among historical and fictional discourses, between nineteenth-century Spain and its reader—then and now—cannot be stabilized, let alone resolved. These relationships constitute an ever more ceaseless, ever more complicated interplay of identity and difference.

NAMING

One of the most obvious ways in which the fifth series resists conventional modes of interpretation is through the use of

153

proper names. Roland Barthes has defined character as a proper
name that substitutes for a relatively stable set of adjectives, or
semes (67–68; see also chapter 1, note 24, of this study). This
"process of nomination . . . is the essence of the reader's activity: to read is to struggle to name" (92). The difficulties involved in naming epitomize those involved in reading, because
to name is to classify, to define the "truth" of the character (67),
and this "truth is what completes, what closes" (76), what
freezes meaning and invites definition. But in the last *Episodios*
the names of characters are continually and literally changing,
thus their truth is not stable and their meaning cannot be
named. The task of forming meanings is frustrated from the
outset of the series in one of the seemingly most elementary
tasks a reader performs: naming a character.

The example that most readily comes to mind is Proteo Liviano, the protagonist and narrator of the last four volumes. Well
into *Amadeo I*, he finally identifies himself: "Yo me llamo, sabedlo ya, Proteo Liviano, de donde saqué *Tito Livio* usado en mis
primeros escritos, y el *Tito* a secas que hoy merece mi prefer-
encia por lo picante y diminuto" (4:500). He is variously called
Tito, Titín, Proteo, Liviano, Tito Livio. Several obvious connotations of these names are immediately apparent: Tito's physical smallness—he is a lightweight; as Proteus his protean nature
is demonstrated through changing roles, opinions, and physical
sizes; Liviano signals his lasciviousness; and, of course, Livio
marks his role as historian: as Ribbans writes, he is "a burlesque
imitation of Livy" ("Literary Presentations," 10). The various
functions of all of these different aspects of Tito will be discussed, but first the naming process itself must be examined. No
other narrator or protagonist in the *Episodios nacionales* incurs
such a nominal instability, although Santiuste/Tuste/Confusio
of the fourth series comes close to sharing this characteristic
(and others) with Tito. If the proper name allows the reader to
postulate the existence of a character, the difficulty of stabilizing
a name makes postulating a character's existence, and thus
maintaining the realist illusion, much more difficult. In this way
the fifth series resists the reader's impulse to posit the existence

of characters who conform to conventional images of people in the world. This is one of the ways in which the breakdown of representational functions in these volumes begins at a more elementary level than has been observed in the third or fourth series.

The function of the character Tito is further confused by two additional factors: his role as first-person narrator and the odd name Tito/Proteo. Barthes discusses the difference between the "I" that is a character, in a realist text for example, and the "I" that is a figure in a modern text such as *A la recherche du temps perdu*. The "I" of a realist text, like "Sarrasine," functions just like the proper name, collecting various attributes under one sign:

> to say I is inevitably to attribute signifieds to oneself; further, it gives one a biographical duration, it enables one to undergo, in one's imagination, an intelligible "evolution," to signify oneself as an object with a destiny, to give meaning to time. On this level, *I* . . . is therefore a character. (68)

This definition is strikingly inadequate to Tito, as subsequent remarks about his biography, evolution, destiny, and relation to time will clearly show. More descriptive of his role in the fifth series is Barthes's definition of figure: "As figure, the character can oscillate between two roles, without this oscillation having any meaning, for it occurs outside biographical time (outside chronology): the symbolic structure is completely reversible: it can be read in any direction" (68). Tito's unchronological method of narration, the absence of cause-and-effect relationships between his fantastic and real experiences, or his historical observations and amorous exploits, tend to dissolve the realist illusion of Tito as a person; he becomes rather "a symbolic ideality" (Barthes, *S/Z*, 58). The dissolution of Tito as character also occurs through his odd name. Barthes writes that to give characters slightly out-of-place, nonpatronymic designations is "to emphasize the structural function of the Name, the Name as pure convention" (95). This serves to call attention to the artifice of language at the very beginning of a text, as Barthes observes: "All subversion [of the realist illusion], or all novelistic submission [to it], thus begins with the Proper Name" (95). Such a subversion of the realist illusion is indeed evident from the outset of the four volumes in which Tito is narrator and protagonist.

While having the widest implications, Tito's is not the only unstable name in the series. To cite just a few examples, there are the host of freed prisoners from Cartagena in *De Cartago a Sagunto* and *Cánovas*, who take part in the canton's uprising and later come to Madrid: David Montoro/Simón de la Roda (4:705), don Florestán de Calabria/Jenaro de Bocángel (4:686), or Pepe *el empalmado*/José Tercero (4:683). Many of the female figures, most of whom are Tito's conquests, have several names: Candelaria Penélope/Rosa Patria (4:587), the superficial and volatile political pamphleteer; Leonarda Bravo/Leona la Brava (4:683)/la dama de la Mula (4:784), the Andalusian prostitute turned influential Madrid courtesan; Silvestra/Chilivistra (4:707), the pathologically lascivious "beata;" and the faithful, humble, if "cursi," Casiana Conejo/Coelho/de Vargas Machuca (4:793)/de Portugal (4:804)/Fabia (4:875). The impulse to create a realist illusion for these figures is thwarted to the point of mockery, not only because of the absurd combinations of such names and nicknames, but also because the phenomenal social transformations of Leona or the split-personality of the hysterical, lustful Chilivistra almost exceed the limits of our imagination. Like Tito's, the excesses of these women defy incorporation into a world somehow like our own. They are caricatures and thus their representational functions are parodic. Their representative and symbolic functions not only parody society in these *Episodios*, but also any attempt to make connections between characters and society or characters and symbolic meanings.

The mythic figure of the last four *Episodios* also appears under different names. Mariclío/Clío/Madre Mariana, the muse of Spanish history, takes on different physical guises, and changes her shoes, depending on her attitude toward the events taking place (see note 14 in chapter 1). She, the divine historian, like Tito, the vulgar historian, reinforces the protean quality of the narration in its contradictions of fiction and history, realism and myth, or interpretation and confusion. Her aids, too—doña Grámatica, doña Aritmética, doña Caligrafía, etc., incur various names and guises according to their functions in the realistic or fantastic narratives offered by Tito. In *De Cartago a Sagunto*, for example, Tito encounters the women he met as Clío's mythical helpers on his fantastic journey to Cartagena in *La primera República*. Now in the real world he sees "la propia Doña Aritmética . . . el mismo demonio transfigurado para volverme tarumba." He asks if it is she, and she reponds, "no me llamo Demetria, sino Augustias." When he speaks to whom he believes to be "la imagen de Doña Geografía," she replies "No me llamo Sofía, sino Consolación" (4:696). These nonsensical interchanges serve to illustrate not just that Tito is unable to distinguish the real from the fantastic, but also that the difference between them is determined only by a name. Doña Geografía/Sofía/Consolación plays a different part according to each name. The reader's perception of her realistic or fantastic role, and consequently of her function in the discourse, is determined by that name, not by something that lies beneath it. What lies beneath the name is a phantom—Tito's phantom nymph or the reader's meaning.

These variations in name serve to question what hitherto seemed to be a natural act—naming and thus defining a character. By inhibiting the naming process, the text also inhibits the ensuing interpretation of that character's functions in plot and theme. From word one, so to speak, these *Episodios* offer resistance to conventional reading patterns. These texts lack what seem to be the basic elements required for creating an intelligible world and thus defy a conventional interpretive effort. The subversive processes observed with terms like "soberano" or characters like Teresa Villaescusa in the fourth series come to dominate the fifth series. In these last *Episodios* not only does a proper name identify conflicting adjectives and a signifier simultaneously relate different and contradictory signifieds, but also multiple signifiers combine in ways that ultimately work to neutralize contradiction itself, as will be described.

Lest it be imagined that this fluctuation of names and its consequent effects pertain to the last four novels of the fifth series alone, therefore supporting the theory of a radical discontinuity between the first two *Episodios* and the last four, one need only recall the case of Nicéfora/Céfora/Verónica of *España sin rey* (4:265), whose fluctuations between Christian and Jew, uncontrollable sensuality and fanatical mysticism, prefigure that of Delfina or Chilivistra in subsequent *Episodios* and repeat that of Dominiciana Paredes from the fourth series. Dominiciana, in turn, along with Donata from the same series and Rafaela Milagro from both the third and the fourth, becomes one of "las tres Parcas/Ecuménicas/ Euménides/Triple Hécate" in the fifth (4:382–83). Céfora is variously labeled "diablesa" or "ángel," "loca" or "histrionisa" (4:266), "inocente" or "hipócrita" (4:268), "tonta" or "cínica," "loca" or "Embustera," "riendo" or "llorosa," belonging to the "mundo" or "religión" (4:269), with a "cara ardorosa" or "de hielo" (4:308). Finally she is "el Diablo mismo en su duplicada encarnación histórica y romántica" (4:352); she is the contradiction of a historical novel. These alternations in the signifiers with which don Wifredo de Romarate or "Gaiferos" (4:289), a burlesque Quijote figure and an inept Carlist intriguer, and the reader attempt to interpret Nicéfora's character and to predict the outcome of the plot make those very efforts problematical. Don Wifredo, "el Bailío," seeks to make sense of Céfora in *España sin rey* in the same way that Tito tries to determine the real or fantastic existence of doña Caligrafía, Mariclío, or his ideal Floriana. As don Wifredo and Tito strive to find the truth of these women, so the reader strives to find meaning in the series. Don Wifredo and Tito are readers of other characters, other names, other words, just as the reader is of their names, the fluctuating signifiers that comprise these texts. The attempts of these characters/readers to resolve the paradoxes of a Nicéfora or of a fantastic world parallel our attempts to make these characters, stories, or relationships between fictional and historical discourses seem natural. Tito's or don Wifredo's inability to resolve such paradoxes to their satisfaction without recourse to otherworldly explanations— Wifredo's telepathy, Tito's mythical messengers—again illustrates how these texts resist the realist, representational impulse. If Nicéfora, like Tito, Chilivistra, don Florestán, Leona la Brava, or Mariclío, is every one of the signifiers that compose her character, and if her character inscribes various aspects of Spain, of writing, and of the *Episodios nacionales*, then the relationships between her character and those aspects incur the same problematical alternations between identity and difference that manifest themselves in *O'Donnell*.

The importance of the Name as a basis for the truth-seeking process in reading can be demonstrated briefly in two passages from the series. When in *España trágica* Vicente Halconero first hears the name of the beautiful young woman he has observed in the garden, he begins to create a reality out of her illusory image: "Al oír esto, sintió Vicente alegría y un cierto alivio de su confusión y pesadummbre, porque el misterio con nombre es misterio que empieza a desemborrarse. Ya no era tan hermética la bella y triste aparición que decía: 'me llamo Fernanda' " (4:368). Halconero thinks that he has the key to Fernanda's story, her text, when he can name her. And paradoxically, her linguistic designation creates the illusion for him that she has become more real. The passage, of course, exemplifies the realist illusion that language is reality, that a name connotes existence. By the third *Episodio*, *Amadeo I*, such self-consciousness of the functional value of the Name subverts that function itself. Tito meets the playful courtesan, "la llamada Graziella," soon to be another of his momentary paramours: "Dióme en la nariz que el nombre de Graziella era postizo, la nacionalidad dudosa, la mujer un misterio, una cifra obscura de interpretación imposible" (4:504). The relationship between naming and interpreting is revealed in all its conventionality and arbitrariness. Along with Graziella's introduction here in chapter 9, Tito enters the fantastic world of nymphs and other-dimensionality, dissolving completely the text's illusion of realism. The inability to name is the inability to interpret, to create meaning, and to make language and reality cohere. Tito's inability to name Graziella ultimately inscribes the reader's incapacity to resolve the fantastic and realistic sequences of the fifth series.

CONSTRUCTS OF PERSONALITY

The subversion of the realist illusion can be seen in other aspects of character. The postulation of a character's existence through a name entails assigning that character a name. This process also involves conditioned expectations and responses to nineteenth-century narrative and especially to the *Episodios*. Yet it is obvious that character development as it is usually conceived leaves much to be expected in the fifth series. When they are not sheer caricatures, the novelistic figures are often insipid, frivolous, or just boring. With few exceptions—the tragic Fernanda Ibero, the quixotic don Wifredo, or the portrayal of a courageous and warm-hearted Nicolás Estevañez, a politician esteemed by Galdós—these characters inspire little sympathy and more frequently dislike, or merely disinterest.

Clearly a conventional identification with the characters is difficult, if not impossible. Since this radically inhibits the easiest and most natural route to making sense of them, the reader must seek other means of creating their "personalities." One obvious way is through symbolism. Fernanda Ibero, for instance, is surely symbolic of various aspects of Spain. But unlike her novelistic predecessor, Lucila, "la celtíbera," she exhibits little evolution or development. Rather, as Rodríguez observes, her "two facets"—innocence and sensibility plus morbidity and violence—are "superimposed rather than successive stages in her development" (182). While this absence of a developmental rationale for her two facets makes of Fernanda a less complex, more static personality than Lucila, it also makes her a more interesting textual figure in another way. A relationship of superimposition, as opposed to evolution, between her two facets focuses attention on Fernanda's symbolic function and on the structure of the symbol itself.

The conventional definition of a symbol is a unified sign, but

the symbol Fernanda reveals that it is an arbitrary union of signifiers. This kind of static symbolism that calls attention to itself
is even more true with Nicéfora. From the outset her portrayal
as a sensual mystic gives her a paradoxical personality, and
nothing occurs to alter this. The paradox functions as a paradox;
there is no denouement, no synthesis. As with the symbols in
the fifth series, the use of paradox unveils the rhetorical figure
and the textual strategy itself.

While at once unrealistic or unnatural, and so calling attention to their narrative functions rather than representing personalities, Fernanda and Nicéfora do present the reader with interesting dualities. Most of the characters that populate the fifth
series, however, like the "cursi" Casiana, Tito's last mistress, or
the frivolous Obdulia, one of his first, lack this attribute and are
"flatly" one-dimensional. Coleridge's observations on allegory
suggest an insight into the strategic function of such pervasive
one-dimensionality in so many of the series's characters. When
a character becomes interesting in his own right, an allegory
fails; accordingly, the best allegories are those in which the
characters are the least interesting (Coleridge, "Allegory," 31,
33). Thus, if the characters in these six volumes tend to be less
interesting as personalities than those of many in the previous
forty, it is perhaps because these last *Episodios* are more allegorical. The question remains, however, as to what purpose the
allegory serves, what symbolic discourse it enables.

Symbols seem to unify different identities into a sign that
comprehends them both. To call a character symbolic is like des-
ignating the Proper Name; a symbol collects often disparate
semes under one economical sign. But allegory calls attention to
both the differences and the identities at the same moment. The
apparent movement of characters in the *Episodios* from realis-
tic-symbolic, to symbolic alone, to allegorical seems to suggest
á progressive self-consciousness of language's inability to be
anything but an arbitrary union of words. Allegory recognizes
the fallacious privileging of the signified idea or world when it
refuses to join signifier to signified, novel to world, and only
gestures to a union of signifier and signifier, word and word.

The failure of allegorical characters such as Casiana or Chilivis-tra to illuminate a transcendental truth about the historical ep-och epitomizes the fifth series's refusal to conform to a conven-tional understanding of the designation historical novel. Even the dualities of symbolic characters like Fernanda or Nicéfora, like the duality of the historical novel, remain fixed in that un-synthesizable yet undifferentiated state, resisting conventional modes of symbolic reading. Further implications of the exten-sive and often complex uses of symbol and allegory in the series will be discussed more at length toward the end of this chapter.

Some characters, not so unconventional from a symbolic or allegorical perspective, offer resistance to the more usual strat-egies of reading in other ways. Vicente Halconero, for example, first appears to conform more or less to the conventions of a realistic character. His personality is fully intelligible, he has no irreconcilable contradictions; he even appears to develop, but he is simply uninteresting, almost unsympathetic, from the mo-ment of his introduction. In *España trágica* he is a youth with a classically beautiful, "casi lampiño," face, but with a body that is "mezquino y endeble." His "cojera" is "casi distinguida"; he has one of those "medias voluntades" and "inteligencias en tres cuartos de madurez" (4:366). A reader's response to this por-trait and to all of Halconero's halfway achievements and near distinction could be disappointment, pity, or even scorn. He is certainly not the protagonist one might hope for or expect. His all-consuming passion for Fernanda ends with her sudden death. He "heroically" challenges Paúl y Angulo to a duel, only to be-come the ludicrous victim of a street fight. He finally resigns himself to a loveless marriage and his own mediocrity. Near the end of *España trágica* he recognizes that "mi alma no estaba fortalecida para ninguna clase de acción. Me faltan los bríos, el arranque, el desprecio de la vida." But he is content with himself and his insipid fiancée, Pilar Calpena, as he reveals when he speaks of "nuestra clase . . . estas familias medianamente ilustres, medianamente ricas, medianamente aderezadas de cul-tura y de educación, [que] serán las directoras de la Humanidad en los años que siguen" (4:460). In comparison with Gabriel

Araceli, Salvador Monsalud, Fernando Calpena, the two Santiago Iberos, characters of action who never quite relinquished their ideals, or even with Pepe Fajardo, who held on to his in theory if not in practice, this *Episodio*'s hero is particularly disappointing, because he is so unconventional.[12] Halconero's contentment with mediocrity thwarts the reader's expectations from previous series and the general literary expectations that a hero seek some goal, and either reach it or, in failing to do so, be devastated. While the reader can readily form a concept of his personality that is not unrealistic or unintelligible, there is always the sense that something is lacking in Halconero's characterization. The attempts to explain what that is and why it is lacking tell more about the reading process than about the character. Culler writes of Frédéric Moreau in *L'Education sentimentale* that

> the novel does not simply portray a banal personality but shows a marked lack of interest in what we might expect to be the most important questions. . . . What is learned and what is missed in his sentimental education? We can, as readers and critics, supply answers to these questions, and this is certainly what traditional models of character enjoin us to do. But if we do so we commit ourselves to naturalizing the text and to ignoring or reducing the strangeness of its gaps and silences. (*Poetics*, 231–32)

In the fifth series this "strangeness" in Halconero and other characters is in fact part of their effect.

The most obvious case of a character that rejects both literary and living models of personality is Tito. Dendle writes that there is "no evolution in the character of Tito Liviano. . . . Tito, like the Spain evoked by Galdós, remains forever fixed in instability and weakness" (153). He combines the worst of Fernanda Ibero and Vicente Halconero: huge, unexplainable mood swings, and a degradation that makes Halconero look positively gallant. Tito is even smaller than Halconero, almost dwarfish, and his handsome, though childish, face is also "casi lampiño." Tito is a degenerated Halconero, just as Halconero is a degenerated reflection of past protagonists. The cycle of degeneration observed in the third series, culminating in *Bodas reales* and continuing through the fourth series, makes itself felt with a vengeance in these last *Episodios*.

Tito first appears in *Amadeo I* as an "hombre chiquitín de cuerpo, grande de espíritu y dotado de amplia percepción para ver y apreciar las cosas del mundo" (4:479). He holds promise as a parodic "pícaro" or Don Juan figure because of his diverse genealogy, his lies and boasting about his age, his amorous conquests, and his apparent powers of perception. Though he is clearly unrealistic, he is possibly consistent with other literary conventions. As Northrop Frye concludes, "All lifelike characters, whether in drama or fiction, owe their consistency to the appropriateness of the stock type which belongs to their dramatic function. That stock type is not the character but it is as necessary to the character as a skeleton is to the actor who plays it."[13] Culler adds that it is not necessary for a character to fit such a role precisely, "but that these models guide the perception and creation of characters, enabling us to compose the comic situation and attribute to each an intelligible role" (*Poetics*, 236). Yet it is precisely such questions of consistency and intelligibility that are problematical with Tito, and with many other characters in the series. Tito is protean and parodic. His behavior and perceptions are often virtually unintelligible to him as well as to the reader. Attempts to interpret his role, to answer questions that the text—as in the case of Halconero or Frédéric Moreau—refuses, cause his personality, such as it is, to disintegrate almost completely. His behavior is so irrational and ridiculous, he is often so delirious or totally unconscious, that he ceases to conform to any literarily or culturally preconceived model, unless of course it is that of the madman, though not Don Quijote. Tito resists those efforts at intelligibility outlined by Frye, with literary types, or Barthes, in grouping semantic features. Perhaps this is his meaning: Tito functions not to present a lifelike personality, but to serve as one more absurd note of discord among the absurdities and discontinuities of the series.

There is another aspect of Tito that thwarts the reader's expectations: he is totally devoid of any conventionally positive qualities. Nothing in this character requires the reader's sympathy. Moreover, he is a protagonist who often does nothing through four *Episodios* where little occurs. Tito's self-descriptions define the personality that is offered to the reader page after page. He first attributes, in *Amadeo I*, all his life's problems to "la menguada talla. . . . Mi defecto era simplemente la pequeñez" (4:480). This smallness reaches the proportions of caricature and absurdity as, for example, at the end of *Amadeo I*, where he says that he and his mistress Obdulia—or "Tita"— "nos convertíamos en gatitos diminutos" (4:578). At the beginning of the next *Episodio*, *La primera República*, he says that "mi estatura parece que tiende a empequeñecerse más cada día; la agilidad de mi espíritu y de mis movimientos toca ya en lo ratonil" (4:581). After failing in his conquest of the ideal beauty, Floriana, a personification of Education, Tito's self-concept further diminishes, since at the end of *De Cartago a Sagunto*, he must compare himself to Floriana's consort, "el divino forjador" (4:678), the personfication of a Spain revitalized through Work:

> Yo, Tito Liviano, el hombre raquítico, enclenque, de ruín naturaleza, residuo miserable de una raza extenuada, politicastro que pretendía reformar el mundo con discursos huecos, con disputas doctrinales, fililíes retóricos y dogmáticos requilorios, me sentí tan humillado, que anhelé con todo mi alma huir de la comparación con aquel ser titánico de infinita grandeza. (4:679)

Surely the reader joins Tito in his self-condemnation after the narration of his repeated and degraded affairs with supercilious women, his bouts of drunkenness, delirium, violent rages, and his outrageous egotism. His smallness corresponds not only to his physique and his "insignificant" personality, but most importantly, perhaps, to his role as historian. He lacks the breadth of vision conventionally expected from someone assigned to witness, interpret, and record the world around him, as Tito has been assigned to do by Mariclío and "el isleño" (4:492).

The "ser titánico," along with his nymph Floriana, in the above passage is obviously a Promethean figure, as the term "titánico" and descriptions of him as an "hombre hercúleo" or as having a physical beauty comparable only to "la estatuaria helénica" illustrate (4:676). The comparison of Tito—Proteo—to this mythical hero is interesting for a number of reasons. The difference in their names in Spanish is marked by a single syllable, yet the difference in their functions is much greater. The "divino forjador" with his "fuego plasmador" (4:678) forges "los caracteres hispanos del porvenir" (4:676), just as Prometeo brings fire and thus civilization to man in classical mythology. Yet the ambiguous ending to the Prometheus myth—was he bound or unbound?—suggests that this fantastic characterization is not an unambiguously optimistic ideal in the *Episodio*. Even such larger than life heroes in the fifth series lend themselves to equivocal definitions, and in this case, as with the series, to equivocal interpretations of their conclusions. Upon first glance, however, Tito's derogatory comparison of himself to the "ser titánico" parallels one the reader might make between Tito's actual development and the literary expectations associated with a traditional hero.

The difference between Tito and his literary predecessors is most explicit in *Cánovas*, when he becomes a sardonic champion of "cursilería":

> Ya he dicho, y ahora repito, que nos habíamos declarado muy a gusto figuras culminantes en la flor y nata, o dígase *crema*, de la cursilería.
>
> Para que mis simpáticos lectores se rían un rato, les contaré lo que hacíamos mi compañera y yo ganosos de afianzarnos y sobresalir dignamente en aquella interesante clase social. Sigo creyendo que la llamada *gente cursi* es el verdadero estado llano de los tiempos modernos, por la extensión que ocupa en el censo y la mansedumbre pecuaria con que contribuye a las cargas del Estado. (4:811–12)

He proceeds to enumerate all the daily tasks and habits that are appropriate to the "cursi." This self-parody is not without political and social connotations. However, Tito's personality, ironic though it might be at this point, is nonetheless one-dimensional, and certainly unrealistic. Although the enumeration of "cursi" activities gestures toward the "*réel*," the fact that Tito knows he is one makes the entire situation implausible, since one of the characteristics of the "cursi" is ignorance of that fact.[14] The effect of this passage is perhaps to parody the "cursi" reader, not to create a likeable or lifelike personality for the protagonist. And, since Tito, "cursi" though he is, considers himself "superior a toda esta turbamulta" of Restoration society, a sort of "contrafigura del señorío enfatuado" (4:812), Restoration society appears even more insipid and degraded than Tito. Moreover, when he says to society, "Miradnos bien. Somos cursis por patriotismo" (4:812), the idea of patriotism itself becomes an object of parody. In passages like these Tito's autonarration is a degraded rewriting of the social, moral, and political values of the entire five series. His narration is even more acutely and broadly critical than the degenerated revisions offered in *Bodas reales*. Considering how the ideas of patriotism or heroism were treated in volumes like *Trafalgar*, even if more ambiguously than commonly acknowledged, Tito appears here as the end of the line of a progressively degenerating and degraded series of protagonists or heroes since Gabriel Araceli. The values that Tito incorporates are likewise degraded, parodic counterparts to those of Araceli, Monsalud, Calpena, Ibero, Fajardo, or even Santiuste. And Tito's text is an absurd rewriting of the discourse of all of Galdós's historical novels.

In passages like the "cursi" speech above, when Tito speaks with irony and seems to see himself and his society, it is certainly tempting to attribute to him the voice of truth, as though he were upon an "olimpo irónico," as Casalduero would say (165). But his irony is deceptive; it does not claim a supreme knowledge of self or Spain. The mere act of detachment is not enough to give the reader or Tito insight into the meaning of individual or society, fiction or history. From the beginning,

Tito has been "diferente de mí mismo" (4:480)—two selves, the waking and the sleeping, the narrator and the actor, the reader and the text, the author and the character, the novelist and the historian, the fantastic voyager and the interpreter of those fantasies. At times he does seem to have reconciled his roles of historian and character, object of irony and ironist, "loco" and "cuerdo," as in the parodic passages on "cursilería" or the final chapters of *Cánovas*. There Tito no longer suffers from blindness or delirium and seems to appropriate the voice of Mariclío when he advises Casiana as Mariclío might have advised him: "Modera tu arrebato bélico, que los tiempos son más de paciencia solapada que de fiereza impulsiva" (4:874). Yet the seeming closure of two selves, of two discourses, leads to no truth about Tito or about the series. Paul De Man writes that "a reconciliation between the ideal and the real as the result of an action or the activity of the mind" is precisely the "assumption that the ironist denies. Friedrich Schlegel is altogether clear on this. The dialectic of self-destruction and self-invention which for him, as for Baudelaire, characterizes the ironic mind is an endless process that leads to no synthesis."[15] The impossibility of a synthesis of two selves or of life and art is Tito's and the historical novel's. Tito's ending is like the ending of Hoffman's *Prinzessin Brambilla*, where the young couple exist "in a state of domestic bliss that might give credence to Starobinski's belief that art and the world have been reconciled in art" (De Man, "Rhetoric," 199–200). Tito's essay into "cursilería" functions in the same way that De Man believes *Prinzessin Brambilla* does: "the bourgeois idyll of the end is treated by Hoffman as pure parody, . . . the hero and the heroine, far from having returned to their natural selves, are more than ever playing the artificial parts of the happy couple." He goes on to describe

> Starobinski's error in seeing irony as a preliminary movement toward a recovered unity, as a reconciliation of the self with the world by means of art, [as being] a common (and morally admirable) mistake. In temporal terms it makes irony into the prefiguration of a future recovery, fic-

tion into the promise of a future happiness that, for the time being, exists only ideally. ("Rhetoric," 200–201)

The future of Tito and of Spain that Mariclío predicts in the chapter following Tito's advice to Casiana, which constitutes the last chapter that Galdós wrote in the forty-six *Episodios nacionales*, only exists ideally. This future is no less ideal, however, than are conventional ideals of character, of fiction and history, or of self and world.

Many questions remain unanswered with respect to nearly all of the characters in the fifth series, not just Tito: what motivates them to act as they do; what do their actions mean; what happens to them as a result of their actions? Attempting to answer these questions according to realist models results in what seem to be failed characterizations. However, it is not the characters that fail, but rather preconceived ideas about them and conventional modes of interpretation. These failures are repeatedly evidenced in critics' comments about the works. Rodríguez, for instance, concludes what is otherwise a thought-provoking and revealing analysis of character in the fifth series with this statement: "When compared with the first four Series, the Fifth seems *less effective* in characterization (189; emphasis mine). He cites the defects of an "unrealistic protagonist," which nonetheless satisfies Galdós's "illustrative intent" of "expressing an era's dissipation and lack of vigor" (189). Rodríguez's dissatisfaction has to do with the conventions and expectations by which he approaches and evaluates the series. He is clearly looking for Galdós's intentions and for fixed connections between narrative and message and between fiction and history. The inability to fix these connections or intentions is what creates misunderstandings about the series's function and value. In order to consider a character or a text "less effective," one must presume to define and delimit effects in the first place. Surely the "lifelike" effect is absent, but perhaps there are other effects that are functional besides this one.

For the purpose of filling the gaps in characters' personalities, the reader must bring something to the text that is not there.

Yet such blank spaces in the fifth series's characterizations are intrinsic to their function, just as in *L'Education sentimentale* or *Prinzessin Brambilla*. It is the sheer absurdity, hollowness, and strangeness of these characters that, together with other irregular aspects of the text, make the fifth series so effectively disorienting. The characterizations that subvert the reading process constitute a critique of the concept of personality itself in narrative. The creation of a personality for a character is another novelistic convention. The relative facility with which the characters of the first four series conform to conventional expectations about personality encourages the reader to have those same expectations in the fifth; hence the readings by Dendle, Rodríguez, or Hinterhäuser. But the characters of the fifth series resist such facile formulation, which is essentially reductive, and so call attention to reduction as an interpretive strategy. This resistance can allow the reader to scrutinize that consistent desire to make sense of literary and material words, and to see that such a desire often excludes elements deemed nonsensical. Perhaps the fifth series suggests that neither fiction nor history, and certainly not its characters, make such good, conventional sense as its reader may desire.

ORGANIZING PLOT SEQUENCES

The desire to fill in the blanks in a character's personality, that is, to organize details—semes—around a proper name in order to satisfy the expectation that a character conform to an image of a real person, is part of the overall effort to organize narrative elements into a meaningful, coherent system or plot. The conventional reading strategy is to organize the diverse elements of a narrative in order to find out what happens and what those happenings mean. The more complex or diverse the narrative, the larger and more challenging the organizational dilemma. Anything in the narrative that "seems insufficiently explained, poses problems, arouses a desire to know the truth," writes Culler, and this desire acts as a structuring force, leading the reader to look for features which he can organize as partial answers to the questions he has asked. . . . This desire to see what happens next does not itself act as an important structuring force, whereas the desire to see an enigma or a problem resolved does lead one to organize sequences so as to make them satisfy. (*Poetics*, 210–11)

Culler's remarks are especially pertinent to the historical novel, since it presents a dual challenge: to organize fictional sequences and to see how these fictional plots elucidate historical plots. The reader's attempts to satisfy both of these expectations encounter virtually insurmountable obstacles in the fifth series.

The difficulties in forming satisfactory narrative organizations or plot sequences can be seen in the comments of nearly all those who have written about these six novels. Dendle observes that "unlike earlier series of *Episodios*, there is little semblance of continuous plot in the fifth series. Coherent intrigue— the representation of an ordered progression of events toward a goal—gives way to an almost haphazard presentation of *faits divers*, the novelistic reflection of a period and a society without transcendence" (153). Several of Professor Dendle's expectations have been thwarted: that the fifth series be like the first four; that there be a continuous plot; that there be coherent, ordered, and goal-oriented intrigue. But in spite of his difficulties with organizing a plot, he does see a relationship of "reflection" between the history and fiction, even in its "haphazardness."

Alfred Rodríguez, too, in his discussion of the plots of the series, sees them as "radical departures from the literary norms of the *Episodios Nacionales*." For him "the existent volumes of the Fifth Series do not measure up to those of the previous four as novels" (181). His expectations are conditioned by the specific literary norms of the *Episodios*; therefore the fifth series seems to him unsatisfactory. He observes that "Neither Halconero's disenchanting biography nor Liviano's aimless movements command a high level of interest, which does not necessarily detract from their successful projection of mood" (181). Amidst this confusion, Rodríguez, like Dendle, still finds a connection between history and fiction, even if it is only in the resulting "mood." The major complaint he has about the last four *Episodios* is almost identical to Dendle's: as opposed to the plots centering on Araceli, Monsalud, and Fajardo, "Tito Liviano has no specific trajectory, no set of personal goals. There is no passion, no ideal to provide cohesion and meaning to his fragmentary existence" (180). A specific trajectory, personal goals, passion, ideals, and cohesion are traditional literary values. It is clear that the fifth series questions the conventions of narrative that organize and attribute meaning to and among plots and characters. Testimony to this is the disappointment felt by some of the best and most sympathetic readers of Galdós, like Brian Dendle and Alfred Rodríguez.

There are those who tend to dismiss, without serious examination, the series's substantial departures from other *Episodios* as owing to a reduced mental capacity in Galdós. Regalado, while refuting such charges, writes that "el desorden está más que en los recuerdos en su adecuada colocación en el proceso narrativo" (496). This assessment is based on the assumption that narrative elements should have an adequate or proper arrangement, another literary convention that invites examination, of course. Adequacy and properness, like order and consistency, are conventional, not intrinsic, aspects of narrative. While this study does not argue with many of the above statements as to the mood created, the difficulty in identifying plots, or their deviance from previous *Episodios*, it does question the value of judging these texts on preconceived models of what makes a successful narrative, historical novel, or *episodio nacional*. Perhaps instead of evaluating these works according to prior expectations, an understanding and appreciation of the novels of the fifth series would be better served by examining how they function, what textual strategies they do employ, and to what effect. Moreover, through an analysis of the texts themselves in conjunction with reader expectations, what one does when one reads them can be better understood and evaluated.

The fifth series offers lessons not only about the processes of reading these texts, but also about how conventional and limited previous readings may have been.

The fifth series thwarts the conventional expectation that a narrative plot enigmatically evolve into some grand meaning or final resolution that explains the entire story, that it reach closure, just as it thwarts the expectation that characters develop and evolve. And just as the reader may conventionally view the elements of narrative in terms of beginnings, middles, and ends, so may historical discourse be approached. The traditional description of the *Episodios nacionales*, consequently, is that they depict the movements of Spain's history through the nineteenth century. In addition, many scholars and critics of the *Episodios* believe that Galdós was trying to teach the present and future through an understanding of the past. This implies that there are certain morals, meanings, or truths to be gleaned from reading nineteenth-century history (or at least Galdós's reading of it) in particular ways. Yet this is simply one more conventional expectation that leads the historian, the historical novelist, or the literary critic to interpret and organize to his or her satisfaction what might be "haphazard" "*faits divers.*" The process of selection and organization is the same regardless of whether the plot or characters are fictional or historical.

Theoreticians as diverse as Hayden White, Michel Foucault, and Jacques Derrida have studied history as language; their insights provide alternative modes for approaching the *Episodios.* Hayden White sees historiography as a process of invention and organization just like fiction:

> In point of fact, history—the real world as it evolves in time—is made sense of in the same way that a poet or novelist tries to make sense of it, i.e., by endowing what originally appears to be problematical and mysterious with the aspect of a recognizable, because it is familiar, form. It does

not matter whether the world is conceived to be real or imagined; the manner of making sense of it is the same. (*Tropics*, 98)

The process that White defines as identical to that of the novelist and the historian is the process by which any reader organizes and interprets narrative. By making the "mysterious" "recognizable," by solving the enigma, the historian, novelist, or reader creates an organization, a meaning, which satisfies the conventional desire for intelligibility. For readers of the fifth series, this process becomes problematical, since there seems to be no familiar form that fully or satisfactorily explains or organizes its plots, characters, and symbols.

The resistance to coherent, conventional organizations in the fifth series resembles Michel Foucault's description of history as a discursive field that must first be viewed "in its nonsynthetic purity" if any sense is to be made of it.[16] By the term "discourse" he designates the organization of things and of the writing of those organizations. And within discourse the relationship between words and things becomes problematical, he writes in *An Archaeology of Knowledge*, a text that rereads his own previous discourse of *The Order of Things*:

> "discourses," in the form in which they can be heard or read, are not, as one might expect, a mere intersection of things and words: an obscure web of things, and a manifest, visible, coloured chain of words; . . . not a slender surface of contact, or confrontation, between a reality and a language (*langue*), the intrication of a lexicon and an experience; . . . in analysing discourses themselves, one sees the loosening of the embrace, apparently so tight, of words and things, and the emergence of a group of rules proper to discursive practice. These rules define not the dumb existence of a reality, nor the canonical use of a vocabulary, but the ordering of objects. "Words and things" is the entirely serious title of a problem; it is the ironic title of a work that modifies its own form, displaces its own data, and reveals, at the end of the day, a quite different task. A task that

consists of not—or no longer—treating discourses as groups of signs (signifying elements referring to contents or representations) but as practices that systematically form the objects of which they speak. (48–49)

Whether it is the discourse of the fifth series or of its interpretation, these practices are not innocent. Any discursive practice—whether of realistic or fantastic literature or of literary criticism—must be analyzed for the preconceived, hidden values that organize it. The series's repudiation of realism reveals the way that realism works; its resistance to interpretation unveils the prejudices and processes involved in that act.

Tito's physical formlessness, his random travels, and disordered, often incoherent, observations prevent the reader from deciding what, if anything, is meaningful in his behavior and comments, and from selecting a name—a structure, a set of rules—for them. Likewise in the early *Episodio, España trágica,* the narration that first appears to recount the death of Prim in the tragic mode becomes a satire through Halconero's ludicrous endeavors at heroism. Moreover, the stress given to the trivial in these *Episodios,* whether of historical or fictional material (Amadeo's or Tito's love affairs, for example), thwarts any "Lukácsian" expectations that the monumental be represented in the historical novel.[17] The chronological confusion, Tito's fantasies, the continual omission or cursory treatment of what might have been expected to play a large part in historical novels about this epoch, indeed offer a narrative field that resists synthesis, structure, and definition. Perhaps this is precisely the point of these texts: to call attention to that very desire to make sense, instead of allowing the reader, unthinkingly, to fulfill it. For Jacques Derrida,

the processes of history and sense are without a simple foundation but are open-ended, non-finalized. History has traditionally been the attempt to impose *a* sense on these processes, to posit an origin or end (*telos*), and thus to reduce what is contradictory, conflictual, and pluridimensional. Nostalgia for the origin and anticipation of the

175

end—that is, all forms of teleology and eschatology whether idealistic or materialistic—work according to the same reductive mechanisms.[18]

These observations offer insight not only into the fifth series, but into many of the volumes that precede it. One need only recall the tasks of Pepe Fajardo or Ventura Miedes as discussed in chapter 2, for instance. The one sought ideal truth and the other an origin to history in Lucila; the futility of their pursuits is that of any endeavor to reduce or subdue what is open-ended and multifaceted in the discourse of language or the world. Likewise, the third series relates over and over a "nostalgia for the origin and anticipation of the end" that leads to the endless frustration, disillusionment, and even death of characters like Fago, Beltrán, Nelet, or Leandra. Derrida's critique of history is applicable to the *Episodios nacionales* overall because it questions any form of representation and the indissolubility of the linguistic sign.

Derrida's rejection of the reductive tendencies of history, like that of White or Foucault, must be ours of those strategies which seek to reduce the *Episodios* to some truth or truths, which seek to make language and things cohere, or which posit some hierarchy between words and worlds that would make these texts re-present an original presence. The fifth series resists just such reduction and closure and forces us to reanalyze its textual process with other than traditional logocentric strategies. In the course of such a reanalysis, we must also reexamine our process of reading and that of all the *Episodios nacionales* as they reread the discourse of nineteenth-century Spain.

Derrida believes that "if today the problem of reading occupies the forefront of science, it is because," for more than a century, the reader has been suspended "between two ages of writing. Because we are beginning to write, to write differently, we must reread differently."[19] This study has attempted to offer alternative readings of the *Episodios nacionales* because they seem to suggest a pervasive awareness of their own diversity and difference. They provide constant rereadings of their own writings, just as *Bodas reales* provides of the third series or the fourth series—Isabel II, politicians, protagonists like Fajardo— provides of the third. The fifth series confronts perhaps only more blatantly the problems of reading and writing; it rereads and subverts the characters, plots, modes, and structures of previous volumes at the same time that it seems to undermine those very subversions themselves. Vicente Halconero, for example, who is considered by many critics to be, at least partially, an autobiographical sketch of the young Galdós, reads works by historians and novelists aware of the problematics of language: Michelet's "admirables *Historias*" or Rousseau's "*Nueva Heloïsa*" (4:367). The specific reference to these works certainly suggests that Galdós was aware of the debates on the limits of language in literature and philosophies of history. The relevance of these texts to the project of the *Episodios nacionales* could not be more obvious. Here, Halconero, "en su fiebre de asimilación empalmaba la Filosofía con la Literatura, y tan pronto se asomaba con ardiente anhelo a la selva encantada de Balzac, *La comedia humana*, como se metía en el inmenso laberinto de Laurent, *Historia de la Humanidad*" (4:367). He devours indiscriminately philosophy and literature, reflecting the interchanging and inextricable weave of the "redundantly hybrid genre" of the *Episodios*.

Carlos Clavería offers an incisive discussion of the possible connections between Halconero's readings and those of a youthful Galdós. He writes that, for Galdós, "esos libros habían hecho sentir la poesía de la Historia . . . de un pasado no demasiado remoto y abierto, con ello, a posibilidades de una novela histórica con substancia—hechos y personas—del propio siglo. La História podría ser vista como trama novelesca" ("Pensamiento," 171). In other words, these works by Lamartine, Theirs, Michelet, and others might offer a design for Galdós's historical novels. Clavería continues with a discussion of further possible sources for Galdós's ideas on history, but quite acutely observes that one cannot know which were most influential, since Galdós obviously "recurrió al recuerdo de un sinfín de lecturas, hechas al azar" (172). Any attempt to identify a source—

a cause or an origin—is ultimately frustrated and even counter-productive, Clavería appears to suggest.

Vicente Halconero is not only an avid reader, but also charts a course of writing for himself:

> No tardó Halconero en tomar grande afición a la literatura concebida y expuesta en forma personal: las llamadas *Memorias*, relato más o menos artificioso de acaecimientos más o menos verídicos, o las invenciones que para suplantar a la realidad se revisten del disfraz autobiográfico, ya diluyendo en cartas todo una historia sentimental, ya consignando en diarios apuntes las sucesivas borrascas de un corazón atormentado. En densas epístolas puso Rousseau su *Nueva Heloïsa*, y en espasmos de amor y desesperación, diariamente trasladados al papel, contó Goethe las desdichas del enamorado de Carlota. De este arte apasionado, melancólico y amarguísimo se prendó tanto el hijo de Lucila, que sin quererlo, y por inopinadas comezones de la edad juvenil, fue inducido a imitarlo. (4:367)

More than a prescription for Halconero's *Memorias*, which leave off with the intrusion of the omniscient narrator at the conclusion to chapter 1 of *España trágica*, this passage describes Tito's four *Episodios* in form—his "memorias," Mariclío's "cartas" and "epístolas"—and content—his "corazón atormentado," "espasmos de amor y desesperación," "arte apasionado, melancólico y amarguísimo." The passage also recalls the memoir structure of the entire first series and the epistolary form of many of the novels of the third series, in particular. It is a prescription for all of the *Episodios*; yet at the same time it unmasks their narrative conventions. The artificiality, degeneration, and parody of the structures, the characters, and the plot developments in the last series call more attention to the "más artificioso" than to the "menos," more to the "invenciones . . . para suplantar a la realidad," than to "acaecimientos verídicos." The progressive and virtually omnipresent references to language as process and artifice in the fifth series illustrate the *Episodios*'s progressive subversion of writing's ability to represent reality. Rather, reality and writing are both infinitely separate and infinitely the same in that they are both representations of a presence that is only ideally structured.

TEMPORAL ORGANIZATIONS

The fifth series constantly questions its ability to signify, and thus it questions the status of its own discourse. As a system of signs, language is sequential and linear, according to Saussure (70). The process and passage of history is also conventionally considered to be a linear phenomenon. Derrida observes that "the process of linearization, as Leroi-Gourhan describes it on a very vast historical scale, and the Jakobsonian critique of Saussure's linearist concept, must be thought together. The 'line' represents only a particular model, whatever might be its privilege."[20] The difficulty in forming plot sequences posed by the last *Episodios* implies a subversion of the conventionally linear, temporal, and spacial structures of both fictional and historical discourses, as can be seen from several textual examples.

The linear conception of history is reductive when it posits an origin and an end, just as are similar concepts of plot in narrative. The fifth series challenges such reduction by continually confusing time sequences or by disallowing the distinction between real time and fantasy time. Tito's journeys, as the enchanted, diminutive passenger in Mariclío's arms returning from Vizcaya to Madrid in *Amadeo I* (chapters 18 and 19), or through a mythic "valle intratelúrico" that assaults all the senses in *La primera República* (chapters 14 through 17), are the most obvious examples of fantasy time. In this fantastic passage through time and space that takes Tito, Mariclío, and a host of women/nymphs from Madrid to Cartagena, Floriana says to Tito: "Borre usted de su mente . . . las palabras *tarde* y *temprano*, que aquí no existe esa forma de apreciar el tiempo" (4:635). In this dream world Tito dreams he is in Congress, "oyendo un discursazo de Salmerón. . . . Aquello se me representaba como un teatro de niños, con figurillas diminutas que se movían con alambres" (4:637). Tito redoubles Calderón's conceit: in a dream world, he dreams of a reality that is nothing more than theater. He also dreams of his life in Madrid and of a decadent Olympus, until not only time, but the distinctions of place, myth, and reality, are inextricably confused. He asks himself: "¿la realidad era lo de allá o lo de acá? ¿Eran éste y el otro mundo igualmente falaces o igualmente verdaderos?" (4:638). Floriana offers an answer to such questions when she says "es ley divina que esto acabe siempre en aquello y aquello en esto, pues nunca se verá el fin definitivo de las cosas" (4:643). Her "divine law" ultimately makes fantasy and reality, past and present, here and there, indistinguishable. Conventional processes of perceiving and organizing time and place, or realistic and fantastic narrative structures, are unable to make sense of such passages. The difficulty in separating a fantastic from a realistic story subverts the narrative convention of a story within a story, or "nested narratives," where the illusion of an inner story makes the "frame story" seem more real. Here the absence of limits between stories frustrates any attempt to form these hierarchies and calls attention to the fact that the language of the fifth series, like that of any narrative, is all one surface (see Barthes, *S/Z*, 90).[21]

Lest it be thought that such questions pertain to the last four *Episodios* alone, one need only recall don Wifredo's "terremoto cerebral" (4:342) allows him to divine don Juan de Urríes's activities with Céfora and with General Prim in other parts of Spain. It also enables him to read letters that are exchanged between Céfora and don Juan, without actually seeing them (*España sin rey*, chapters 26 to 30). Don Wifredo puts together the pieces of don Juan and Céfora's love affair: "Seguro de poseer ya la clave entera, apresuróse el Bailío a construir a su modo toda la historia, con potente imaginación y lógica un tanto poemática" (4:351). Imagined history or poetic logic, these passages question the divisions between history and fiction, logic and fantasy. The fantastic mental abilities of don Wifredo, "el Bailío," are simply called "su lógico artificio" (4:345). The narrative offers no explanation as to how or why he finds answers through such irrational means, just as it offers no explanation for Tito's powers of metamorphosis or his telepathic contact with mythic and even historic figures like Cánovas. Rodríguez writes: "Liviano is the exclusive channel for a world of mythological fantasy that is never quite assimilated into the basic realism of the *Episodios Nacionales*. The extraneous matter, which Galdós originally felt compelled to justify in realistic terms, as dream content, soon becomes an independent element of the work" (180–81). Yet this "basic realism" was disturbed from the very first volume of the series through don Wifredo. Moreover, the label of "extraneous matter" privileges realism over nonrepresentational forms of discourse. Rodríguez goes on to identify "an open bifurcation of [Tito's] novelistic activities: one direction represented by the dissipated woman chaser; the other by the official historical observer. The two activities, even when simultaneous, coincide but superficially, thus weakening the novelistic fibre of the last Episodios" (181). Clearly the terms "novelistic fibre" require further definition and explanation, just as does Montesinos's assertion that *Cánovas* is not really a novel (284). The reference to the "superficial coincidence" of Tito's activities, or the confused mixture of fantasy and realism, illustrates the reader or critic's desire to see coincidence or make connections more than it defines the merits of the series. One might better read these "bifurcations" in plots, times and places for what they do in the text: they force the reader to admit at least the possibility of nonrational explanations, and to realize how conventional expectations of rationality may limit one's abilities to perceive. Neither don Wifredo nor Tito is confined to limitations imposed by conventions of rationality or dimensionality, nor need the reader be, at least while reading their texts. To limit interpretations of the characters and events of the fifth series to familiar modes of realistic or rational explanation is to limit one's understanding and appreciation of the texts. Just as they stretch the limits of comprehension here, so they may seek to reveal the arbitrariness of those limits in narrative, and perhaps in the world.[22]

The fifth series's resistance to temporal, spatial, or rational limitation is epitomized chiefly in Mariclío and her followers;

she is able to change shape, to cross boundaries of space and time. As the muse of history, she is not subject to reduction by order or logic. Her presence is both eternal and momentary: "Se va como viene, sin saludar a nadie y diciendo 'Hasta ahora.' Y el 'ahora' quiere decir *siempre*" (4:492). Time does not function for Mariclío in the conventional way, nor does it for Tito. He says of himself immediately prior to the above passage, "Necesito el desorden; la estricta cronología pugna con mi temperamento voluble y mis nervios azogados" (4:491). From the moment Tito introduces himself in chapter 2 of *Amadeo I*, he admits the

> falta de método . . . en mis escritos, los cuales aparecen reñidos con el orden cronológico. Este defecto mío radica en el fondo de mi naturaleza, y sin darme cuenta de ello refiero los acontecimientos invirtiendo su lugar en el tiempo. Si nunca me ha entrado en el cerebro la Aritmética, tampoco hice migas con la Cronología, y sin pensarlo refiero lo de hoy antes que lo de ayer, y la consecuencia antes que el antecedente. . . . Va siempre por delante lo que hiere mi imaginación con más viveza. (4:479)

Hierarchies of time and place, cause and effect, yesterday and today, are inverted here. Whatever strikes Tito's unconscious, thoughtless fancy of the moment takes precedence. He goes on to describe his ancestry at length, concluding that "debo declarar que de la heterogeneidad de mis fundamentos genealógicos he salido yo tan complejo, que a menudo me siento diferente de mí mismo" (4:480). The heterogeneity of Tito is not reducible, nor is that of the fifth series. Heterogeneity and other-dimensionality are functional values of the series in its plots, characters, structures, and symbols. Tito, time, fantasy, or history are not stable identities but continually shifting differences. The novelistic elements are not limited by beginnings and endings, chronologies, or simple oppositions. Even the notion of a dialectical structure of time is questioned, since Hegelian dialectic proposes a transcendence of contradiction, a making sense, and a moving forward through time.[23]

Regalado García observes that from *El caballero encantado* (1909) on, there is an important change in Galdós's concept of history: "Su visión lineal de la historia . . . y su creencia en el progreso sufren en ella modificaciones. . . . La visión de la historia como presente, pasado y futuro cede a la de un tiempo simultáneo, en la que el pasado y el presente se unifican" (489). But it is not quite simultaneity that the fifth series demonstrates because "simultaneity coordinates two absolute presents, two points or instants of presence, and it remains a linearist concept" (Derrida, *Grammatology*, 85). Synchrony as well as diachrony is a system of differences that posits a linearity and a hierarchy even if that hierarchy can be reversed. But the diversity of the fifth series, like Foucault's discursive field of history, resists organization in such ways. Tito's narrative employs a haphazard selection of details—words—from a nonsynthetic field of discourse—historical or fictional. The correlations between events or moments are arbitrary and can dissolve as soon as they are made. Just as the way in which one combines words is not sheerly linear, but broadly structural, so are the ways in which one combines moments.

The "Efémeras" that bring Tito messages from Mariclío epitomize the random combination of events and times that constitutes a history that forever erases itself. They are "mensajeras veloces" with "alas eternas," whose "memoria no dura más que un día" (4:827). The notion of memory is also linear since it posits the identities of present and past. To deny the duration of memory here is not only a rejection of a linearist concept of temporality, but also implies that Spain learns nothing from her past. Likewise, the "ends of history" are merely another illusion (see Dendle, *Mature Thought*, 183). At another point Tito defines as "*Efémera*, nombre que quiere decir historia de cada día, el suceso diario, algo así como el periódico que nos cuenta el hecho de actualidad" (4:796–97). The simile of "Efémera" as a newspaper casts doubt on the validity of the "historia de cada día," since this series, even more than previous ones, questions the authority of journalism, particularly through the journalist Tito. Here, as throughout his narrative, Tito wonders whether

what he perceives is fantasy or reality. The choice of the name
"Efémera" evokes the entire problematics of truth, presence,
and the possibility of knowing anything absolutely; it is an ad-
jective used to describe "la fiebre que dura por lo común un día
natural."[24] The knowledge of history comes to Tito as if in a
brief fever, which, as soon as it is over, leaves one doubting the
perceptions during that time. Tito suffers numerous fevers;[25]
for example, in *De Cartago a Sagunto*: "aprecié en mí un estado
febril, y ello fue causa de que la pesada modorra me trajera vi-
siones fraguadas en mi propia caldera cerebral, imágenes absur-
das que al desvanecerse no dejaron rastro en mi memoria"
(4:744). He has no memory of his dreams nor rational knowledge of his real or dream selves. Dreams and reality are thus no
more than sets for the acting out of his stupified roles as historian or character, observer or observed. Dream and reality, historian and character, observer and observed become indistinguishable as they refuse to form identities or sequential
structures.

The difficulty in perceiving temporal and spatial differences,
truth and falsehood, is seen throughout the series, not only in
obvious aspects like Tito's experiences during his fantastic journeys. For instance, Tito visits Cánovas at Efémera's behest and
is charged with a mission by him. All during the visit (*Cánovas*
chapters 4 and 5) and afterwards, Tito doubts the reality of what
transpires.[26] The scene thus fuses fiction with history, especially
when Cánovas lauds Tito's unpublished pages on the Cartagena
uprising. He says to Tito:

> Y usted pensará: "¿cómo puede este señor haber leído mis
> escritos si aún no han tenido la sanción de la letra de
> molde?" Pues si no lo sabe, le diré que tengo una loca afi-
> ción a los estudios históricos. A mí llegan diversos papeles
> interesantes, trozos de la Historia viva que aún destilan
> sangre al ser arrancados del cuerpo de la Humanidad. Yo
> los leo con avidez; los ordeno, los colecciono. . . . ¿Cómo
> llegaron a mí los escritos de usted? No lo sé, ni me importa
> saberlo. (4:800)

Cánovas equates Tito's unpublished, illogically acquired history with published, conventional history. The writings of the one are interchangeable with the other. At another point in the narrative when Tito visits Cánovas, the minister has read a journalistic piece supposedly written by Tito, but which Tito has no memory of writing. Reading takes precedence over writing here in a topsy-turvy discourse that is read before it is written. After this episode (chapter 14 of *Cánovas*) Tito decides that

> En cuanto a la entrevista con Cánovas y a la intervención de las *Efémeras* buenas y malas, diré que esto lo trasladaba yo a la esfera de mis relaciones ideológicas con *Mariclío*, estableciendo una especie de equilibrio entre lo cierto y lo dudoso, y saboreando los puros goces que encontré siempre en la verdad de la mentira. (4:839)

As with the "soberana modestia/hipocresía" of *Narváez* or the "buenos/malos" politicians of *Bodas reales*, these last *Episodios* equivocate between certainty and doubt, truth and lie. The elusive equilibrium of these terms marks the space between history and fiction that is the text of the fifth series.

The fifth series is as historical as official history is fictional. But Cánovas's voracious reading, ordering, and collecting of documents—living or dead, published or not, written or read—will ultimately have no effect on his own course of history. Mariclío tells Tito about his extensive library, saying,

> Todo esta ciencia arcaica y este fárrago, . . . ¿le sirven al buen don Antonio para consumar y sutilizar sus artes de estadista y gobernador . . . o sería el mismo sujeto que descuella hoy al frente de los negocios públicos si estuviera privado del continuo trato con los 30.000 volúmenes que adornan las paredes de esta noble vivienda? . . . Voy creyendo que esto no es más que un bello delirio de coleccionista . . . monomanía que satisface los amores de la erudición platónica, con poca o ninguna eficacia en el arte de aplicar las sabidurías trasnochadas al vivir contemporáneo. (4:865)

Cánovas the bibliophile is not unlike the half-made Ventura Miedes of the fourth series or the collector of memorabilia, Beltrán de Urdaneta, of the third series. Perhaps even more than they, Cánovas's "bello delirio de coleccionista" for "toda esta ciencia arcaica y este fárrago" illustrates the final degeneration of the antiquarian historian described by Nietzsche:

> Antiquarian history degenerates from the moment that it no longer gives a soul and inspiration to the fresh life of the present. The spring of piety is dried up, but the learned habit persists without it and revolves complaisantly round its own center. The horrid spectacle is seen of the mad collector raking over all the dust heaps of the past. He breathes a moldy air; the antiquarian habit may degrade a considerable talent, a real spiritual need in him, to a mere insatiable curiosity for everything old; he often sinks so low as to be satisfied with any food, and greedily devours all the scraps that fall from the bibliographical table.
>
> Even if this degeneration does not take place . . . there are dangers enough if it becomes too powerful and invades the territories of other methods. It only understands how to preserve life, not to create it; and thus always undervalues the present growth. . . . Thus it hinders the mighty impulse to a new deed and paralyzes the doer. (20)

Cánovas's collection seems to have no relationship with his Spain's present or future. Like O'Donnell and unlike Teresa Villaescusa, Cánovas is unable to put into practice the theory he reads in books. His reading, then, is an activity without relation to his reality; it is not representational. In like fashion, perhaps, the fifth series has no representational value; it does not tell us the meaning of the epoch, nor what will become of Spain. After reading these *Episodios*, the reader is still left in the dark, so to speak, like the Tito who goes blind. The fifth series obscures and confuses instead of illuminating the Spain to which its readers may assume it refers. This is one more way in which these volumes resist the literary conventions commonly associated with the historical novel.

The lack of historical or representational illumination in the series is epitomized most obviously in Tito's blindness, during which he writes that his existence "no era más que una sombra encerrada en ancha caverna . . . llegué a perder, según he podido apreciar, la conciencia de la realidad" (4:831). Tito's uncertain perception is a functional aspect of many of his roles and activities in the series. With respect to his fictional role, he suffers extreme fits of jealousy that make him think that his faithful mistress, Casiana, is unfaithful (*Cánovas*, chapters 13 and 14). And he confuses Casiana, Leona, and the "Efémeras." The confusion among these figures prohibits the reader from making distinctions between them, which therefore puts into question their separate identities. Their "facciones," like their names, are confused; their signifiers cannot be fixed since their texts consist of a constantly shifting play of difference. Tito's inability to distinguish among these characters and their functions as realistic or fantastic, modest or lascivious, is parallel to the reader's inability to make common sense of the various elements of these *Episodios*.

Like his incapacity to distinguish light from dark, character from character, Tito is unable to make sense of time during his blindness: "Recluso en mi habitación, sumido en intensa obscuridad, yo no distinguía los días de las noches, ni un día de otro, ni apreciaba el principio y fin de cada semana. Era para mí el tiempo un concepto indiviso, una extensión sin grados ni dobleces" (4:831). Tito perceives no distinguishing points in time, just as he perceives no differences in characters. Time is without dimension just as its concept is indivisible. Like a cloth without texture, his text "produces no relief."[27] His physical blindness corresponds to most of 1877 (4:839), yet his sense of time was confused before he went blind, too: "¡1877! La cifra pasó fugaz por mi mente. Menos que los años me interesaban los meses y los días, pues el tiempo había llegado a ser para mí un concepto caótico" (4:828). All notions of linear, progressive history or sequential time in which things change, evolve, and move forward are subverted through Tito's fantasies, his literal blindness, the confusion of time and space throughout his four volumes, and through the absence of rational explanations for these things. The fifth series suggests that the ways in which we conventionally perceive history, lineally or dialectically, are simply more conventions, more fantasies.[28] A mythic view is as meaningful as a rational view; Tito's unpublished memoirs are as influential as real history books. In fact, the conventions of logic, truth, fantasy, reality, time, and space are as mythical as any others.[29]

Tito's blindness obviously suggests that which Galdós underwent while writing *Amadeo I;* both the textual and the extra-textual blindness have inspired much critical controversy, as seen in the debates about the "unfinished" series or the appropriateness of its fantastical elements. The remarks about Galdós's abilities and intentions, and their effects on his work, are based, inevitably, on other texts whose origins and truths are as ambiguous as the intertextual relationships in the *Episodios.*

Josette Blanquat, in "Documentos galdosianos: 1912," cites an interview with Galdós by Javier Bueno, published in the "revista parisiense de lengua española *Mundial-Magazine* . . . julio de 1912 (num. 15)." In the interview, which took place in June of 1912, Javier Bueno writes of a depressed and pessimistic Galdós and quotes him as saying, "estoy casi ciego y esperando que hagan una operación en los ojos." Blanquat also cites the July 11 edition of *El País* that announces Galdós's recovered sight, health, happiness, and serenity.[30] Thus, during the time that Galdós is composing *Cánovas,* one document suggests a blindness and dispair that would support the opinion that he could not or would not continue with the *Episodios;* another document optimistically expresses a state of health and mind that would permit him to continue.

Brian Dendle publishes a more recent collection of documents as the "Appendix" to his "Galdós en *El año político.*" This collection contains an interview, published by Gómez Carrillo in *El Liberal,* between Galdós and Alfonso XII on 7 January 1914, during the performance of Galdós's play *Celia en los infiernos*. Galdós is quoted as responding to the king's question about his work in this way: "Preparo, además de un drama . . . un nuevo tomo de los *Episodios Nacionales*; el tomo número 47. Se titula *Sagasta*, y termina justamente en la fecha del nacimiento de V. M., en Mayo de 1886."[31] This document, then, suggests that Galdós was preparing and able to continue with the fifth series in 1914.

These documents may support or refute arguments about Galdós's abilities or intentions, because their truth is always in the eyes of the interpreter. In an article in the same volume as Dendle's, Vernon Chamberlin and Jack Weiner, together, translate another interview with Galdós, this time by a Russian journalist. The interview took place sometime between 1884 and 1885 and was published in St. Petersburg in 1889. The translation reads that Galdós said to Isaak Ia. Pavlovskii:

> Spain is a country which has been slandered, primarily by French writers, such as Dumas. It has preserved many peculiarities, but they are not easy for a foreigner to grasp. Therefore, those who write about Spain compose fictions rather than tell the truth. The one man who faithfully described our country was Washington Irving, but his book has become obsolete.[32]

So this 1984 English translation of an 1889 Russian translation of Galdós's 1884 or 1885 words would support the view that, for Galdós, the truth of Spain resides in fiction, thus implying that all of his writings about Spain are fictional, which is to say true. Galdós's preference for one romantic writer over the other recalls Clavería's claim that he was always influenced by the romantics. It also provides a self-parody of Galdós's endeavors, as, for instance, with the presence of Dumas at the end of *Bodas reales*.

The documentation inside and outside of the *Episodios nacionales* provides a wealth of possible interpretations. Yet the problems incurred by placing too much credence on documents are everywhere apparent, in critics' texts as well as throughout

Galdós's novels, as has been demonstrated. Geoffrey Ribbans defends the "symbolic burning of the document" in a literal instance in *España trágica* ("Literary Presentations," 9). There, Halconero apparently possesses a list of Prim's assassins, which Lucila finds and destroys. Lucila, the symbol of Spain, burns that trace of a truth that can never be known. Had the document been preserved—written in order to be read—as with Valvanera and Juan Antonio's "documento" in the third series, would it have been any truer than the multiple translations that portray Galdós's intent to write *Sagasta*? These documents are written in blindness, because the presence of Galdós, the past and the person, is not recuperable. But blindness may not be a handicap if one does not equate sight, or insight, with truth, or reality. The reinscription of blindness in the fifth series reveals how blindness itself may be a metaphor for writing and reading.

In chapter 18 of *Amadeo I* Galdós first resorts to dictation. Only one paragraph of the chapter is dictated (beginning with "Sin otra forma"), but it marks the entrance of Tito and Mariclío into the world of fantasy.[33] Mariclío aids Tito's escape from Viscaya and the irritated parents of his former fiancée Facunda. He describes a dark room and limited perception: "no pude distinguir," "no supe si," "inciertas blanduras," and so on. Of Mariclío he says, "la reconocía tan sólo por la voz, pues su figura se perdía en las tinieblas" (4:546). In this brief paragraph, after which Galdós's hand resumes the story, the personification of history fades from sight and is distinguishable only by a voice. This barely audible trace of history subsequently dissolves, too.

Returning to Madrid, as though on a fantastic journey, Mariclío tells Tito of the frustrated attempt at civil war that she witnessed in Viscaya. Tito listens, but is unable to retain the sense of her history:

> De la boca de la *Madre Mariana* salieron con limpia dicción nombres de esos que se resisten a permanecer en la memoria del oyente. . . . Pronunció otros nombres, que yo, con atención muy afilada, intenté clavar en mi memoria.

Pero entraban en ella y al instante salían a perderse en el ambiente ahumado y tenebroso de aquella estancia. . . .

Turbado yo y soñoliento, pude formular en mi magín este razonable juico: "El suceso que la puntual *Mariclío* trata de referirme es de aquellos que se desvanecen en la Historia, y a los treinta o más años de acaecidos, no hay memoria que los retenga. . . . El humo y la penumbra borran todo hecho que no tuvo eficacia, y de él sólo quedaba un epígrafe, la etiqueta de un frasco vacío." Yo vi el letrero: *Convenio de Amorebieta,* y ante él la *Madre Mariana* y su humilde interlocutor bostezábamos. (4:547)

This *Convenio* leaves not even the paradoxical trace that the *Convenio de Vergara* did in the third series. The "nombres" and "letreros" that seem to mark historic events fade from memory as soon as they are uttered or written. The signfier not only has no signified—"frasco vacío"—but disappears itself. This passage comments on Tito's entire narrative, since in chapter 5 "el isleño" asked him to write the history of this period from some thirty years in the future, relying on his good memory. This is precisely what Tito is now doing, but as he says, there is no memory after thirty years that can retain such a history. The passage also prefigures the conclusion to the series, where Mariclío falls asleep, retreating totally from consciousness and history, as she is on the verge of doing now. This chapter will examine both of these key passages at greater length below. At those moments, like this one, where the hand and the voice of the writer seem to separate, where fantasy takes over history, and memory and words fade, the text reinscribes its own endeavor. It is an endeavor, moreover, that seeks to erase itself as it is written, just like the history it cannot remember.

Chapter 19 continues to relate Tito's fantastical experiences as an ever more minute passenger inside Mariclío's pocket, unable to see. It is here, again in a dictated passage (beginning "—Pronto veremos") that Mariclío retains Tito as her aid: "Tu vista y oído son excelentes órganos de observación. Pequeño eres; más pequeño, casi imperceptible, serás cuando me sirvas en calidad de corchete, confidente y mensajero'' (4:549). Tito, invisible, will be able to see all, albeit what he sees is not worth observing, let alone recording, the text repeatedly implies. This is a curious inversion of a writer, perhaps, who in blindness can now see all. As Gilman writes, Galdós's recourse to Tito allows him a ''liberation from the constriction of identity'' (''Memories,'' 48).

Tito's commentary on his new role, his strange, indescribable sensations—''Mis sensaciones se perdieron en un sopor delicioso y rosado, tirando a violeta. . . . No sé cómo expresarlo'' (4:550)—describes a liberation not only from the strictures of identity, but from the conventions of historical discourse and realism. They also tell the reader how to read this text:

> Al llegar a este punto, el más delicado, el más desaprensivo de esta historia, me detengo a implorar la indulgencia de mis lectores, rogándoles que no separen lo verídico de lo increíble, y antes bien lo junten y amalgamen; que, al fin, con el arte de tal mixtura, llegarán a ver claramente la estricta verdad. A riesgo de que no me crean, les digo que me encontraba en la plena conciencia de mi yo espiritual y físico; y era yo mismo en mi ser inmanente; . . . todo lo que supe sabía, y mi memoria se armonizaba con mi entendimiento; . . . yo iba por las calles saboreando la inefable dicha de que nadie me viera ni en mi diminuta persona reparara; yo disfrutaba el placer de verlo todo sin ser visto, y de ejercitar el don de la crítica, el don de la burla, más precioso aún, sin que nadie por ello me molestase; yo podía reírme a mansalva de todo ser viviente, del Rey para abajo, y no encontraba freno ni obstáculo a mi observación fisgona. (4:550)

Tito's burlesque truth, this history, is a clear vision of what has already been said to leave no memory. Thus Tito's memories of himself and the folly he observes are evanescent impressions. His definition of ''la estricta verdad'' makes blindness and writing interchangeable terms. Moreover, Tito's insistence on his self-identity also serves to undermine that identity as memory.

It therefore undermines these texts as memoirs that reveal only the fictions that are, perhaps blindly, taken for history or autobiography.

THE REPETITION OF HISTORY

The mixture of the true and the incredible in the above passage recalls the chronological mixture and the mixture of discourses that Tito has defended in previous passages. This confusion of modes and times subverts conventional readings of both symbolic and temporal structures in radical ways. The conventional perception of the discourse of history or fiction as linear necessarily posits concrete differences between moments and meanings; a perception of a beginning and an end requires a distinction between them. In addition to chaotic chronology, distortions of time and space, and the various literal and figural manners of obfuscation and obscurity presented in these volumes, the fifth series resists differentiation of, and distinction among, its diverse elements through the constant use of repetition. Through repetition many elements that at first appear to be very different from each other become quite similar. For example, characters like Fernanda, Nicéfora, Donata, Delfina, Chilivistra, Wifredo, Tito, Halconero, and Segismundo García Fajardo are all distorted repetitions of each other. This distorted repetition occurs in plots, too, like the duels between don Enrique de Borbón and the duque de Montpensier (*España trágica*, chapters 8 and 9), Paúl y Angulo and Felipe Ducazal (*España trágica*, chapter 15), the near duel between Paúl y Angulo and Halconero (*España trágica*, chapter 14), and Tito's with Alberique, the former lover of his current mistress, Cabeza (*Amadeo I*, chapter 8). There are repetitions in love plots, replete with their triangular configurations: in *España sin rey*, don Juan de Urríes is unofficially involved with Nicéfora and officially with Fernanda, whom he replaces with a richer fiancée while still retaining Nicéfora on the side; in the same novel, don Wifredo maintains a platonic love for Fernanda and a sensuous desire for the prostitute "Paca la Africana"; Halconero's idealized passion for Fernanda in *España trágica* is replaced by a convenient engagement to Pilar Calpena, during which he maintains his relationship with a mistress, "la Eloísa." The succession of Tito's monotonous affairs is an exaggerated multiplication and degeneration of the more conventional, if only slightly more interesting, love plots of the fifth series: for a while Tito maintains a relationship with three different women at once (*Amadeo I*, chapter 12). Specific scenes repeat each other, too; for example, the visions of don Wifredo, Halconero, and Tito of the Cortes have very similar circumstances; exceedingly bored with the theatricalized proceedings, the characters turn to the real or imaginary contemplation of women (4:273, 366, 816, 825). Most notable in the series is the endless repetition of the same events and attitudes that are called history.

If Spain's history is only a repetition or distortion of itself, if there is no effective change, no functional difference between past and present, then there is no progress, no movement, no lesson that is to be learned.[34] This repetition is observable in numerous instances. In *Cánovas*, Tito and Segismundo García Fajardo watch Alfonso XII's "triumphant" entry into Madrid— into the Restoration—on 20 March 1876 in front of the troops that subdued the Carlists (again). Segismundo offers his "juicio histórico del Rebelde" when he says of the First Carlist War: "A los siete años de un batallar tenacísimo, los dos ejércitos, fatigados," decided to reconcile and say *"el Todos somos unos."* However, he continues, although this "huevo de Vergara fue ciertamente un huevo de paz . . . aquí la paz es el huevo de que sale otra generación con la misma estúpida manía." The most recent truce with the Carlists is also only a false peace: "Llaman paz a una tregua cuya duración no podemos apreciar todavía." What is more, the ideas that seemed to be so different between the two causes are one and the same:

> todo queda lo mismo. . . . El borbonismo no tiene dos fases, como creen los historiadores superficiales, sino una sola. Aquí y allá, en la guerra y en la paz, es siempre el mismo, un poder arbitrario que acopla el Trono y el Altar

. . . una política de inercia, de ficciones y de fórmulas men-
tirosas extraídas de la cantera de la tradición. (4:824)

If all is illusion, fiction, and lie, then so are the spatial, temporal,
political, or moral distinctions called here and there, then and
now, us and them.

Passages that equate what are conventionally deemed opposites—war and peace, past and present, Carlists and Alfonsists—
occur as early in the series as the first volume, *España sin rey*.
There Cánovas attends one of Eufrasia's dinner parties. The
presence of Eufrasia introduces the codes that have repeatedly
traversed her character since *Bodas reales* and throughout the
fourth series—adultery, degeneration, and deceit—into the
weave of the fifth series and the character Cánovas. He remarks,
"Don Carlos, antes de disparar el primer tiro, tendrá que irse a
su casa, porque el carlismo dejará de ser tal, y cambiando de
ideas, ha de cambiar necesariamente de nombre; se llamará *Alfonso XII*" (4:315). In *De Cartago a Sagunto*, Tito observes
Congress at the moment when General Pavía orders its dissolution. He laments that even such crises in Spain are not truly
tragic, but a "comedia desabrida y fácil."[35] The farcical outcome
of so serious an event as a military intervention in the government is symptomatic of Spain's illness: "El grave mal de nuestra
Patria es que aquí la paz y la guerra son igualmente deslavazadas
y sosaínas" (4:715). Prim in *España trágica* says: "Prefiero . . .
el tiempo de guerra declarada . . . a esta paz guerrera en que nos
sentimos cercados de enemigos, sin saber por dónde han de ata-
carnos . . . ; paz que no es paz, sino un estado rabioso" (4:413).
Just as there is no difference between war and peace—they are
equally inane—so the various governments brought to and
from power by such wars and truces are indistinguishable. The
Restoration is only a repetition of previous problems because
"todo lo ponen al revés" (4:716) and "los tiempos . . . se retro-
traen y vuelven las cosas al estado que tenían años ha" (4:828).
Such repetition is not particular to the nineteenth century; even
Spain's so-called glorious past is implicated when don Juan de
Urríes recounts the opening of Carlos v's tomb: "Creíamos ver

la Historia que volvía . . . no sé decirlo . . . el pasado que se nos ponía delante . . . tampoco acierto a expresarlo" (4:317). Urríes cannot articulate that difference that is history or the past, since these terms have no identity.

Like the differences among monarchs through the ages, the differences in ministries and ministers are merely momentary, superficial; all are the same in the end. The "turno pacífico" will spell no change for Spain either, the conclusion of the series illustrates. Vicente Halconero, now a deputy, reappears in *Cánovas* and says to Tito: "El turno se impone, y la tocata liberal ha de sustituir a la tocata conservadora. Espero yo que entre ambas músicas haya bastante diferencia, así en lo fundamental como en lo externo" (4:872.) The substitution of one term or one "tocata" for another, however, will not distinguish the external from the fundamental if all is one surface. In fact Maclío's last letter to Tito states that Halconero's hope is futile: "Los políticos se constituirán en casta, dividiéndose, hipócritas, en dos bandos igualmente dinásticos e igualmente estériles, sin otro móvil que tejer y destejer la jerga de sus provechos particulares en el telar burocrático" (4:876). The differences in politics and political rhetoric are as indistinguishable as the fiction and history that are woven together in the texts of the *Episodios nacionales*. The "jerga" of the politicians, like war and peace, or then and now, are terms or signifiers that seem to make differences, or lead to progress and change. But they are still only arbitrary markers in a system without absolute identities. What appears to mean one thing today may mean something else tomorrow in the continual "tejer" and "destejer" of the discourse of history. If today is like yesterday, if war is peace and history is fiction, then there are no differences, just endless and meaningless repetitions. The fifth series seeks a reevaluation of the processes of history by equating them explicitly with language. Thus both the history that is written in these volumes and the discursive strategies themselves are subject to the same questions, the same unraveling.

The series's reinscription of its own textuality is obvious from the first volume of the series, *España sin rey*. Fernanda writes

to her fiance Urríes, a deputy in the congress formed after the September Revolution:

> Estoy celosísima de las Cortes, que me parecen unas ja-
> monas habladoras y emperifolladas. Dices que vais a hacer
> una Constitución. Por Dios, no te metas en eso. . . . En
> todo caso, coge una de las viejas, y con algún garabatito
> aquí y otro allá, la presentas como nueva. Me ha contado
> mi madre que el famoso caballero don Beltrán de Urdaneta,
> cuando ya chocheaba, no tenía más entretenimiento que
> hacer Constituciones. Todas las noches escribía una, y al día
> siguiente hacía con ella pajaritas. (4:255)

If each constitution is a repetition of those already written, the difference between old and new or past and present dissolves. The senile Beltrán and the congressmen like Urríes are both authors of documents that are written to be destroyed. Beltrán and Spanish politicians, senility and government, writing and destroying, thus become interchangeable. These repetitions, these constitutions, are already senile texts that are forgotten and useless as soon as they are written. Spanish politics endlessly rewrites as it forgets its own stagnant history. The metaphor of Congress and its constitutions as talkative, gaudy women in the above passage also includes the code of sexuality in the textual network of politics, history, and language itself, much as occurred in *O'Donnell*. Women, constitutions, senility, writing, forgetting, even Fernanda's chatty letter and Fernanda herself are interchangeable elements in the text of this historical novel where one "tocata" sounds the same as the next.

The codes of sexuality, politics, and language intertwine to include characters, plots, themes, and structures throughout the series, most obviously through Tito in his roles as Don Juan, political satirist, orator, journalist, and historian, and through the letters he receives from Mariclío. While the names Beltrán and Fernanda come to connote antiquarianism and senility or naive loquacity and romantic infatuation, and so likewise do the constitutions, letters, politics, history, and fiction that are associated with them, in Tito these elements take on even more ve-

hemently parodic and condemning associations. Tito's ever more degraded and repetitive love affairs become inextricably linked to the other political, amorous, historical, or fictional elements of the last four volumes, so that these elements in turn become absurdly repetitive and degraded.

Many seemingly diverse narrative aspects come together in repetition and degradation in the final *Episodio, Cánovas*, where nothing has changed, including the constitution, as Tito says:

> Y ahora, lector mío, a mi modo *continuaré la Historia de España*, como decía Cánovas. En cuanto terminaron los desabridos festejos, las Cortes enredáronse en el arduo trajín de fabricar la nueva Constitución, la cual, si no me sale mal la cuenta, era la sexta que los españoles del siglo xix habíamos estatuído para pasar el rato. (4:825)

Not only will this constitution be a refabrication of the five previous ones, but it will suffer the same "sistemática violación de aquella ley, como violadas y escarnecidas fueron las cinco Constituciones precedentes. En el propio estado de pérfida legalidad seguiría viviendo nuestra nación año tras año" (4:825). As soon as it is written, this constitution is violated, ignored. Its function is to be without function except as a mark of deferral. As a historical document this constitution of signifiers, like the ones before it, requires no signified value. There is no functional relationship between the words of its text and the Spain it appears to address. The reading, then, of this writing is indeed "different": the constitution serves to deconstitute itself at the moment that it becomes a historical document.

The "desabridos festejos" that celebrate the historical event of this document have marked the writing of other constitutions, other governments, too. Decorated balconies testify to such a ludicrous simulacrum of meaning, movement, or change in history, as Tito observes prior to the above passage:

> ardió Madrid en fiestas, conforme al ceremonial de alegría pública que amenizaba nuestra Historia desde que volvió del destierro Fernando *el Deseado*, en 1814. Vestían los bal-

cones abigarradas percalinas, las más de ellas de respetable ancianidad, pues ya figuraron en el regocijo de 1860, cuando entraron las tropas vencedoras de Africa, y en el regocijo del 68, entrada de Serrano, vencedor an Alcolea. . . . La iluminación pública era la misma que esmaltó las noches en diferentes ocasiones de júbilo, como el nacimiento del Príncipe y las Infantitas o la traída de aguas del Lozoya. (4:825)

The biting irony of these words is underscored by the choice of "el Deseado," instead of "vii," by the repetition of "regocijo" and "vencedor," and by the sardonic juxtaposition of the royal births to the entrance of the waters of Lozoya. These balconies are like the words of history, as Tito observes when they are illuminated to celebrate Amadeo's abdication and the "new" Republic: "aparecieron iluminados casi todos los balcones. . . . Eran como letras, palabras y conceptos de una página histórica, escrita con hachones y farolillos" (4:577). This celebration is just as meaningful as that marking Fernando "el Deseado's" entry, as well as every new government and every new constitution. These celebrations, like the constitutions, are meaningless repetitions of each other that provide no real illumination. They are done to be undone, constituted to be deconstituted, just like the adornments for Isabel II's wedding procession at the end of the third series. The capacity of the Madrileños to forget the ephemerality of each constitution, government, and historical event as they triumphantly celebrate the next is the same as that which calls for the systematic forgetting of each constitution as soon as it is written. It is don Beltrán's senility; it is the memory of the "Efémeras"; it is Spain's history, as Tito says in *Amadeo I*:

No sé si mis lectores tendrán interés en conocer el Ministerio de conciliación, presidido por el duque de la Torre. Eran los de siempre, ni mejores ni más malos que los anteriores y subsiguientes. ¿Qué hacían? Ir viviendo, ir trazando una historia tediosa y sin relieve, sobre cuyas pági-

199

nas, escritas con menos tinta que saliva, pasaban pronto las aguas del olvido. (4:487)

This passage equates history with life and the written word— saliva and ink. All will soon be forgotten because there is no "relieve" to mark a difference or a point of reference that interrupts the tedious procession of history or writing. These lines describe the relationship of repetition and difference where the one process is indistinguishable from the other, as the old is from the new or the good from the bad. All triumphs, identities, or meanings rest on the ephemeral and arbitrary perspective of the moment.

The interchangeability of terms for times, for events, for governments, and for constitutions is seen among politicians, too, here, as was observed in the third and fourth series. In *Amadeo I*, Tito relates the "terrible pelea" between

zorrillescos y sagasteros. Cada uno de los jefes de estas dos revoltosas taifas dio al país su manifiesto. Leílos yo, y la verdad, no encontré gran diferencia entre una y otra soflama. . . . Los padres de las criaturas, que parecían mellizas, Zorrilla y Sagasta, se avinieron a nombrar un Jurado . . . de arbitraje

to resolve the differences between the twin "manifiestos/soflamas/criaturas" (5:503). They finally decide that "entre el programa de Sagasta y el de Zorrilla no había un comino de diferencia" (4:507). Mariclío observes, belittles, and records all of this (*Amadeo I*, chapter 9), but tells Tito:

Obligada estoy . . . a mencionar todo lo que hace esta gentezuela; pero escribo sus nombres con una saliva especial que me dio mi padre para estos casos. . . . Esta saliva tiene una virtud preciosa. Lo que con ella escribo se lee hoy, se lee mañana; pero luego se borra y no llega a la posteridad. (4:508)

The changes in political rhetoric, manifestos, or constitutions are merely words that have no transcendental significance, no

functional value other than ephemeral difference, just like the terms "Zorrilla" and "Sagasta" themselves. The lack of "relieve," substance, or texture is underlined by the numerous instances in the fifth series where politicians are referred to as "figurines"[36]; they are fakes, signifiers without real significance, like the papier-mâché facade of Atocha in *Bodas reales*. Their rhetoric is written with the saliva/ink of forgetfulness, like don Beltrán's endless, senile rewriting of constitutions. Mariclío's history, like Tito's *Episodio*, must be written, but only in order that it be forgotten. The documents of Mariclío, Beltrán, or the "gentezuela" will teach men nothing really; perhaps the fifth series teaches its readers only to "reread differently" by forgetting the illusions that the texts of history endlessly defer and repeat.

Yet repetition does imply a difference—distortion: even a reflection is not self-identical, but a simulacrum. The phenomena of repetition and difference can be observed in other elements besides the paper documents of the fifth series. In *De Cartago a Sagunto*, for example, Tito praises "la perfección del cuño" of the new "duros" fabricated in Cartegena, "cuya ley superaba en una peseta a la ley de los duros" made in Madrid. They are minted, moreover, by "buenos chicos," condemned "por monederos falsos" (4:681). These new coins function in the same way that Spain's six constitutions do: one "ley" surpassing the next. Yet a "duro" in Cartagena functions like a "duro" in Madrid. Though one is the distortion of the other, their function is the same; the coins only achieve their difference from each other because of that likeness. It is ironic, of course, that these coins are made by professional forgers, especially considering the choice of the term "ley." Counterfeiting coins or constitutions achieves the same effect: to make different what is identical is simultaneously to make identical what is different.

The battleships in *De Cartago a Sagunto* incur this repetition in difference just like the coins:

> el cantón creyó deber patriótico cambiar el nombre del
> barco en que íbamos, pues aquello de *Fernando*, con añadi-

dura de *el Católico,* conservaba el sonsonete del destruído régimen monárquico y religioso. Para remediar esto, buscaron un nombre que expresase las ideas de rebeldía triunfadora, y no encontraron mejor mote que el estrambótico y ridículamente enigmático de *Despertador del Cantón.* (4:682)

The function of the ship is the same, regardless of its new name. Moreover, this "rebeldía" will be no more lastingly "triunfadora" than were any of those "vencedores" celebrated by Madrid's endless series of decorated balconies. Nor is the "régimen monárquico y religioso" destroyed, as the Restoration and the entrance of foreign friars in *Cánovas* reveals. Changing the "sonsonete" or "mote" of a ship, a coin, a character, or a constitution brings no more than the illusion of difference, the fiction of change, the distortion of the "ridículo y estrambótico." The metaphor, hyperbole, and catechresis of passages like these, or the degeneration, decadence, and degradation of the characters of the fifth series, and the parody, irony, and allegory of the narration itself describe the endless and distorting phenomena of repetition and difference that constitutes the relationship between fiction and history.

Because such historical events are manifested chiefly through words alone, the fate of Cartagena's rebellion has been repeated throughout the century. As Mariclío says in *La primera República* about the canton uprisers, "Creen estos inocentes que las revoluciones se hacen con discursos frenéticos" (4:669). Cánovas, in the last *Episodio,* believes that revolution and violence take Spain backwards rather than forwards: "Las alargadas y las violencias nos llevarían hacia atrás, en vez de abrirnos paso franco hacia un adelante remoto" (4:838). In *España trágica,* Segismundo predicts a true revolution for Spain if Prim is assassinated: "en prólogo épico estamos. Pronto aparecerá lo que faltó en las abortadas revoluciones del 54 y del 68: el elemento trágico" (4:441). But Segismundo's expectations of tragedy, revolution, and real change are disappointed just as Tito's are when he views the tragicomedy of Pavía storming Congress, as discussed above. Such frustrated rebellion finds a parallel in Segismundo himself. In *Cánovas*, he leaves his wealthy home for a bohemian life, where he must be fed and clothed by Tito. Finally he fully integrates himself into the social, political, and even religious farces of Restoration Spain. Segismundo, like Halconero and Tito, personifies the trajectory of aborted revolutions on both large and small scales. As he says of one of his early conquests, another sensuous "beata," Donata of the fourth series, "Yo no había pretendido más que un triunfo sin consecuencias. Llegué, vencí, y a mi camarachón a continuar viviendo la Historia de España" (4:438). Triumph without consequences, rebellion without change, this is Segismundo's personal objective, just as it is Tito's in his numerous conquests. The comparison of these frivolous sexual affairs to the affairs of the state of Spain is explicit in the repetitions of Cánovas's phrase "continuando la Historia de España."[37]

When we compare such passages as the above with the final words of Mariclío, perhaps we must read a new irony into her forecast for the future of Spain, as she says

> Alarmante es la palabra Revolución. Pero si no inventáis otra menos aterradora, no tendréis más remedio que usarla los que no queráis morir de la honda caquexia que invade el cansado cuerpo de tu Nación. Declaraos revolucionarios, díscolos si os parece mejor esta palabra, contumaces en la rebeldía. En la situación a que llegaréis andando los años, el ideal revolucionario, la actitud indómita si queréis, constituirán el único síntoma de vida. (4:876)

Considering the function that words, especially the word "revolution," have in the series, it is difficult to disentangle this last paragraph from the play of repetition and difference that has preceded it. A word may be alarming or terrifying, but it is still a word. To use a word, to declare oneself "revolucionario," or merely "díscolo," or "contumaz" is only to display an ideal, an attitude, or a symptom, not to act. Tito sees this about Spain and about himself when he writes in *Amadeo I* with regard to the rumors he hears:

No daba yo gran crédito a tales monsergas. Mil veces había llegado a mis oídos el susurro de alzamientos . . . sin que los hechos correspondieran a las risueñas esperanzas. El optimismo de los revolucionarios sencillotes y pillines, que creen lo que sueñan, es un fenómeno habitual en tiempos turbados. Manteníame yo escéptico, convencido de que no había más revolución que la formulada en ardientes discursos, revolución puramente teórica y verbal. Por eso yo, sempiterno hablador, era el primer revolucionario de la época y el primer oráculo de un resurgimiento que no quería venir. (4:556)

Revolution may be a happy hope or a believed dream, but as a verbal theory, it is only illusion. Tito is a revolutionary without a cause, the only kind there is: a signifier devoid of signified value. Not only are words divorced from actions, but also from univocal concepts, as has been seen in numerous passages of repetitive political rhetoric. The signifier is without a material reference as Tito is without relation to the world; it is also without a signified, as Tito is without coherent meaning. Signifieds or conventional concepts tend to disappear altogether in the fifth series, making the reader's efforts to make the text intelligible, to form signs, so problematic. The gap between words and sense is almost as great as that between words and deeds in the *Episodios*. These gaps not only question the relationship of text to world, but of writing to reading.

In *Amadeo I* Tito observes that "No había en España voluntades más que para discutir, para levantar barreras de palabras entre los entendimientos, y recelos y celeras entre los corazones" (4:514). These barriers to sense pertain to the global relationship between the fifth series as a different kind of writing and, consequently, to its rereader. They also pertain to another aspect of the novels' irrationality, the specific plot of the character Tito, who suffers mad, violent attacks of jealousy (*Cánovas*, chapters 13–15, for example), who lacks will, and who is the narrator of these *Episodios*. He writes of himself:

escribo facilmente, ajustándome a las ideas que se me piden. Escribo en republicano, escribo en conservador y hasta en *neo* si fuera menester. Pero esto es, como si dijéramos, producción inconsciente de mi ser . . . que brota de mí sin más valor que el de un juego de palabras. Dentro de mí quedan mis convicciones inalterables. (4:515)

Tito's writing is different: it is a play of words that has no consciousness of its writer. The notion of an original relationship between author and text or even thought and word is demythified. Such passages frustrate every attempt to join signifiers to signifieds, to create any meaning at all for this series. In the hand of a character like Tito, even the terms "ser" or "convicciones inalterables" lack sense. Ultimately the entire project of the Series comes into question, as Tito writes:

No cesaba yo de interrogarme así: "¿Estaré yo un poco demente, o siquier tocado de tenaces manías, la manía de mi proteísmo, que consiste en escribir con distintos criterios y aparente convicción; la manía de mi esencial criterio inmanente, de tendencias atrozmente revolucionarias?" Y otra cosa pregunto a los que me leen y a mí mismo: "¿Todo lo que cuento es real, o los ensueños se me escapan del cerebro a la pluma y de la pluma al papel? ¿Las amorosas conquistas que me sirven de trama para la urdimbre histórica, son verdaderas o imaginarias? ¿Creo en ellas porque las imagino, y las escribo porque las creo?" (4:521)

Tito as character and writer, this text's history and fiction, and the revolution it proclaims come together here. Tito's mania is both protean and revolutionary, subject to constant change, seemingly endless difference. He is Proteo Liviano, "el primer revolucionario de la época" (4:556). Yet he is also, like that revolution, only endlessly repeated words. Like the fictional plots that intertwine with the "urdimbre" of history, the distinctions between reality and dream, truth and imagination, reader and writer, character and narrator, dissolve in passages like these.

Tito as character or narrator, writer or reader, is no more revolutionary than those six constitutions:

Llevado y traído por fatal corriente misteriosa, yo era el campeón de todas las causas. En corto tiempo enaltecí con

mi fácil pluma el federalismo intransigente, el federalismo
templado, la monarquía conservadora de Serrano y Sagasta
y la monarquía democrática de Ruíz Zorrilla. Era yo, pues,
un caso peregrino de proteísmo; y ved, amigos, como esta
mi voluble constitución mental venía consagrada desde mi
nacimiento y bautismo por mi nombre y cognomen. Yo me
llamo, sabedlo ya, Proteo Liviano, de donde saqué el *Tito
Livio* . . . y el *Tito* a secas. (4:500)

Tito questions the relation of himself to his writing and finds
that there can be no fixed identity, whether he writes of himself
or of himself writing. Even his name marks the constant shifting and mutability of signifiers, not a stable, signified sign.
Whether it is Proteo or Tito, five constitutions or six, written or
imagined documents, a verbal revolution or a revolutionary
mania, all is a text without relief. The terms and categories of
Tito, narrator, historian, character, rhetoric, politics, sexuality,
society, history, fiction, and the fifth series of *Episodios nacionales* become interchangeable and ultimately indistinguishable
in their repetitive pursuit of an intelligible reality, a meaning, a
past, or a present that continually resists differentiation and signification.

SEEKING SYMBOLS

The entire project of the fifth series—its fictional and historical
allusions, its relationships between fantasy and realism, truth
and lie, word and idea, writing and interpretation or text and
reader—becomes an open-ended process of repetition and difference through passages like those cited above. These categories refuse to form distinct boundaries and correlatively conventional oppositions. Just as the reader's efforts to distinguish
these categories in order to make sense of them are undermined,
so other types of discursive relationships resist coherent for-
mulations.

Roland Barthes, A. J. Greimas, Claude Lévi-Strauss, along with
many others, have discussed how symbolic meaning is based on

a structure of antithesis. When a text offers two situations, events, or characters that seem to be opposed, the reader attempts to organize these oppositions into a coherent structure that encompasses the antithesis. Culler writes of this process:

> The presentation of two heroines, one dark and the other fair, sets in motion an experiment in extrapolation in which the reader correlates this opposition with thematic oppositions that it might manifest: evil/good, forbidden/permitted. . . . The reader can pass from one opposition to another . . . determining which are pertinent to larger thematic structures which encompass other antitheses presented in the text. (*Poetics*, 255–56)

Antithesis forces the reader to interpret; the space between the antithetical poles is the space of interpretation. The interpretation that most comprehensively includes and makes sense of these oppositions within the organization of the text is said to be a correct one. It has already been seen, however, that many of the terms of the fifth series—even the modes of fantasy and realism—resist antithetical structuring either because they are repetitions of each other or because they are inextricably merged. Consequently, the space of interpretation is not delimited, being at times both invisible and open-ended. This frustrates from the outset the endeavor to stop the play of meaning, or to begin it in the first place. The difficulty involved in forming antithetical relationships in these *Episodios* is perhaps most obvious with characters.

As has been seen, Vicente Halconero, Tito Liviano, even don Wifredo or Segismundo, all demonstrate aborted revolutions, the absence of cause and effect relationships between their words and their deeds or even between their words and their thoughts.[38] Other characters, seemingly unlike them at first, are quite similar. In *De Cartago a Sagunto*, Mariclío tells Tito that all of Chilivistra's stories, which have motivated the travels of Tito and Chilivistra during a large part of the *episodio*, have been lies: "mito el administrador . . . mito es también ese marido errante, y por fin, personaje de leyenda es el hijo que busca"

(4:764). According to Mariclío, this mythmaking makes of Chilivistra

> un perfecto símbolo de la vida española en el aspecto político, y estoy por decir que en el militar. . . . Inventa con lozana imaginación fábulas absurdas y acaba por creerlas. . . . En ella habrás observado que al fuego del sentimentalismo sustituye rápidamente el hielo de los negocios menudos, todo sin criterio fijo, sin noción alguna de la realidad.
> . . . con el sistema puramente *chilivistril*, y conforme al voluble proceso mental de tu amiga, gobiernan a España las manadas de hombres que alternan en las poltronas o butacas del Estado, ahora con este nombre, ahora con el otro.
> . . . También ellos inventan historias para domar las fieras oleadas de la opinión y acaban por creer lo que engendró su propia fantasía. Tus gobernantes son creadores de mitos, y mostrándolos al pueblo andan a ciegas, sin saber lo que quieren ni adónde van. (4:764–65)

This description of Chilivistra and the politicians recalls Tito's self-description of his "voluble constitución mental" (4:500), as cited above, and all his mood swings, lasciviousness, and storytelling. The voluble Chilivistra, the alternating politicians, and the protean Tito are all alike. None of them can separate fantasy from reality; their lies are taken for truths even by themselves because none of their words or actions are based on fixed criteria or a sense of reality. They are mythmakers who move without direction since in blindness they perceive no differences. Tito's literal blindness is only a hyperbolic manifestation of the inability to see clearly through the web of myth and lie. The history that Tito writes, these *Episodios*, are no more than myth, as he often suggests. Tito's or Chilivistra's names may change, like the names of governments or governors, but these fluctuations have no rational explanation, form no real opposition; their lack of antithesis closes off the space of interpretation, prohibits "progress" in the discourse of politics or interpretation.

The back-and-forth movement of the government—in its "turno," constitutions, revolutions, or restorations—is at once an open-ended and a stagnant structure. Each repetition implies what came before and what will come after, but does not provide a new interpretation. Without contradiction or antithesis, there can be no dialectic to these political formations, to the temporal structure of history, or to the relations among plots and characters. The fiction does not contradict the history of the fifth series, it merely repeats it endlessly. In this "historia sin relieve" (4:487), there are no gaps to be filled.

Many of the other characters in the series resemble Chilivistra and Tito. With their mood swings, hysteria, or delirium, don Wifredo, Delfina, Nicéfora, Donata, and even Fernanda Ibero are only slightly paler reflections of the more obviously burlesque characters.[39] Male or female, rich or poor, idealistic or degraded, historical or fictional, the characters of the fifth series provide a monotonous procession of repetitions. An effort, therefore, to organize and synthesize their oppositions into a comprehensive thematic meaning for the series is pointless. The interpretations offered of these figures as symbols are only symbols themselves—illusions, myths, a series of repetitions and differences—where no meanings—signs—are stable. Tito, Chilivistra, and Spain's governors are mythmakers and inventors of history. But myth and history are equally words that only seem to contain a momentary significance. These mythmakers, or liars, are writers, and whether their discourse is fiction, history, or interpretation, it is still repetition.

It is relatively easy to condemn the myths created by often parodic, rather demented characters like Tito and Chilivistra, Nicéfora and don Wifredo, or the slippery political maneuverings depicted in these volumes, without always questioning the myth- (or history-) making process of the fifth series and its interpretations. But from the first volume, *España sin rey*, these processes are undermined in their seemingly conventional, more apparently natural contexts. Fernanda Ibero, for example, is a more sympathetic character than later protagonists because she conforms, at least superficially, to the expectation that a protagonist have some goal or ideal; yet she is a mythmaker just like Tito. She thinks longingly of Santiago Ibero and Teresa

209

Villaescusa of the fourth series as representing the triumph of happiness and true love after suffering and travail. They represent for her all that she lacks and desires, after her aborted engagement to Juan de Urríes:

> "Quizás mi destino y el de mi hermano sean igual destino."
> . . . Santiago y Teresa eran para ella un símbolo más admirado que comprendido, un mito que representaba la humana vida en su primordial concepto. Veíalos como un grupo de clásicas figuras, imponentes por su belleza y noble gravedad. Sin que hubiera en torno a ellos palabras escritas ni grabadas leyendas, algo decían. . . . Invisibles trompetas de oro daban al aire estas voces: "Energía, Dignidad, Amor, Justicia," y algunas más que no se oía bien. (4:357)

Fernanda admires these symbols but does not understand them. Her symbols are therefore not so different from the symbol "revolución"—a word that is functional only in that it marks the absence of a referent. It is an incomplete sign, lacking meaning because its conventional application cannot be distinguished from those terms it is presumed to oppose—peace, monarchy, or restoration. Fernanda's myth seeks to represent essential and original humanity—"la humana vida en su primordial concepto." Yet representation is always severed from the primordial or originary. She cannot make present the origin or truth of her ideal world, of Santiago and Teresa, she can only re-present them. In this way her representation becomes the origin/ source of imitation.[40] Her symbol-making calls attention to the unbridgeable distance between symbols and truth, writing and material reality, signifier and signified. Indeed, it is the impossibility of making present a life, a meaning or a moment in time that her symbols illustrate. They are statues, classics, frozen and lifeless. These are the representations that give rise to further representations in an endless endeavor to uncover an absolute truth that is no more than words, visible or invisible, written or imagined, with saliva or ink.

As with myths of rationality, origin, or linear history, Fernanda represents her myth in terms of beginnings and endings.

She desires to solve the enigma of her life, to seek the opposite of what she has, to chart her plot and to interpret, just as do readers of her text. In order to make sense of and organize what perhaps has no sense or organization, she must create symbols to fill the void she perceives in her life, her text, which is what the reader may do with the fifth series when it seems meaningless. Even without the written word as evidence, "sin que hubiera en torno a ellos palabras escritas," Fernanda forms her symbols: "Energía, Dignidad, Amor, Justicia." Even without textual evidence the reader may form symbols to fill in the gaps between images, the spaces between the lines of these *Episodios*. Fernanda seeks to transform people—Santiago and Teresa—whose lives are open-ended, whose history is not finished, into classics—complete, authoritative, perfectly meaningful texts. Likewise, the interpreters of these texts may seek to infuse characters—mere words—with a symbolism that tells classic stories, histories, or myths. But a classic is defined by its name; to name is to stop the play of meaning. Fernanda's project is an emblem of how making symbols, defining classics, and naming in themselves arbitrarily close off the signifying process.

The activities of naming, classifying, and symbolizing animate other characters, too. Vicente Halconero seeks to make Fernanda into the classic figure of "Polimnia . . . escultura famosa" (4:373) or into an "imagen de la interesante reina Alceste" (4:376, 365). He also makes his mother, Lucila, into a classic figure, just as Fajardo and Ventura Miedes did in the fourth series, when he sees her as "Melpómene, Musa de la Tragedia" (4:372). Tito views Floriana as "una estatua de imponderable belleza" (4:634) and "Efémera" as a "figura estatuaria" (4:796, 836). The process of transforming characters into classic figures emblemizes the way readers often try to stop the play of words, to close the book and name its meaning. By transforming Santiago into a classic figure named Dignity, Fernanda has defined him to her satisfaction, closed his book, and posited an ending to her own. This desire to make what is real into what is classic, that is, originary, complete, and transcendental, allows lives or stories, histories, or myths, to appear meaningful. As

Frank Kermode writes, "to make sense of their span . . . [people] . . . need fictive concords with origins and ends."[41] Fernanda sees herself as moving toward Dignity and Justice, just as readers may conventionally see themselves as moving toward some meaning or moral in the fifth series, or at the very least toward an enlightening view of history. But Fernanda's, Halconero's, or Tito's symbols, or any of those of the fifth series, are only names that collect often disparate narrative elements into manageable myths. Whether a single symbol or a theme, which is "the name we give to forms of unity which we can discern in the text or to the ways we succeed in making various codes come together and cohere" (Culler, *Poetics*, 224), they are words, without transcendental coherence or even linear temporality. If "plot is but the temporal projection of thematic structures" (*Poetics*, 224), and theme is but a collection of symbols, and symbols are merely names given to something perhaps difficult to understand, then the entire project of the fifth series (or of any text), from its individual words to the meaning it may proffer as history, becomes problematic.[42]

The conventions of sense making that seek to organize the fifth series can be divided into two types: empirical recuperation and symbolic recuperation. Empirical recuperation relies on causal connections. It is assumed that "anything noted is probably notable and significant," writes Culler (*Poetics*, 225). Thus, in the fifth series, the reader naturally expects the historical events mentioned to be important, the fictional events and characters to somehow illuminate the history, the problems posed to be gradually solved through the plots of the narrative. The efforts to recuperate empirically in these *Episodios*, to seek causal explanations for events such as Tito's diminutive stature and amorous exploits, his ability to metamorphize or his underground journey, his magic pen and telepathic powers, his ability to obtain government jobs for his numerous acquaintances, Halconero's knowledge of Prim's assassins, or don Wifredo's "terremoto cerebral," nonetheless all encounter obstacles, as has been seen. These events are not rational or realistic and they are often unconnected to other activities in the narrative. So the reader, like Fernanda, must revert to symbolic recuperation, which "operates where causal connections are absent or where those which could be called upon seem insufficient to account for the stress which an object or event receives in the text, or even when we do not know what else to do with a detail" (Culler, *Poetics*, 225). Since there are so many instances in the fifth series when elements resist empirical recuperation, most readers consider it highly symbolic. Dendle, for instance, writes of the later *Episodios* that "novelistic characters embody aspects of the national soul; they symbolize (with corresponding lack of individuality) rather than respond to, the historical context" (184). But symbolic recuperation is just one more type of organization or truth finding, that is, of closure. When readers like Brian Dendle or Mariclío say that Chilivistra symbolizes Spain's political system, or that Fernanda Ibero and Tito Liviano symbolize Spain's ills, they attempt to reduce the text to a manageable size. But this effort at symbolic recuperation is undermined, too, just as is the attempt to see meaning in history.

The fifth series places the reductive impulse of the symbolizing project in the foreground in many instances. *La primera República*, for example, opens with Tito writing

> Ansío penetrar con vosotros en la selva histórica que nos ofrecen los adalides republicanos en once meses del 1873. . . . La historia de aquel año es, como he dicho, selva o manigua tan enmarañada, que es difícil abrir caminos en su densa vegetación. . . . Es en parte luminosa, en parte siniestra y obscura, entretejida de malezas con las cuales lucha difícilmente el hacha del leñador. (4:581)

He goes on to equate history with a labyrinth, too, replete with its images of light and dark. These metaphors and analogies likewise describe the relationship between text and reader. The textual jungle or labyrinth is a reinscription of the *Episodios*. Their dense and tangled weave continually presents obstacles to the reader who would see clearly, who would "penetrar" and "abrir caminos." The image of the reader or interpreter as a "leñador," ax in hand, is an image of reduction. In order to get through the text, to open paths of meaning and illumination in this web of words, he must chop down what he deems supplementary or superfluous—"malezas." But these "malezas" are as much a part of the jungle or text as any other element, only more obscure. Whether the "leña" is history, representation, or workable symbols and themes, and the "maleza" is fantasy, absurdity, or unincorporated detail, the choice of what remains and what is cut out entails a value judgment. To cut out, devalue, or ignore the "maleza" of the text also devalues or ignores what is equally a functional part of the labyrinthine discourse of the fifth series.

As if to express the impossibility of the task of the "leñador," Tito soon abandons these metaphors along with the images of light and dark. He is unable to find the way out of the entanglement of fiction and history or to delimit a *chiaroscuro* in this *Episodio* or in the series. His open-ended metaphors describe an open-ended text. Tito cannot make sense of his history; the reader cannot comfortably separate the light from the darkness, the meaningful from the trivial. Consequently, there are no antitheses to synthesize into stable symbols that form manageable themes and plots. The reader wanders through this narrative jungle just as Tito wanders through the streets of Madrid: "Sin saber cómo ni dónde, cual cuerpo inconsciente lanzado por el acaso a los laberintos callejeros" (4:789). He is unable to chart his course, pursue his meaning, or to complete a journey even as "insignificant" as Leandra's in *Bodas reales*; she at least "dominó sin brújula" her neighborhood in Madrid.

The fantastic underground world where Tito travels also displays this resistance to a clearly delimited symbolic structure. There "la luz siempre era la misma, y la temperatura inalterable" (4:637). The bulls that inhabit it are "todos del mismo color y estampa; parecían hermanos" (4:636). Tito grows bored with this world: "pensando que aquel mundo en que había caído era un tantico monótono y sosaína, me dormí profundamente" (4:637). Without "chiaroscuro," antitheses, or classical oppositions, there is no space for interpretation, difference, movement. Tito's experience of boredom here is like his and Halconero's in the congress (4:366, 816). At times one cannot help but liken the characteristics of these political or fantastical worlds and of Tito and Halconero's reactions to them to the experience of reading the fifth series and the history it represents.

The last words of Mariclío to Tito, the last words of the forty-six *Episodios nacionales*, are, "Yo, que ya me siento demasiado clásica, me aburro . . . , me duermo" (4:876). At the moment that she writes of her great fears and small hopes for Spain, Mariclío retreats out of sheer boredom to the unconsciousness of sleep. But her description of an idealized future and her self-description are caught up in the process of representation that is either writing history or history as writing. "El ideal revolu-cionario, la actitud indómita . . . constituirán el único síntoma de vida" (4:876). Whether it be called ideal, attitude, or symp-tom, what she describes is not life. And like Fernanda's, Tito's, or Halconero's invocations of classic figures, Mariclío's charac-terization of herself as "clásica" is an emblem of how history is always already written. Mariclío, who represents in this series the muse of history, the ideal historian, the eternal always— "ahora quiere decir *siempre*"—has gradually subverted her own representational role in this last *Episodio*, as she fails to appear in person to Tito in *Cánovas*. (The closest he comes to her is having a whiff of her perfume—"los tomillos del Monte Hy-meto." [4:836, 839].) She finally erases any trace of her pres-ence—the presence of history—in this last sentence of the se-ries. She has revealed that history, the ideal, or the present moment are only representations: classics.

To see history as classic is to see it as a representation of what is already a representation—words, statues, books—but one that has forgotten its status as a representation in the process of becoming the source of new ones. To be classic is to become originary in the moment of forgetting that a classic can only be a representation of what is not present.[43] This describes the se-nility of the classic Beltrán and the violation of each classic Span-ish constitution. As Mariclío sleeps, historical consciousness ceases; her sleep calls attention to the artificiality of that con-sciousness, the myth of our ability to perceive reality or presence through words, signs, and symbols, or the historical novels of the fifth series. There are only words for words, representations of representations. Mariclío's final words as she retreats into sleep epitomize this process of forgetting, of losing consciousness of the representational process as soon as it begins, that characterizes writing itself.

Such a loss of consciousness or forgetting, seen so frequently in Tito as well as in other figures, is also a loss of a sense of difference between sleeping and waking, fantasy and reality, words and things. And without difference there is no need for interpretation. As Mariclío foresees little for Spain but a repetition of the past, she also becomes conscious of her eternal status as representation. In like fashion, these texts illustrate that perhaps any meaning in history or any relationship of difference between fiction and history is a false consciousness. It fosters the belief that some essential meaning can be captured, some truth can be made present, or something classic can be discovered through interpretation. The attempt to symbolize, interpret, or define classics reveals a desire for closure, for a solution to enigmas, for an end to the game of words. But even as the fifth series ends, as the book closes, as history becomes classic, the reader may glimpse the impossibility of ever really closing that book or of stopping the game of language that has no origin or end, because it is a continuous process of substitution of words for words, "continuando la historia de España." The game of the fifth series is ended as arbitrarily as it began— somewhere in what is called the middle of a series of representations without an origin or an end, a past or a future, or a moment of truth.

At the end of the fifth series, Mariclío steps back, away from her text of history, as she refuses a consciousness of what is still to be written. Her retreat has a counterpart in Tito and in the textual "Galdós," and it is the last word, so to speak, on a text that continually resists conventional and comfortable modes of signifying. One of the most controversial ways in which these *Episodios* resist signification is precisely this association between Mariclío, Tito, and Galdós.

The retreat from a consciousness of history at the end of the series was foretold early on, in chapter 5 of *Amadeo I*. There, after first beginning to learn about Mariclío, in a preliminary reference to her as *Tía Clío*, Tito falls ill with a fever. He describes how his "buen camarada el isleño" cared for him when he was ill, and then returns thirty-seven years later, asking him to write the history of the period for him. "El isleño" or "el gaunche," the writer from the Canaries that suggests Galdós himself, says:

> Una promesa indiscreta oblígame a escribir algo de aquel reinadillo de don Amadeo. . . . Tu memoria es excelente. . . . Hazme ese libro, y con ello quedará saldada la deuda de caridad que tienes conmigo. Puedes observar el método que quieras. . . . Por este trabajo te pagaré lo que dió Cervantes al morisco aljamiado, traductor de los cartapacios de Cide Hamete Benengeli. (4:493)

Tito accepts, reminding the reader

> que el isleño me autorizó a contar la historia como testigo de ella, figurándome en algunos pasajes . . . como lo que en literatura llamamos héroe o protagonista. A mi observación de que yo tendía, por temperamento y volubilidad natural, a la mudanza de opinión y a variar mi carácter y estilo conforme a la ocasión y lugar en que la fatalidad me ponía, contestó que esto no le importaba, y que la variedad de mis posturas o disfraces darían más encanto a la obra. (4:493)

Obviously, not all critics have found these texts to be enchanting. Most recently, Geoffrey Ribbans writes that Tito's "individual characteristics . . . seem at odds with his allegorical role and irrelevant and distracting in the historical context. It is not surprising therefore that critics have not been kind to these innovations" ("Literary Presentations," 10). On the other hand, Stephen Gilman defends such innovations, in an article in the same volume.

Throughout his "Memories of Remembering," Gilman at-

tempts to "make sense of [Tito's] peculiar symbiosis with Galdós," of "Galdós' curious self-caricature" (49). He seeks an explanation for why Galdós removed "himself from events by
turning over the narrative to a grotesquely 'hybrid' alter ego"
(47), and sees it as a "liberation from the constriction of identity" and as a "transference of memories [that] endows the process of remembering with acute self-awareness" (48). As in
Proust, this "first-person novelistic self-displacement" allows
"memory itself" to become "the subject rather than the more
or less trivial (and for the most part unresolved) mysteries that
are remembered" (49). As observed in the passage above, the
memory of history, for Mariclío, is a process of forgetting. This
may well be the case for "el isleño" and Tito as well. Gilman
writes of them that "their most striking characteristic in common is their identification with and rejection of historical consciousness" (48). "El isleño's" regret about his promise, Tito's
disregard for chronology, fact, or logic, and Mariclío's retreat
into sleep all imply such a "rejection of historical consciousness."

The value for the reader of these complex texts and their ambiguous attitude toward history seems to lie more in what they
say about reading memories, fictions, or histories than in their
possible representations of reality. Neither Gilman nor Ribbans
sees the fifth series as painting a realistic picture of Spain. Yet if
these texts are not realistic, they must be something else. For
Gilman they are more like works of Proust than Balzac: "The
'recherche' could now in a sense be Proustian" (47; see note 10
of this chapter). For Ribbans, on the other hand, these different
narratives "take too far the dissastisfaction Galdós came to feel
with realist narrative" (14). These differences of opinion between two of the most lucid and seminal Galdós scholars clearly
illustrate how difficult texts have always both alienated and fas-
cinated their readers.

The fifth series's capacity to fascinate and alienate is what
makes it remarkable, problematic, and ultimately revealing of
the diverse relationships possible between text and reader,
words and interpretations. A Cervantine lesson is offered once

again. As the "aljamiado traductor," Tito is a hybrid of races, languages, and translations. In the Cervantine analogy, "el isleño" is the "segundo autor" but Cide Hamete and his "cartapacios" are absent. Tito, then, is translating from a manuscript—history as real—that does not exist. The textual retreat from historical consciousness is reinscribed in this analogy where Tito must make a translation without an original; he must translate a past that he did not really experience, because he does not exist. There is not even the illusion of original documentation as with Fernando Calpena.

The last sentence of chapter 5 of *Amadeo I*, where "el isleño" appears to hand Tito his task, seems to move forward to 1908. Tito writes: "Vacilé un instante, mirando al cielo y a los tranvías que de un lado a otro pasaban, y acepté, y con un apretón de manos sellamos nuestro compromiso" (5:493). The "tranvía" suggests the back-and-forth movement of translation, of the relationship of the past to the present, of the signifying process overall in its constant play of identity and difference. Tito appears to be translating the past, 1871, from the standpoint of 1908. Yet is it Tito's 1908 creation that gives the illusion of 1871 or is it the illusion of 1871 that posits a Tito and an "isleño" of 1908? Which text, time, narrator, or perspective is original? This ostensible glimpse into the future of "tranvías" and "isleños" illustrates the indeterminacy between self and other, real and imaginary, past and present, history and fiction. All documents, memories, histories, and fantasies can only be distinguished arbitrarily, since they rely on the same textual processes.

FORMING ALLEGORIES

The space between 1908 and 1871, between Tito and "el isleño," between the memory and the memoir, between the "segundo autor" and the "aljamiado traductor" where Cide Hamete and his document are absent, mark a sort of limbo, much like Mariclío's boredom and sleep, the final words of the series. This is like the interpretive limbo that exists when narrative elements in texts like the fifth series refuse to take on an antithetical, differentiated, structure. The symbolic relationships that can be formed in such texts are often isolated, stagnant, or refuse to cohere into an enlightening novelistic whole: the statues are frozen and lifeless; the labyrinth has no exit; Nicéfora, Delfina, Chilivistra, and Tito are ludicrous repetitions of each other. There is little satisfaction in organizing these symbols, characters, themes, or plots in either a literal or figurative sense. Thus the frustration of many critics who tend to explain their dissatisfaction by way of an "unfinished Series," or Galdós's age and exhaustion (e.g., Hinterhäuser, 298, or Rodríguez, 177). Montesinos's annoyance with these works leads him to write of a "manía alegorizante," an "enfermedad de vejez," and a "deformación senil" (327).

It is precisely the fifth series's refusal to provide satisfaction that has been the subject of this chapter. The lessons in reading that these volumes offer are surely as valid as any other lessons that might be gleaned from previous series. These volumes are deformations in many ways, but that term need not take on a rigidly pejorative sense. To de-form is to open up, perhaps to new formations, new definitions and symbols. Their senile—repetitive and forgetful—formations are one more discursive strategy among the many observed in the *Episodios nacionales*, only less natural because less expected and customary. Culler writes that "many works challenge this process of naturalization, prevent us from feeling that the pursuit of symbolic readings is imminently natural" (*Poetics*, 229). These types of works may be broadly called allegorical, according to Coleridge:

> We may then safely define allegoric writing as the employment of one set of agents and images with actions and accompaniments correspondent, so as to convey, while in disguise, either moral qualities or conceptions of the mind that are not in themselves objects of the senses, or other images, agents actions, fortunes, circumstances, so that the difference is everywhere presented to the eye or imagination while the likeness is suggested to the mind. (30)

This likeness and difference is what is illustrated by the play of repetition and distortion, by the open-ended symbols and the alternations between realism and fantasy throughout the series.

The mode of allegory appears to be a most appropriate, rather than a "maniacal," description of the series. In fact the constant difficulty in forming seemingly natural symbols is intrinsic to allegory. Culler writes:

> The symbol is supposed to contain in itself all the meaning we produce in semantic transformations. It is a natural sign in which *signifiant* and *signifié* are indissolubly fused, not an arbitrary or conventional sign in which they are linked by human authority or habit. Allegory, on the other hand, stresses the difference between levels, flaunts the gap we must leap to produce meaning, and thus displays the activity of interpretation in all its conventionality. Either it presents an empirical story which does not itself seem a worthy object of attention and implies that we must, in order to produce types of significance that tradition leads us to desire, translate the story into another mode, or else it presents an enigmatic face while posing obstacles even to this kind of translation and forces us to read it as an allegory of the interpretive process. (*Poetics*, 229–30)

Obviously Tito's story is unworthy of the reader's interest, and so to a large extent are the stories of Halconero and even Fernanda. Attempting to translate these characters and plots into more productive terms still leads to frustration since they provide little enlightenment of the epoch. As Tito says, the history of the period is a dense and tangled jungle, difficult if not impossible to penetrate. The traditional impulse to see illuminating connections between fiction and history surely encounters obstacles in these volumes. And, as this study has sought to show, the obstacles are part of their effect. Labeling these novels allegories, however, in no way resolves their meaning or provides a self-assured interpretation. Because, as Culler writes of other problematic texts, one might tell oneself:

221

If the work makes sense it will be as an allegory, but we cannot discover a level at which interpretation may rest and thus are left with a work which, like *Finnegans Wake*, *Locus Solus* or even Flaubert's *Salammbô*, flaunts the difference between signifier and signified and seems to take as its implicit theme the difficulties or the factitiousness of interpretation. Allegory, one might say, is the mode which recognizes the impossibility of fusing the empirical and the eternal and thus demystifies the symbolic relation by stressing the separateness of the two levels, the impossibility of bringing them together except momentarily and against a background of disassociation, and the importance of protecting each level and the potential link between them by making it arbitrary. Only allegory can make the connection in a self-conscious and demystified way. (*Poetics*, 230)

If it seems difficult to form symbols, themes, and plots in the fifth series, it is perhaps because these last *Episodios* have included the very efforts of the reader in their tangled and labyrinthine weave.

The fifth series frustrates the desire to connect signifier to signified, novel to history. Its reinscription of its own resistance to interpretation has been observable from the outset, for instance in the program of reading Halconero plans for himself, as discussed above. The inclusion of *La Nouvelle Héloïse* in his list of required readings suggests the complexities involved in autobiography, memoir, and allegory that pertain to this series and that have been discussed at length by theorists like Derrida and De Man. In *Allegories of Reading*, with reference particularly to *La Nouvelle Héloïse* and generally to all narrative, De Man writes:

Any reading always involves a choice between signification and symbolization, and this choice can be made only if one postulates the possibility of distinguishing the literal from the figural. This decision is not arbitrary, since it is based on a variety of textual and contextual factors (grammar, lexicology, tradition, usage, tone, declarative statement, diacritical marks, etc.). But the necessity of making such a decision cannot be avoided or the entire order of discourse would collapse. The situation implies that figural discourse is always understood in contradistinction to a form of discourse that would not be figural; it postulates, in other words, the possibility of referential meaning as the *telos* of all language. (209)

Yet the *Episodios*, as well as many other of Galdós's works, have demonstrated repeatedly the truth of Derrida's claim of the " 'literal' meaning of writing as metaphoricity itself" (*Grammatology*, 15). One cannot get out of these texts and into the world. There is no guarantee of transcendence, no complete and stable sign, no origin, no end to discourse.

The above citations illustrate that the allegory of the impossibility of joining words to things or of forming symbols pertains not only to the more fantastic and discontinuous passages of the fifth series, but equally to the more realistic sections of *España sin rey* and *España trágica*. The fifth series is necessarily not only an allegory of its own reading, but of any reading, however seemingly natural or representational. The fifth series, then, becomes by extension a reevaluation of the reading and writing processes of all of the *Episodios nacionales*, even the most conventionally representational. De Man writes that one must always

> question the status of referential language. It becomes an aberrant trope that conceals the radical figurality of language behind the illusion that it can properly mean. As a result, the assumption of readability, which is itself constitutive of language, cannot only no longer be taken for granted but is found to be aberrant. There can be no writing without reading, but all readings are in error because they assume their own readability. Everything written has to be read and every reading is susceptible of logical verification, but the logic that establishes the need for verifica-

tion is itself unverifiable and therefore unfounded in its claim to truth. (*Allegories*, 202)

Merely because it seems easier, more natural, to verify or find truth—to interpret or symbolize—by assuming a real or historical referentiality for more conventional narratives does not mean that these are valid readings. In fact, the impossible reading that the last *Episodios* offer may be the only valid reading. If history is writing, and writing is metaphor, then there is no escape from representation and "semblance." Mariclío's last words predict the future of Spain in more words—"Declaraos . . . inventáis otra palabra." When she describes herself as classic, as she falls asleep, she returns to the archetypal state of representation that the unconscious activity of sleep—dreaming—brings. There is no return to a prerepresentational state, to presence, to a type of immediate knowledge or wisdom of things—even if those ideals persist. Mariclío's reversion to a more unproblematic state of representation in sleep as the final word of the *Episodios nacionales* redefines writing and history as the representation of representation. It is a commentary on all of the *Episodios* in this series as well as in the first four.

The distancing of history from her own text, from her knowledge of herself, is only the final statement of the series's self-consciousness of the problematics of interpretation. Mariclío has given Tito the job of recording, of narrating Spain's history, just as has "el isleño." This is not the first time that the *Episodios nacionales* have employed a first-person narrator and a self-consciously autobiographical, perhaps "Rousseauian," style for relating and interpreting history. Virtually the entire first series is a pseudo-autobiography in which the octogenarian Gabriel Araceli narrates his youth. From the first chapter of the first *episodio*, the notion of autobiography is displayed in all its fictionality. Autobiography is one more myth, like history. The narration of the self can never be that self, as Ginés de Pasamonte reasoned in 1605. Autobiography, memoir, is thus always allegorical.

Yet even if the relationship between Araceli and his text is ultimately the same as that between Tito and his, they have different effects. In *Episodios* that come before the fifth series, the reader is permitted to make natural, or referential associations, even if those associations eventually come apart. These conventional associations can no longer be made in Tito's narrative because Tito is different from Gabriel Araceli and the numerous first-person narrators that follow him throughout the course of the forty-six *Episodios*. In his 1984 study of *La corte de Carlos IV*, Germán Gullón writes that by the second novel of the first series, Gabriel has taken a new posture "de clara autoridad," "responsabilizándose de la visión histórica novelada," and that "se convierte en narrador con principios, con 'honor,' y por tanto merecedor de confianza." In sum, "el honor le salva y su liberación lo convierte en narrador digno de confianza, eco fiel de la moral del autor implícito que noveliza la historia condenando lo que debe ser condenado."[44] While these statements raise questions about such intentional interpretations, they also attest to how distant critics' perceptions of Tito's function are from those of Gabriel's. Yet who is to say which protagonist is more real than the other?

One of the characteristics of Tito that makes him have such a different effect on readers is his lack of conventional honor or principles, illustrated by his degraded conquests. Even more disturbing is his blatant refusal to take responsibility for what he writes, for example, "escribo en republicano, escribo en conservador" (4:515, 500). He is clearly without authority because of his depravity, because of his semi-conscious or unconscious states, and because of his refusal even to claim a knowledge of what he writes (for example, with Cánovas, or the magic pen that writes Elena Sanz's biography, and numerous other instances). Tito repeatedly states that he is unaware of having written what others think he did write, that he is able to write in any style (or to speak in any style, as for example in his speech on the "República hispanopapista" in *Amadeo I*, chapter 17), and to address any audience about any ideas, without feeling compelled to believe those ideas. He also is unable to tell himself or his readers if what he perceives, experiences, says, or writes is true or false, fantasy or reality. "El isleño" and Mari-clío have both stepped back from their texts and relinquished their authority to Tito, a totally unreliable narrator who in turn relinquishes his authority over his own narrative.

All of the repetitions and discontinuities seen in character development, temporal and spatial structures, realistic and fantastic modes of narration, and in plot sequences are epitomized in Tito Liviano's refusal to understand his own text. Tito is the mark of the fleeting difference between truth and lie, knowledge and madness, reading and writing, sense and nonsense. As a text stands to its translation or a self to its other, as with Fernando Calpena or José Fago in the third series, Tito is forever "diferente de mí mismo" (4:480). De Man observes that the confusion that results from "Rousseau's assertion that he does not know whether he or his fictional characters wrote the letters that make up *Julie* makes little sense. The situation changes when we realize that R. is merely the metaphor for a textual property (readability)" (*Allegories*, 203). If Tito, like the "R." of *La Nouvelle Heloïse*, is a metaphor for readability, and if he cannot even read himself, let alone his own text, then he is a reinscription of the most complex aspect of allegory. "Allegorical narratives tell the story of the failure to read" (De Man, *Allegories*, 205). This is Tito's failure and it often is the reader's, too, in the fifth series.

Tito is one more word in the continuum of the discourse, but he is also the narrator of that discourse by the convention that allows the reader to separate the two, to make into a hierarchy what is one surface, without relief. He is what is read and he is also a reader, so he is an allegory or a metaphor for both reading and writing, for the *Episodios nacionales* and for the reader. If he is both at the same time, he makes reading a repetition of writing, or writing a repetition of reading, where neither act has priority over the other. As we read and interpret these writings, readings, and interpretations that are called novels, histories, or *Episodios nacionales*, our writings and readings are reread and rewritten in a never-ending series of representations whose original presentation can never be identified. The truth of one interpretation is the lie of another. These texts, these interpretations, are like Tito who no longer knows the difference between fantasy and reality, but establishes "una especie de equilibrio entre lo cierto y lo dudoso . . . saboreando los puros goces que . . . [encuentra] . . . siempre en la verdad de la mentira" (4:839).

Conclusion

Benito Pérez Galdós was an astute reader of his own literary signs. His novels demonstrate this repeatedly as each one seems to reread and reinterpret the ones written before. Montesinos observed in 1968 that "Galdós va aprendiendo de su misma experiencia . . . y, por ello entre sus fuentes hay que contar sus propias obras" (86). According to Gilman, this is "the most important critical statement that has been made about the art of Galdós" (*Art*, 34). Not only did Galdós learn to write from Cervantes and other Spanish Golden Age authors, the romantics, and numerous European novelists, but also from constant reflection on his own verbal creation. His continual experimentation with and refinement of diverse narrative strategies for over five decades enabled him to create texts whose range of sophistication and perspective are unsurpassed in the Spanish novel.

In the last three series of *Episodios nacionales*, each successive volume constitutes a rewriting of the previous ones in diverse ways. These intertextual connections among *Episodios* are clearly observable in the relationships among Galdós's other works as well. The last twenty-six *Episodios* rewrite many of the strategies found in the *Novelas contemporáneas*, the *Novelas de primera época*, and, of course, the first two series of *Episodios nacionales*, not to mention those seen in his stories and dramas. Yet this continual refinement does not imply that only Galdós's later works achieve such a sophisticated scope of narrative technique and perspective. Even his early works, notably the first twenty *Episodios nacionales*, display many of the same self-conscious strategies observed in the last volumes. Galdós was from the beginning to the end of his career a revisionist—of the literature written before his own, of the ways in which literature and history can be read, and, above all, of the ways in which one may read oneself.

Galdós's persistent reexamination and revision of his own work seems to me to indicate a continual search for narrative methods that would allow him to portray events whose ultimate meaning or truth he had come to doubt. His historical novels question the possibility of gathering lessons from history in the conventional sense, offering instead lessons on how to read what is labeled history, whether in books or in oneself. Galdós constantly experiments with different definitions of historical truth and of the nature of reality. Within the plots of his novels, the characters debate and argue the interpretation of the events around them. At the same time, the novels almost invariably offer multiple versions or views of the same events, from which no single definition of their status as objects of knowledge emerges. Historical knowledge thus becomes an elusive prey that necessarily either seems to escape language or be created by it.

The last three series of *Episodios* offer a progressively more deliberate challenge to the conventions of representation, whether in literary or historical discourse. These volumes become more like those of Proust and Joyce than those of Flaubert and Tolstoy. They therefore occupy a transitional position between nineteenth-century realist literature and the various attempts to produce antirealist literature in the twentieth century. Reading these *Episodios* in this light also implicitly forces one to reevaluate the representational validity of Galdós's earlier, seemingly more realistic historical novels, too. The artistic techniques observable after 1898 did not spring from a void. Even in the first chapter of the first *Episodio*, written in 1873, it is clear that what the reader is about to experience is art, not life.

Near the conclusion to a highly self-conscious chapter 1 of *Trafalgar*, the narrator, the octogenarian Gabriel Araceli, gives us a tongue-in-cheek introduction of himself and his project of relating the events of his youth:

No me exija el lector una exactitud que tengo por imposible, tratándose de sucesos ocurridos en la primera edad y narrados en el ocaso de la existencia, cuando cercano a mi fin, después de una larga vida, siento que el hielo de la senectud entorpece mi mano al manejar la pluma, mientras el entendimiento, aterido, intenta engañarse buscando en el regalo de dulces o ardientes memorias un pasajero rejuvenecimiento. Como aquellos viejos verdes que creen despertar su voluptuosidad dormida engañando los sentidos con la contemplación de hermosuras pintadas, así intentaré dar interés y lozanía a los mustios pensamientos de mi ancianidad, recalentándolos con la representación de antiguas grandezas.

Y el efecto es inmediato. ¡Maravillosa superchería de la imaginación! Como quien repasa hojas hace tiempo dobladas de un libro que se leyó, así miro con curiosidad y asombro los años que fueron; y mientras dura el embeleso de esta contemplación, parece que un genio amigo viene y me quita de encima la pesadumbre de los años. (1:184)

This metafictional display of the strategies of memory, art, and textual self-inscription does not suggest a naive realism or representationality by any means. At the very beginning of the *Episodios nacionales*, the reader learns that exact recall and an accurate depiction of reality are impossible, because the past is past and the memory deceives, if only to delight. What Gabriel remembers, too, however inaccurately, is not life, but its simulacrum: "hermosuras pintadas." He does not recall the past, but represents it. He does not relive his youth, but imagines it. His life, literally, is like a book. It would be the reader's own senile self-deception to view this book as a life or a past.

The passage from *Trafalgar*, like countless others in the volume and in the first two series, could well form part of any of the *Episodios* examined in this study. The image of the ancient, handicapped, senile "viejo verde" recalls Beltrán, Santiuste, Tito, and even "el isleño," suggested again in "el genio amigo." The first series is not so different from the last in its self-referential examinations of art, memory, the self, and the past. Nor is it necessarily more or less senile. The enfeebled hand inscribed in *Trafalgar* and the enfeebled hand that can be seen in the manuscripts of the last *Episodios nacionales* are cut of the same mold, refined and revised, reread and rewritten, but curi-

ously, a repetition and a prefiguration, simultaneously, of each other. Gabriel, the narrator of 1873 or the boy of 1805, seems to look forward to Tito and "el isleño" of 1871 or 1908, at the same time that those characters and narrators of the fifth series look back to the first. It is as though the reader, too, must read backwards, revising interpretations of Galdós, just as he constantly revised his own work, and like Mendizábal say, "A ver qué me cuenta."

The attempt to categorize Galdós's works into naively realistic or fantastically allegorical, historical or fictional, even optimistic or pessimistic, according to their chronology or titles, is to delimit categories that in the end, upon rereading, are untenable. Tito's aversion to chronology and realism, if extreme, serve as a warning to us as we attempt to evaluate Galdós's works. Ribbans, writing about the fourth series and the *Novelas contemporáneas* treating Isabel II's reign, cites Galdós's "sense of distance" and concern with providing "a wide spectrum of points of view":

> This is why any attempt to isolate categorically Galdós's own opinions is so hazardous. No political view, no representative figure, not even such partial "reflectors" as Beramendi, is offered as a model: such a tidy solution would be to rewrite history as *Confusio* attempts to do. At every turn in the political maelstrom Galdós seeks to allow the diverse and heterogeneous forces at work to act and speak for themselves and to enable the reader to reflect and arrive at his own conclusions about the agonized recent history of his country.[1]

Differences in the treatment of historical material that Ribbans perceives between the *Episodios* and *Novelas contemporáneas* notwithstanding, his assessment of these texts' continual effort to allow the reader to interpret for himself could easily apply to all of Galdós's work.

The diverse and heterogeneous forces that Ribbans sees in Galdós's view of history are cited by Clavería as well. He writes of the nineteenth-century consciousness of history, "conciencia

que se había ido cimentando lo mismo sobre colecciones de documentos e interpretaciones subjetivas de sucesos pretéritos que sobre rigor filológico o esquemas abstractos de pensamiento." But it was also many other things: "no sólo recuento y reconstrucción del pasado, sino pasión y dialéctica política y religiosa, reflejo de ideologías dispares, de prejuicos y preocupaciones del presente, arte literario, filosofía, filosofía de la historia. . . . Todo eso iba a ser la Historia para Galdós." Above all, "no esperábamos del novelista una concepción precisa y definida de la Historia" ("Pensamiento," 170). More than in history, according to Clavería, Galdós was interested in what is now called "intra-historia."

Rejecting Unamuno's certainty that Galdós borrowed the concept of "intra-historia" from him, Clavería instead shows how it can be observed in Galdós's earliest works, for example, *Juan Martín "el Empecinado"* (1874) of the first series. Whether Unamuno's *Paz en la guerra* (1897) inspired Galdós's *Luchana* (1899) of the third series, or Galdós's previous novels inspired Unamuno, is ultimately a question that, if still argued, can no longer be so easily put to rest. In rereading Galdós, one finds continual experimentation with narrative technique, constant self-referentiality and a counterrealism that, coupled with a pervasive intrahistorical perspective, makes the effort to distinguish sharply between Galdós and the Generation of 1898 untenable. The attempt to delimit literary movements, to define where one begins and where one leaves off, like attempts to delimit genres or to locate original sources, is an endless pursuit. This is demonstrated repeatedly within the *Episodios nacionales* and without, as Clavería argues with regard to the impossibility of knowing all the sources and influences that contribute to the genesis of the *Episodios*. He shows that it is equally difficult to trace the origin of the concept of "intra-historia":

> "intra-historia" podía llegarse independientemente por distintos caminos: Michelet. . . . Otro camino hacia "intra-historia" encontramos en la consideración histórica de "moeurs", "gouvernmement intérieur", "usages", que in-

icia, en el siglo xvii, Voltaire. . . . Y, a la par con estos historiadores, otros escritores y pensadores europeos. . . . Sirvan de ejemplos ilustres, el ensayo, de 1830, *On History*, de Thomas Carlyle; *Die Welt als Wille und Vorstellung*, que es de 1841, de Schopenhauer; y papeles póstumos del último Nietzsche, de fines de siglo, en que pueden encontrarse esbozos de una idea que se estaba imponiendo a la época: la idea de la "intra-historia." ("Pensamiento," 176)

Scholars like Clavería and Ribbans appear to reject that fevered search to secure absolute sources, origins, or perspectives, to locate the indisputable right way of defining Galdós's work. Such a search was the object of ridicule in the *Episodios* in characters such as José Fago, Beltrán de Urdaneta, Ventura Miedes, Pepe Fajardo, or Tito Liviano. The *Episodios* constantly suggest that the unselfconscious pursuit of the past, in oneself, in documents, or in the world, is a futile and destructive endeavor. Witness the effects that Fernando Calpena's knowledge of his origin, Juana Teresa's documentation of Pilar's sin, and Miedes's etymological obsession produce.

In his introduction to *The Use and Abuse of History*, Nietzsche describes how the weight of history, the constant memory of the past, can destroy life and happiness. One must be able to forget in order to live happily:

in the smallest and greatest happiness there is always one thing that makes it happiness: the power of forgetting, or, in more learned phrase, the capacity of feeling "unhistorically" throughout its duration. One who cannot leave himself behind on the threshold of the moment and forget the past, who cannot stand on a single point, like a goddess of victory, without fear or giddiness, will never know what happiness is; and, worse still, will never do anything to make others happy. (6)

An obsession with the past that creates personal unhappiness and an inability to make others happy surely characterizes Fago, Nelet, Beltrán, and Leandra in the third series. Their incapacity to live "unhistorically" is like Spain's refusal to give up the illusions of her past. The perpetuation of the same traditions that provide Isabel II with a poor education and a weak husband spell unhappiness for her and the nation, as the fourth series reveals.

The characters and plots of the third and fourth series clearly demonstrate the life-threatening, when not death-bringing, effects of an obsessive pursuit of the past. Thus, Tito's forgetfulness in the fifth series may not be such a pessimistic commentary on Spain as many scholars believe, but rather the only way of looking toward a different life in the future. Nietzsche writes: "there is a degree of sleeplessness, of rumination, of 'historical sense,' that injures and finally destroys the living thing, be it a man or a people or a system of culture" (7). The fifth series of *Episodios* rejects this destructive sleeplessness, and instead offers the life-giving forgetfulness of Mariclío as the conclusion to *Cánovas*. This conclusion has the effect, perhaps, of suggesting, as Nietzsche says,

> we must know the right time to forget as well as the right time to remember, and instinctively see when it is necessary to feel historically and when unhistorically. . . . the unhistorical and the historical are equally necessary to the health of an individual, a community, and a system of culture. (8)

Galdós's retreat from historical consciousness at the end of the *Episodios nacionales*, after revealing the dangers of its excess, can be read as a retreat into life and out of representation, the fictional bondage called history.

Galdós's historical novels provoke the kinds of questions that Nietzsche puts to his reader:

> History, so far as it serves life, serves an unhistorical power. . . . The question how far life needs such a service is one of the most serious questions affecting the well-being of a man, a people, and a culture. For by excess of history life becomes maimed and degenerate, and is followed by the degeneration of history as well. (12)

The *Episodios nacionales* have clearly shown how history degenerates. Their successive historians, Beltrán, Fernando Calpena, Cristeta del Socobio, Pepe Fajardo, Ventura Miedes, Santiuste, Halconero, and Tito, to name but a few, degenerate as they each pursue their historical tasks. The history they seek to write or document reveals progressively more idiosyncratic and repetitive, sometimes senile or nonsensical, even mad, characteristics. The zealous attempts to document Fernando's origin become parodic in Miedes's efforts to document the origin of the Spanish race, and ultimately absurdly sardonic in Tito's documentation of himself and his story. The relationships among these historians also degenerate as one character dissolves into another from volume to volume. The fictional and historical protagonists of the *Episodios*, as well as numerous secondary characters, mark a series of degenerative repetitions, just as do its plots of love and political intrigue. An excessive pursuit of a historical truth or of a sure knowledge of the past is always destructive in Galdós's works. In order to escape the bonds of history, one must self-consciously acknowledge the limitations imposed by it. Yet these limits and bonds, like those that define and unite fiction and history in Galdós's novel histories, like all representations and idealizations, are products of the imagination.

Notes

INTRODUCTION

1. C. P. Snow, *The Realists: Portraits of Eight Novelists* (London: Macmillan, 1978), 167–94.

2. James R. Stamm, *A Short History of Spanish Literature* (New York: New York University Press, 1984), 150.

3. Martin Seymour-Smith, ed., *Novels and Novelists: A Guide to the World of Fiction* (New York: St. Martin's, 1980), 34.

4. Some recent translations of major *Novelas contemporáneas* by Benito Pérez Galdós are *Our Friend Manso*, trans. Robert Russell (New York: Columbia University Press, 1987); *Torquemada*, trans. Frances M. López-Morillas (New York: Columbia University Press, 1986); *Fortunata and Jacinta: Two Stories of Married Women*, trans. Agnes Moncy Gullón (Athens: University of Georgia Press, 1985); *Torquemada in the Fire*, trans. Nicholas Round (Glasgow: University of Glasgow, 1985); *The Shadow*, trans. Karen O. Austin (Columbus: Ohio University Press, 1980). Karen Austin has also completed translations of *Angel Guerra*, *Realidad*, and *La incógnita*, which are under consideration for publication.

5. Alfred Rodríguez, *An Introduction to the "Episodios Nacionales" of Galdós* (New York: Las Américas, 1967), 104. References to this and all critical works will be made parenthetically in the text by page number.

6. Stephen Gilman, *Galdós and the Art of the European Novel: 1867–1887* (Princeton, N.J.: Princeton University Press, 1981), 55.

7. Robert Alter, *Partial Magic: The Novel as a Self-Conscious Genre* (Berkeley: University of California Press, 1975), 97–98.

8. Robert C. Spires, *Beyond the Metafictional Mode: Directions in the Modern Spanish Novel* (Lexington: University of Kentucky Press, 1984), 25–32. This study is one of the most useful treatments of the genre for the whole tradition of the Spanish novel.

9. John W. Kronik, "Feijoo and the Fabrication of Fortunata," in *Conflicting Realities: Four Readings of a Chapter by Pérez Galdós*, ed.

Peter B. Goldman (London: Támesis, 1984), 40, first published as "Galdosian Reflections: Feijoo and the Fabrication of Fortunata," *Modern Language Notes* 97 (1982): 272–310. See also his "*Misericordia* as Metafiction," in *Homenaje a Antonio Sánchez Barbudo: Ensayos de literatura española moderna* (Madison: University of Wisconsin Press, 1981), 37–50.

10. Kronik, "*Misericordia*," 37–38.

11. See Ricardo Gullón, "La história como materia novelable," in *Benito Pérez Galdós: el escritor y la crítica*, ed. Douglass M. Rodgers, 2d ed. (Madrid: Taurus, 1979), 403–26; reprinted from *Anales galdosianos* 5 (1970): 23–37.

12. Ricardo Gullón, " 'Los Episodios': la primera serie," in *Benito Pérez Galdós: el escritor y la crítica*, ed. Douglass M. Rodgers, 2d ed. (Madrid: Taurus, 1979), 379–402; reprinted from *Philological Quarterly* 51.1 (1972): 292–312.

13. Hayden White, *Tropics of Discourse: Essays in Cultural Criticism* (Baltimore: Johns Hopkins University Press, 1978), 130.

14. Gÿorgy Lukács, *Studies in European Realism*, trans. Hannah and Stanley Mitchell (London: Merlin, 1962); Peter Bly, *Galdós's Novel of the Historical Imagination: A Study of the Contemporary Novels* (Liverpool: Francis Cairns, 1983).

CHAPTER ONE

1. Claude Lévi-Strauss, *Tristes Tropiques*, trans. John Russell (New York: Criterion, 1961), 61.

2. Jean Baudrillard, *The Mirror of Production*, trans. Mark Poster (St. Louis, Mo.: Telos, 1975), 47.

3. This is Brian Dendle's thesis, for example, in *Galdós: The Mature Thought*, Studies in Romance Languages, no. 23 (Lexington: University Press of Kentucky, 1980).

4. Rodríguez, *Introduction*, 125. Juan Bautista Avalle-Arce, in his definitive study, "*Zumalacárregui*," writes: "Las relaciones de Fago con su pasado adquieren las dimensiones de una verdadera obsesión, que llega a expresarse en los términos de una trágica paradoja vital: Fago quiere huir del pasado, al mismo tiempo que empeña su vida en la búsqueda de Saloma Ulibarri. Pero los términos de la paradoja son in-

abarcables por la vida, y así Fago se deshace en la empresa." *Cuadernos hispanoamericanos* 250–52 (Oct. 1970–Jan. 1971): 366.

5. Dendle, *Mature Thought*, 39. See note 3. Hereafter, all references to Dendle will be cited parenthetically in the text.

6. Benito Pérez Galdós, *Episodios nacionales*, 4 vols., ed. Federico Carlos Sainz de Robles, 1st ed., 3d reprint (Madrid: Aguilar, 1979), 2:861. All quotations from the *Episodios nacionales* will be from this edition and will be cited parenthetically within the text by volume and page number. For similar fluctuations between terms like "Providencia," "acaso" and "lógica" see, for example, 2:856–57, 861–62, 884. Fluctuations among these terms occur throughout the series.

7. Friedrich Nietzsche, *The Use and Abuse of History*, trans. Adrian Collins, Library of Liberal Arts (Indianapolis, Ind.: Bobbs-Merrill, 1976), 15.

8. The free indirect style or free indirect speech is used extensively in the descriptions of Zumalacárregui in order to foster ambiguity. On the theory and function of the free indirect style see Roy Pascal, *The Dual Voice* (Manchester, Eng.: Manchester University Press, 1977). Peter Bly discusses the ambiguous treatment of Zumalacárregui from another perspective in "Emphasizing the Idiosyncratic: Galdós's problems in *Zumalacárregui*," *Anales galdosianos* 21, in press.

9. Manfred Frank, "The Infinite Text," *Glyph Textual Studies 7* (Baltimore: Johns Hopkins University Press, 1980) 71–72.

10. See Rodríguez's different discussion of this plot linkage, *Introduction*, 110–18.

11. Roland Barthes identifies five codes, hermeneutic, proairetic, semic, symbolic, and referential, which function as "a kind of network, a *topos* through which the entire text passes (or rather, in passing, becomes text)." *S/Z*, trans. Richard Miller (New York: Hill and Wang, 1974), 20. All parenthetical references to Barthes are from this work.

12. See Rodríguez's excellent examination of this and various aspects of Marcela (*Introduction*, 115, 123, 137–38).

13. Joaquín Casalduero, *Vida y obra de Galdós*, 4d ed. enl. (Madrid: Gredos, 1974), 139.

14. See the discussions of Beltrán by Dendle, *Mature Thought*, 56–57, and Rodríguez, *Introduction*, 122–23.

15. "La tradición" here is like Mariclío in the fifth series in some ways. Mariclío has many, not always unconventional, prefigurations. For example, Lucila Ansúrez Cordero Halconero from the fourth series is the symbol of the Spanish race, as will be discussed in chapter 2. She changes her shoes or goes barefoot according to the situation, just as does Mariclío according to the importance of the history she is recording. Ricardo Gullón writes that Mariclío, in the fifth series, "ha substituido en estos episodios el alto coturno apropiado para narrar lo acontecido en *Trafalgar* o en *Gerona*, por zapatillas, alparagatas o—cuando más—borceguis" (*"La historia,"* 28). Shoes have sexual connotations, too, as when Lucila puts on red shoes, which in turn are coveted by Dominiciana Paredes (see chapter 2, n.7). These types of associations among the discursive, historical, sexual, and feminine codes can be observed throughout the *Episodios*.

16. Claude Lévi-Strauss, *The Savage Mind*, trans. George Weidenfeld and Nicolson Ltd. (Chicago: University of Chicago Press, 1973), 257; see also 256–64.

17. See chapter 14 of this novel especially. There are numerous passages in the third series where the codes of food and war come together. This type of conjunction will be more fully discussed with reference to the fourth series.

18. See Irving Wohlfarth's enlightening discussion of this topic in "The Politics of Prose and the Art of Awakening: Walter Benjamin's Version of a German Romantic Motif," *Glyph Textual Studies 7* (Baltimore: John Hopkins University Press, 1980), 131–48.

19. All definitions of "translation" are taken from *The Compact Edition of the Oxford English Dictionary*, vol. 2 (Oxford: Oxford University Press, 1971), 266.

20. See Dendle's discussion of "Galdós's final sarcasm" (78).

21. There are numerous repetitions of words like "acertijo" and "enigma" in the series, for example, 2:235–36; 3:95, 100, 122–23, 631.

22. Avital Ronell, "Why I Write Such Good Translator's Notes," *Glyph Textual Studies 7* (Baltimore: Johns Hopkins University Press, 1980), 229–32.

23. See chapter 2 for practical suggestions of ways in which one might read some of the *Episodios* in the context of "the woman as text." As the series proceeds, Fernando confuses the letters of his future

wife, Demetria, with those of his mother, Pilar. This confusion has particularly interesting connotations for a Freudian analysis of this character, perhaps, and the women he views as his other/texts.

24. Barthes discusses how narrative is not a hierarchy of meaning of "nesting narratives" or "a narrative within the narrative." "Since narrative is both merchandise and the relation of the contract of which it is the object, there can no longer be any question of setting up a rhetorical hierarchy between the two parts of the tale, as is the common practice" (*S/Z*, 90). All parenthetical references to Barthes are from this work.

25. Fernando restores mental and physical health to Zoilo Arratia twice, in chapters 12 and 29, and to don Sabino in chapter 27. All three times he gives them words of comfort and common sense as well as "cordero" or "carne."

26. "When identical semes traverse the same proper name several times and appear to settle upon it, a character is created" (Barthes, 67).

27. This is a discrepancy, perhaps, because in *Mendizábal* Fernando does not know English (2:901).

28. Gilbert Smith observes: "From the first moment of the text, the narrator is selecting and manipulating as he creates aspects of the surface structure and as he creates the discourse, the modal aspect of the text. . . . a feature of the surface structure—the placement of letters—creates a modality in the text." Furthermore, "titles are the only words of the narrator in the text, and they establish a modal communication between the narrator and the ideal reader." "Hermeticism and Historical Fiction: *La estafeta romántica* of Galdós" (Paper presented at the Southeastern Conference on Romance Languages and Literatures, Rollins College, Winter Park, Florida, February 1983).

29. See n. 16.

30. This "strategy of frustration" reaches "epic" proportions at the end of *Los Ayacuchos*. Fernando and Demetria must again wait to be married while Calpena rescues Santiago Ibero from taking priestly vows and brings him back to marry Gracia. Demetria calls this the seventh labor of her Hercules (3:349). The episode suggests another curious analogy to Nietzsche: Hayden White writes of a "Zarathustra-like Superman," which for Nietzsche is the reconciliation of the self with the self: "history is not, therefore, a dialectical movement tending toward an absolute beyond time and space. The only 'absolute' which

Nietzsche recognized was the free individual, completely liberated from any spiritual-transcendental impulse, who finds his goal in his ability to outstrip himself, who gives to his life a dialectical tension by setting new tasks for himself, and who turns himself into a human exemplar of the kind of life which the Greeks thought could be lived only by the gods." *Metahistory: The Historical Imagination in Nineteenth-Century Europe* (Baltimore: Johns Hopkins University Press, 1975), 345. Calpena is a complicated parody of this concept of self-perfection, not only with respect to Nietzsche, but to progressive interpretations of history and to the journeys of the third series. Moreover, Fernando does not set himself this task; Demetria does. He must be coaxed into his godlike status. At the very end of the novel, too, there is a parody of this mythic motif. Santiago duly rescued, he and Fernando journey back to the brides-to-be, retracing many of Calpena's movements with Espartero (for example, 3:402; see chapters 34 through 38 of *Los Ayacuchos*). But they are delayed by a number of events, including Santiago's desire to grow back his mustache before he sees Gracia (3:401). Finally, both men are filled with irrational and repeated apprehensions that the women are only "mitos." The marriages take place between the final, unwritten embrace and the narrator's promise to tell more about the "gloriosa y fecunda" matrimonial era in the future.

31. Throughout the series there are insistent references to God, Chance, Providence, and similar terms as charting courses for the characters (see n.21 above). From Fago's glimpse of "Mé" to this moment, and to the story of Isabel II's marriage in *Bodas reales*, as will be discussed, these allusions and questions about the direction of life are inextricably associated with the literal processes of textuality in letters, "Mé," archives, narrators, etc.

32. George Krzywicki-Herbert, "Polish Philosophy" in *The Encyclopedia of Philosophy*, ed. Paul Edwards (New York: Macmillan, 1967), 6:363–70.

33. One of the heroes of *Trafalgar* reappears in the fifth series, interestingly enough. And while there is an obvious difference between the tone of the first and last series, which the repetition of this character fosters, even the first series is perhaps less optimistic, more antithetical, than traditional interpretations would admit, as Peter Bly has argued in "For Self or Country?: Conflicting Lessons in the first series of *Episodios nacionales?*" *Kentucky Romance Quarterly* 31.2 (1984): 117–

24. I hope to provide an extensive reevaluation of the frst series in a study nearing completion.

34. In "El pensamiento histórico de Galdós," Carlos Clavería cites this sentence as an example of Galdós seeking a causal explanation of history. *Revista nacional de cultura* 121–22 (Mar.–June 1957): 170–77. He seems to miss completely the irony here, as in similar passages that he quotes, such as "la Historia grande, integral." He does go on to assert that Galdós did not think that all history was attributable to known causes, but to mysterious or unknown forces. But his example of this—Galdós's portrayal of O'Donnell, "la figura del general-político, el espíritu de la Unión liberal, el *Zeitgeist* del momento" (174)— also ignores the irony, even sarcasm, of that novel and the paradoxes and ambiguities in the figure of O'Donnell and the notion of "Unión liberal." These aspects will be discussed in chapter 2.

35. See also Rodríguez's discussion of her, 124–25.

36. Narváez's lack of culture, a certain mediocrity, is emphasized on several occasions. He is, for example, one of "esas ilustraciones chicas o . . . eminencias enanas" (3:418). See Narváez, chapter 4 passim.

37. Gÿorgy Lukács, *The Theory of the Novel: A Historico-Philosophical Essay on the Forms of Great Epic Literature*, trans. Anna Bostock (Cambridge: MIT Press, 1971), 103.

38. The prominent use of the term "soberana" here and elsewhere in the series suggests that this term, to be discussed in chapter 2, was already forming part of the puzzle not yet written. Apropos the conception of the *Episodios*, see Rodolfo Cardona, "Apostillas a los 'Episodios nacionales' de B. P. G., de Hans Hinterhäuser," for some fascinating discoveries in Galdós's library housed in the Casa-Museo Pérez Galdós. Particularly interesting are Cardona's listing of tentative titles for the *Episodios*, including indications of erasures. *Anales galdosianos* 3 (1968): 119–42.

39. Frank (72), quoting Derrida, "The Retrait of Metaphor," *Enclitic* 2 (Fall 1978): 7.

CHAPTER TWO

1. Alfred Rodríguez comments on the differences in the treatment of history in all of the five series, although he sees no change in Galdós's approach to history. See his chapter 2, especially 26–31, and Ma-

deleine de Gogorza Fletcher's critique of this position in "Alfred Rodríguez and the *Episodios* of Galdós," *Anales galdosianos* 3 (1968): 179–83. With reference to the fourth series in particular, Dendle describes a dramatic change: "The treatment of history in the fourth series is, indeed, skimpy to the point of casualness" (79). Joaquín Casalduero also mentions differences in style and tone of the fourth series several times, for example: "Por la ironía, por la serenidad, por la penetración histórica, por la creación de personajes, la cuarta serie quizá sea la mejor junto con la quinta que dejó de terminar" (188). Casalduero's reference to "penetración histórica" is obviously inconsistent with Dendle's claim that there is less "treatment of history." This study seeks to avoid such discrepancies by examining more closely the function of terms like history itself.

2. Hans Hinterhäuser discusses the changes in the fourth series, which he sees through the more "realistic" depiction of women characters and which he attributes to the fuller, more credible account of their sexual activity. *Los Episodios nacionales de Benito Pérez Galdós* (Madrid: Gredos, 1963), 335–37. One can consider this change to be consistent with the preoccupation with morality in the fourth series, and especially with the role of women as protagonists.

3. See Casalduero's examination of what he calls the "desdoblamiento de Galdós" in Pepe Fajardo and Santiuste (154).

4. The physical description of Lucila Ansúrez (3:634) perhaps recalls the features of the Dama de Elche, discovered in 1897, a symbol of an idealized past.

5. See Geoffrey Ribbans's perceptive critique of Isabel II's "identification" with the "pueblo" in "The Portrayal of Queen Isabella II in Galdós' *Episodios* and *Novelas contemporáneas*," "*La Chispa '81*": *Selected Proceedings*, ed. Gilbert Paolini (New Orleans: Tulane University Press, 1981), 280.

6. Lucila is also identified in this and later novels by such names as Illipulicia, Cigüela, Lucichuela; these variations, like those in the names of other characters throughout the fourth series, are indications of the indeterminate and unstable identities in these *Episodios*. This aspect of characterization will be discussed at length in chapter 3 with reference to the fifth series. In the final series the wildly fluctuating terms make the difficulty in creating stable identities an object of the discourse itself.

7. The exchange is even more apparent in later novels. In *Los duendes de la camarilla*, for example, Dominiciana appropriates Lucila's red shoes, and ultimately her lover, Bartolomé Gracián. There are suggestions, too, that Gracián becomes Eufrasia's, and even Isabel's, lover. (See chapter 1, n.15.)

8. See Dendle's excellent discussion of the fourth series's "obsessive" concern with clericalism and the religious question (89–91).

9. The same might be said in *Prim* of Santiago Ibero's illness, which results from reading history books: "llegó a encenderse hasta el rojo con las increíbles hazañas de Hernán Cortés, y de ensueño en ensueño, o de locura en locura, acabó por la de querer imitarlas o reproducirlas en nuestro tiempo" (4:10).

10. See Ribbans's discussion of Isabel II's responsibility for the "Ministerio relámpago" and other fiascos of her reign, in "The Portrayal" (281–84).

11. Antonio Regalado García, discusses Galdós's treatment of Isabel II in his *Benito Pérez Galdós y la novela histórica española: 1868–1912* (Madrid: Insula, 1966), 424–33. He concludes that "su juicio del reinado de doña Isabel, por la que sentía debilidad, es suave con exceso" (425). The oversimplification is due in part, no doubt, to the fact that Regalado bases his remarks on Galdós's article about Isabel II, which recalls his actual interviews with her, rather than on the novels he claims to be analyzing. This is the kind of misrepresentation that leads him to further conclusions such as this: "El lector común, no analítico, debió de sentir con la cuarta serie emociones similares a las de la primera, pues sobre ambas se eleva el mito colectivo del pueblo, mito falso y adormecedor que velaba la realidad de los graves problemas sociales planteados" (433). But surely the critic must seek interpretations more profound than those of the "lector común, no analítico." Paul Olson observes that Regalado "subordinates text to context" ("Galdós and History," *Modern Language Notes* 85 [1970]: 274–79), and Peter B. Goldman identifies several contextual confusions and misreadings of the sort cited above ("Historical Perspective and Political Bias: Comments on Recent Galdós Criticism," *Anales galdosianos* 6 [1971]: 113–24). See also Ribbans's response to this question in "The Portrayal," 283–84.

12. At another point in her conversation with Fajardo, Isabel asks, "¿No crees tú que la Crónica mía, la de mi reinado, será bella?" and

receives the reply, "Bella será . . . pero ¿quién asegura que no será también triste?" (3:714). It is tempting to assume that Galdós, drawing on his schoolboy Latin, is offering a pun on the two meanings of *bellum*—"lovely" and "war."

13. One can consider all historical discourse to be rhetorical, as White argues in *Metahistory*: "Thus, the historian necessarily 'constructs a linguistic protocol' by which he 'prefigures' a field of interpretation" (30). See Peter De Bolla's excellent review of White's work on the rhetoric or narrativity of historical discourse in conjunction with Dominick LaCapra's work on the use of the reading strategies of literary criticism for a self-conscious history writing in "Disfiguring History" (*Diacritics* [Winter 1986]: 49–58). De Bolla argues that "if we attempt to construct a historical rhetorics, one which takes account of the specificity of a text's prefigurative construction, we may be able to exploit the folding in of the present within the past characteristic of White's 'imaginative' rhetoric along with the exchange of the past with the present of analysis characteristic of LaCapra's transferential relation. This would obviate the need for the gesture towards an authenticating external discourse—imagination or, even more generally 'literature' in White's tendency and deconstruction in LaCaptra's—since the technology of reading would be present to the object of study and refigured within the analytical discourse" (55).

14. Geoffrey Ribbans, " 'La história como debiera ser': Galdós's speculations on Nineteenth-century Spanish history," *Bulletin of Hispanic Studies* 59 (1982): 271.

15. There are numerous references to light in *Narváez* and the fourth series. Many of them function like the following, which describes the value of Gambito's news about Lucila for Fajardo: "de ellas resulta una luz desigual, que tan pronto esclarece el asunto como la rodea de mayores tinieblas" (3:716).

16. Etymologies are exploited frequently in *Narváez*, as with the names of Eufrasia (3:682–83) and Narváez (3:644, 652), and most self-consciously when the history of the denomination "pollo" is traced (3:668).

17. Rodríguez insists that there was no significant change in Galdós's view of history (29–30). Fajardo's remarks at the beginning of *Narváez* certainly militate against such a conclusion. Rodríguez's view, like those cited in note 1 above, exemplify the kind of judgments that result

from the arbitrary adoption of "fiction" or "history" as fixed categories.

18. Barthes suggests that the structure of the network of codes that constitutes the text nonetheless admits a "multivalence" and "partial reversibility" of its terms in the text (20). (See also chapter 1, n. 11). The following pages explore instances of such reversibility. For further discussions of the nature of codes, see Jonathan Culler, *On Deconstruction: Theory and Criticism after Structuralism* (Ithaca, N.Y.: Cornell University Press, 1982), 32–34.

19. Dendle's discussion of the events of this period is most useful (117–21).

20. Geoffrey Ribbans writes in "La historia" that Teresa decides at the end of *O'Donnell* to be "kept in relative opulence by Manuel Tarfe" (267). However, it is not Tarfe who will be her next lover, as he says to her himself: "¿Cómo has de ignorar tú que alguna persona de grandísimo poder y de riqueza desmedida te solicita . . . vamos, pide tu mano para llevarla al altar que no tiene santos?" (3:1052). Tarfe goes on to encourage Teresa to accept an official rich lover and keep him unofficially: "Teresa, ¿no podrías conciliar la ambición y el amor? Ello es sencillísimo: aceptas lo que los ricos te dan, y me quieres a mí. La riqueza mía es corta. . . . No puedo sastisfacer tu ambición" (3:1053). But Teresa rejects this proposal: "Rebelóse Teresa contra la profunda inmoralidad que esta proposición envolvía" (3:1053). The suggestion at the very end of the novel is that Teresa's next lover is to be the financier Salamanca: "Teresa se metió por un callejón que, a su parecer, debía conducirla . . . al mismo sitio donde estuvo sentada con Tarfe. Pero se había equivocado . . . y . . . fue a parar junto al palacio de Salamanca, cuyo grandor . . . contempló largo rato silenciosa, midiéndolo de abajo arriba y en toda su anchura con atenta mirada" (3:1057).

21. Rodríquez recognizes these paradoxical parallels, but finds in them a resolution that this study rejects. He writes that Teresa's "decision to take on a rich lover . . . constitutes the most honest solution to the materialistic vocation of the period, ethically superior, without question, to economic matches and their subsequent adulteries, however discreet and palatable to a corrupt society" (245).

22. Rodríguez writes that "the suicide of Captain Villaescusa . . . exemplifies the nature of military solutions" (165). See n.21.

23. See my discussion of Benina's ironic transcendence in *Galdós and the Irony of Language* (Cambridge: Cambridge University Press, 1982), 60–63.

24. The cycle of favors here is interesting: Teresa asks Tarfe to obtain jobs for Centurión and others; Tarfe "dirigió sus tiros contra doña Mañuela" (3:1047), instead of against her husband himself. She in turn convinces O'Donnell to grant the favors, after receiving various "folletines nuevos" from Tarfe, who "sacrificaba por las noches sus más agradables ratos de casino y teatros para leerle a doña Mañuela pasajes de febril interés" (3:1048). The sequence of male/female and words/jobs merits further consideration.

25. Both Dendle (120–37 passim) and Ribbans ("La historia," 267–74) have particularly illuminating discussions of Santiuste.

CHAPTER THREE

1. See Rodríguez's discussion, for example, 193–94.

2. Stephen Gilman, "The Fifth Series of *Episodios nacionales*: Memories of Remembering," *Bulletin of Hispanic Studies* 63 (1986): 50.

3. José F. Montesinos, *Galdós* (Madrid: Castalia, 1972), 3:245.

4. Miguel Enguídanos, "Mariclío, musa galdosiana," in *Benito Pérez Galdós: el escritor y la crítica*, ed. Douglass M. Rodgers (Madrid: Taurus, 1979), 428.

5. H. Chonon Berkowitz, *Pérez Galdós: Spanish Liberal Crusader* (Madison: University of Wisconsin Press, 1948), 344.

6. Geoffrey Ribbans, "Galdós' Literary Presentations of the Interregnum, Reign of Amadeo and the First Republic (1868–1874)," *Bulletin of Hispanic Studies* 63 (1986): 14.

7. For an interesting discussion of this bias, see Pierre Macherey's penetrating critique of the critical exercise in *A Theory of Literary Production*, trans. Geoffrey Wall (London: Routledge & Kegan Paul, 1978).

8. I will clarify my remarks on allegory during the course of this chapter. For a theoretical discussion of the particular usage of the term allegory to which I refer, see Samuel Coleridge, "Allegory," *Miscellaneous Criticism*, ed. Thomas Middleton Raysor (Cambridge: Harvard

University Press, 1936), 28–32; Paul De Man, *Allegories of Reading: Figural Language in Rousseau, Nietzsche, Rilke, and Proust* (New Haven, Conn.: Yale University Press, 1979), 188–245; and Jonathan Culler, *Structuralist Poetics* (Ithaca, N.Y.: Cornell University Press, 1975), 229–39. I discuss Galdós's use of irony and parody at some length in *Galdós and the Irony of Language.*

9. This question can be considered from any number of perspectives: for example, reader response theory, as in Wolfgang Iser, *The Act of Reading: A Theory of Aesthetic Response* (Baltimore: Johns Hopkins University Press, 1978); structuralist, as in Barthes, *S/Z*; Marxist, as in Fredric Jameson, *The Political Unconscious: Narrative as a Socially Symbolic Act* (Ithaca, N.Y.: Cornell University Press, 1980). These three works are particularly useful because of their combination of extensive applied criticism and wide theoretical discussion.

10. Culler cites a similarly disconcerting effect on a reader of Flaubert who expects a Balzac novel (*On Deconstruction*, 79 n.13).

11. Victor Shklovsky, "La construction de la nouvelle et du roman," *Théorie de la littérature*, ed. T. Todorov (Paris: Seuil, 1965), 170–96.

12. See Rodríguez's valuable discussion of Halconero, 179–80 and 183–84.

13. Northrop Frye, *Anatomy of Criticism: Four Essays* (Princeton, N.J.: Princeton University Press, 1971), 172.

14. Enrique Tierno Galván, "Aparición y desarrollo de nuevas perspectivas de valoración social en el siglo XIX: lo cursi," *Revista de estudios políticos* 42 (1952): 85–106. Regarding the enumeration of realistic detail, see Roland Barthes, "L'effet du réel," *Communications* 11 (1968): 84–89.

15. Paul De Man, "The Rhetoric of Temporality," *Interpretation: Theory and Practice*, ed. Charles Singleton (Baltimore: Johns Hopkins University Press, 1969), 173–209.

16. Michel Foucault, *The Archaeology of Knowledge and the Discourse on Language*, trans. A. M. Sheridan Smith (New York: Harper, 1972), 26.

17. See Gÿorgy Lukács, *The Historical Novel*, trans. Hannah and Stanley Mitchell (London: Merlin Press, 1976). Also see David Carroll's essay on Lukács, "Representation or the End(s) of History: Dialectics and Fiction," *Yale French Studies* 59 (1978): 201–29. Carroll

discusses both Lukács's early work on irony and his later Marxist writings. He demonstrates that Lukács's early "idealism" and his later "dialectical materialism" are equally representational.

18. David Carroll, "History as Writing," *Clío* 7 (1978): 443–61, a review of Derrida's *Of Grammatology*.

19. Jacques Derrida, *Of Grammatology*, trans. Gayatri Chakravorti Spivak (Baltimore: Johns Hopkins University Press, 1976), 86–87. All parenthetical references to Derrida are from this text. This question of reading and writing differently is a hotly debated one: since when did writing require different reading and how differently are those foundation texts like Rousseau read? Andrew Parker, in " 'Taking Sides' (On History): Derrida Re-Marx" (*Diacritics* [Fall 1981]: 57–74), criticizes Frank Lentricchia's attack on Paul De Man, together with his privileging of Derrida's readings of nineteenth-century philosophies of history in *After the New Criticism* (Chicago: University of Chicago Press, 1980). Massino Verdicchio in "A Reader Like Phaedrus" (*Diacritics* [Spring 1984]: 24–35), criticizes Culler's *On Deconstruction* for privileging Derrida's reading of Rousseau; he prefers De Man's reading in *Blindness and Insight: Essays in the Rhetoric of Contemporary Criticism* (New York: Oxford University Press, 1971). Verdicchio believes that Derrida continues the logocentric fallacy by ignoring the presence of the "literary" in Rousseau, which De Man has defined as "any text that implicitly or explicitly signifies its own rhetorical mode and prefigures its own misunderstanding as the correlative of its rhetorical nature; that is, of its 'rhetoricity' " (*Blindness and Insight*, 136). Furthermore, claims Verdicchio, De Man does not seek to describe the moment at which logocentrism was abandoned, and because Derrida does, he is caught in his own ideological construct (35). These critics are caught, too, perhaps, in the ideological constructs of overdetermined terms like "logocentrism," "literary," and "deconstruction," much as Alter is with the term self-conscious. One does read differently because writing is different. The name of this type of writing is as arbitary as the moment of its beginning. Galdós's writing is different, too, and those who would rigidly classify his *Episodios* as histories or novels, realism or fantasy, cannot but be caught in the ideological construct of naming and defining itself.

20. Derrida, *Grammatology*, 86. The line can be straight or circular, continues Derrida: "If one allows that the linearity of language entails this vulgar and mundane concept of temporality (homogeneous, dom-

inated by the form of the now and the ideal of continuous movement, straight or circular) which Heidegger shows to be the intrinsic determining concept of all ontology from Aristotle to Hegel, the meditation upon writing and the deconstruction of the history of philosophy become inseparable" (86; see also 72–73). The concerns of literature, linguistics, history, and philosophy are inextricable in the *Episodios nacionales*.

21. Tito's underground journey recalls in many details that of Nelet, as discussed in chapter 1, but contains more unintegrated narrative elements. In this and many aspects the fifth series "is a kind of *reductio ad absurdum*," as Gogorza Fletcher writes in *The Spanish Historical Novel: 1870–1970* (London: Támesis, 1973), 48. Stephen Gilman, in "*El caballero encantado* and the Redemption of Spanish History," a paper presented at the 1984 MLA Convention in Washington, D.C., observed numerous connections between the dream episodes of the fifth series and those of *El caballero encantado*, connections that deserve further study.

22. See Carlos Clavería, "Sobre la veta fantástica en la obra de Galdós," *Atlante* [London] 1 (1953): 78–86, 136–43. In this early study Clavería shows how the fantastic has always been present in Galdós's work and that, in spite of its multiple forms, it has the same unifying criteria (82). He discusses the probable influence of Hoffman and Poe, arguing that the fantastic vein comes largely from romantic literature. He sees Galdós as parallel to the rest of European writers in the variety of fantastic themes and motifs he employs. This, coupled with the Cervantine influence and the pre-Freudian strain that Kercheville first pointed out, makes Galdós much more than a realist, and he should be studied as such, argues Clavería (143). See also his specific remarks on the fifth series, 137–38.

23. See Carroll's discussion of this notion in his review of Derrida in "History as Writing."

24. *Diccionario manual e ilustrado de la lengua española*, Real academia española, 2d ed. (Madrid: Espasa-Calpe, 1981), 609. For an interesting commentary on the *Efémeras'* effect on narrative structure, see Ricardo Gullón, who writes that "su presencia transforma el espacio novelesco, pues al atravesarlo en incesantes vuelos lo convierten en lo que Juan Ramón Jiménez llamó 'los espacios del tiempo,' espacios de movimiento puro en los cuales todo se halla en incesante trance de mutación y cambio; el narrador habla de 'átomas aglomerados por el

Tiempo,' con los cuales 'se forma la verdad histórica', otra gran sombra" ("La historia," 33).

25. Wifredo, Halconero, and Fernanda also suffer fevers from time to time.

26. 4:802. See also chapters 4, 5, 14, 15, and 21. Enguídanos has a good discussion of this aspect.

27. Derrida, 145. See his critique of the "supplement," in ". . . That Dangerous Supplement . . ." (*Grammatology*, 141–64).

28. Dendle writes that Tito's confusion is the novelistic reflection of the incoherence of history (*Mature Thought*, 174).

29. Derrida: "The access to pluridimensionality and to a delinearized temporality is not a simple regression toward the 'mythogram'; on the contrary, it makes all the rationality subjected to the linear model appear as another form and another age of mythography" (87).

30. Josette Blanquat, "Documentos galdosianos: 1912," *Anales galdosianos* 3 (1968): 143–50.

31. Brian Dendle, "Galdós in *El año político*," *Anales galdosianos* 19 (1984): 87–107.

32. Vernon Chamberlin and Jack Weiner, "A Russian View in 1884–85 of Three Spanish Novelists: Galdós, Pardo Bazán, and Pereda," *Anales galdosianos* 19 (1984): 111–19.

33. I examined the manuscripts of the *Episodios nacionales* in the Biblioteca Nacional in 1986 and 1987. The dictated folios of the *Amadeo I* manuscript are 331–34, 347–71, and 373–497, out of 500.

34. Dendle admits that there is no final teaching, but assumes there would be if the series were complete (157 n.18). This assumption draws the conclusions that a teaching is necessary for effectiveness and that the series should be completed in a certain way.

35. The series, like previous ones, is filled with literary metaphors, which serve the parody. Also parodic in this scene are the several references to the "padres de la patria," who reveal their cowardice as they flee ignominiously from the Cortes. Compare this to the "crises" and "contracrises" of *Narváez*.

36. With these and many other passages using terms for statues, the codes of religion and politics, as well as life and artifice, or person and

doll, theater and reality, converge and become indistinguishable. See also 4:273, 305, 309, 316, 323, 241, 514, 581, 603, 618, 637, 681.

37. This phrase is repeated often in various contexts, e.g., 4:796, 825, 845.

38. Consider also don Wifredo as an aborted Carlist revolutionary, Segismundo's acknowledgement of his failure in Paris, Halconero's failing to act the way he believes he should and falling ill when he does act, as in the duel with Paúl y Angulo.

39. Regarding the symbolic value of these characters, see Rodríguez (182–89, 190–91) and Dendle (159–79 passim). For Dendle, Tito and Fernanda both represent Spain, Tito being merely a more exaggerated manisfestation of its problems. In regard to the hysteria of the characters, Gilman observes that in the fifth series " 'histeria' is immediately associated with 'historia' on at least two occasions" ("Memories," 51).

40. Regarding art as a copy of a copy, see Barthes (*S/Z*, 55) and Derrida (*Grammatology*, 101).

41. Frank Kermode, *The Sense of an Ending* (New York: Oxford University Press, 1969), 7.

42. See Barthes on the birth of thematics (*S/Z*, 92–93). In the "classic text," themes can be formed when the "skid of names" is "arrested" and the work is closed. The difficulty in halting the skid of names in the fifth series gestures to an "infinite thematics": "Only an infinite thematics, open to endless nomination, can respect the enduring character of language, the production of reading, and no longer the list of its products."

43. See Barthes, "The masterpiece" (*S/Z*, 114–15).

44. Germán Gullón, "Narrativizando la historia: *La corte de Carlos IV*," *Anales galdosianos* 19 (1984): 45–52.

NOTE TO THE CONCLUSION

1. Geoffrey Ribbans, "*Historia novelada* and *Novela histórica*: The Use of Historical Incidents from the Reign of Isabella II in Galdós's *Episodios* and *Novelas contemporáneas*," *Hispanic Studies in Honour of Frank Pierce*, ed. John England (Sheffield, Eng., 1980): 143.

Bibliography

Alter, Robert. *Partial Magic: The Novel as a Self-Conscious Genre.* Berkeley: University of California Press, 1975.

Avalle-Arce, Juan Bautista. "*Zumalacárregui.*" *Cuadernos hispanoamericanos* 250–52 (October 1970–January 1971): 356–73.

Barthes, Roland. "L'effet du réel." *Communications* 11 (1968): 84–89.

———. *S/Z.* Translated by Richard Miller. New York: Hill and Wang, 1974.

Baudrillard, Jean. *The Mirror of Production.* Translated by Mark Poster. St. Louis, Mo.: Telos, 1975.

Berkowitz, H. Chonon. *Pérez Galdós: Spanish Liberal Crusader.* Madison: University of Wisconsin Press, 1948.

Blanquat, Josette. "Documentos galdosianos: 1912." *Anales galdosianos* 3 (1968): 143–50.

Bly, Peter. "Emphasizing the Idiosyncratic: Galdós's Problems in *Zumalacárregui.*" *Anales galdosianos* 21. In press.

———. "For Self or Country?: Conflicting Lessons in the First Series of *Episodios nacionales?*" *Kentucky Romance Quarterly* 31.2 (1984): 117–24.

———. *Galdós's Novel of the Historical Imagination: A Study of the Contemporary Novels.* Liverpool: Francis Cairns, 1983.

Cardona, Rodolfo. "Apostillas a los *Episodios nacionales de B.P.G.,* de Hans Hinterhäuser," *Anales galdosianos* 3 (1968): 119–42.

Carroll, David. "History as Writing." *Clío* 7 (1978): 443–61.

———. "Representation or the End(s) of History: Dialectics and Fiction." *Yale French Studies* 59 (1978): 201–29.

Casalduero, Joaquín. *Vida y obra de Galdós.* 4th ed., enl. Madrid: Gredos, 1974.

Chamberlin, Vernon, and Jack Weiner. "A Russian View in 1884–85 of Three Spanish Novelists: Galdós, Pardo Bazán, and Pereda." *Anales galdosianos* 19 (1984): 111–19.

Clavería, Carlos. "El pensamiento histórico de Galdós." *Revista nacional de cultura* 121–22 (March–June 1957): 171–77.

———. "Sobre la veta fantástica en la obra de Galdós." *Atlante* [London] 1 (1953): 78–86, 136–43.

Coleridge, Samuel. "Allegory." *Miscellaneous Criticism.* Edited by

Thomas Middleton Raysor. Cambridge: Harvard University Press, 1936.

Culler, Jonathan. *On Deconstruction: Theory and Criticism after Structuralism*. Ithaca, N.Y.: Cornell University Press, 1982.

———. *Structuralist Poetics*. Ithaca, N Y.: Cornell University Press, 1975.

De Bolla, Peter. "Disfiguring History." *Diacritics* (Winter 1986): 49–58.

De Man, Paul. *Allegories of Reading: Figural Language in Rousseau, Nietzsche, Rilke, and Proust*. New Haven: Yale University Press, 1979.

———. *Blindness and Insight: Essays in the Rhetoric of Contemporary Criticism*. New York: Oxford University Press, 1971.

———. "The Rhetoric of Temporality." In *Interpretation: Theory and Practice*, edited by Charles Singleton, 173–209. Baltimore: Johns Hopkins University Press, 1969.

Dendle, Brian. "Galdós in *El año político*." *Anales galdosianos* 19 (1984): 87–107.

———. *Galdós: The Mature Thought*. Studies in Romance Languages, no. 23. Lexington: University Press of Kentucky, 1980.

Derrida, Jacques. *Of Grammatology*. Translated by Gayatri Chakravorti Spivak. Baltimore: Johns Hopkins University Press, 1976.

———. "The Retrait of Metaphor." *Enclitic* 2 (Fall 1978): 7.

Diccionario manual e ilustrado de la lengua española. Real academia española. 2d ed. Madrid: Espasa-Calpe, 1981.

Enguídanos, Miguel. "Mariclío, musa galdosiana." In *Benito Pérez Galdós: el escritor y la crítica*, edited by Douglass M. Rodgers, 427–36. 2d ed. Madrid: Taurus, 1979.

Foucault, Michel. *The Archaeology of Knowledge and the Discourse on Language*. Translated by A. M. Sheridan Smith. New York: Harper, 1972.

Frank, Manfred. "The Infinite Text." *Glyph Textual Studies* 7, 70–101. Baltimore: Johns Hopkins University Press, 1980.

Frye, Northrop. *Anatomy of Criticism: Four Essays*. Princeton, N.J.: Princeton University Press, 1971.

Gilman, Stephen. "*El caballero encantado* and the Redemption of Spanish History." MLA Convention, Washington, D.C., 1984.

———. "The Fifth Series of *Episodios nacionales*: Memories of Remembering." *Bulletin of Hispanic Studies* 63 (1986): 47–52.

————. *Galdós and the Art of the European Novel: 1867–1887.* Princeton, N.J.: Princeton University Press, 1981.

Gogorza Fletcher, Madeleine de. "Alfred Rodríguez and the *Episodios* of Galdós." *Anales galdosianos* 3 (1968): 179–83.

————. *The Spanish Historical Novel: 1870–1970.* London: Támesis, 1973.

Goldman, Peter B. "Historical Perspective and Political Bias: Comments on Recent Galdós Criticism." *Anales galdosianos* 6 (1971): 113–24.

Gullón, Germán. "Narrativizando la historia: *La corte de Carlos IV.*" *Anales galdosianos* 19 (1984): 45–52.

Gullón, Ricardo. "La historia como materia novelable." In *Benito Pérez Galdós: el escritor y la crítica,* edited by Douglass M. Rodgers, 403–26. 2d ed. Madrid: Taurus, 1979. Reprinted from *Anales galdosianos* 5 (1970): 23–37.

————. " 'Los Episodios': la primera serie." In *Benito Pérez Galdós: el escritor y la crítica,* edited by Douglass M. Rodgers, 379–402. 2d ed. Madrid: Taurus, 1979. Reprinted from *Philological Quarterly* 51.1 (1972): 292–312.

Hinterhäuser, Hans. *Los Episodios Nacionales de Benito Pérez Galdós.* Biblioteca románica hispánica. Madrid: Gredos, 1963.

Iser, Wolfgang. *The Act of Reading: A Theory of Aesthetic Response.* Baltimore: Johns Hopkins University Press, 1978.

Jameson, Fredric. *The Political Unconscious: Narrative as a Socially Symbolic Act.* Ithaca, N.Y.: Cornell University Press, 1980.

Kermode, Frank. *The Sense of an Ending.* New York: Oxford University Press, 1969.

Kronik, John W. "Feijoo and the Fabrication of Fortunata." In *Conflicting Realities: Four Readings of a Chapter by Pérez Galdós,* edited by Peter B. Goldman, 39–72. London: Támesis, 1984. First published as "Galdosian Reflections: Feijoo and the Fabrication of Fortunata." *Modern Language Notes* 97 (1982): 272–310.

————. "*Misericordia* as Metafiction." In *Homenaje a Antonio Sánchez Barbudo: Ensayos de literatura española moderna.* Madison: University of Wisconsin Press, 1981. 37–50.

Kryzwicki-Herbert, George. "Polish Philosophy." In Vol. 6 of *The Encyclopedia of Philosophy,* edited by Paul Edwards, 363–70. New York: Macmillan, 1967.

LaCapra, Dominick. *Rethinking Intellectual History.* Ithaca, N.Y.: Cornell University Press, 1983.

Lentricchia, Frank. *After the New Criticism*. Chicago: University of Chicago Press, 1980.

Lévi-Strauss, Claude. *The Savage Mind*. Translated by George Weidenfeld and Nicolson Ltd. Chicago: University of Chicago Press, 1973.

——. *Tristes Tropiques*. Translated by John Russell. New York: Criterion, 1961.

Lukács, Gÿorgy. *The Historical Novel*. Translated by Hannah and Stanley Mitchell. London: Merlin Press, 1976.

——. *Studies in European Realism*. Translated by Hannah and Stanley Mitchell. London: Merlin, 1962.

——. *The Theory of the Novel: A Historico-Philosophical Essay on the Forms of Great Epic Literature*. Translated by Anna Bostock. Cambridge: MIT Press, 1971.

Macherey, Pierre. *A Theory of Literary Production*. London: Routledge & Kegan Paul, 1978.

Montesinos, José F. *Galdós*. 3 vols. Madrid: Castalia, 1972.

Nietzsche, Friedrich. *The Use and Abuse of History*. Translated by Adrian Collins. Library of Liberal Arts. Indianapolis, Ind.: Bobbs-Merrill, 1976.

Olson, Paul R. "Galdós and History." *Modern Language Notes* 85 (1970): 274–79.

Parker, Andrew. " 'Taking Sides' (On History): Derrida Re-Marx." *Diacritics* (Fall 1981): 57–74.

Pascal, Roy. *The Dual Voice*. Manchester, Eng.: Manchester University Press, 1977.

Pérez Galdós, Benito. *Episodios nacionales*. 4 vols. Edited by Federico Carlos Sainz de Robles. 1st ed., 3d reprint. Madrid: Aguilar, 1979.

——. *Fortunata and Jacinta: Two Stories of Married Women*. Translated by Agnes Moncy Gullón. Athens: University of Georgia Press, 1985.

——. *Our Friend Manso*. Translated by Robert Russell. New York: Columbia University Press, 1987.

——. *The Shadow*. Translated by Karen O. Austin. Columbus: Ohio University Press, 1980.

——. *Torquemada*. Translated by Frances M. López-Morillas. New York: Columbia University Press, 1986.

——. *Torquemada in the Fire*. Translated by Nicholas Round. Glasgow: University of Glasgow, 1985.

Regalado García, Antonio. *Benito Pérez Galdós y la novela histórica española: 1868–1912.* Madrid: Insula, 1966.

Ribbans, Geoffrey. "Galdós' Literary Presentations of the Interregnum, Reign of Amadeo and the First Republic (1868–1874)." *Bulletin of Hispanic Studies* 63 (1986): 1–17.

———. "'La historia como debiera ser': Galdós's Speculations on Nineteenth-century Spanish History." *Bulletin of Hispanic Studies* 59 (1982): 267–74.

———. "*Historia novelada* and *Novela histórica*: The Use of Historical Incidents from the Reign of Isabella II in Galdós's *Episodios* and *Novelas contemporáneas.*" *Hispanic Studies in Honour of Frank Pierce*, edited by John England, 133–47. Sheffield, Eng.: 1980.

———. "The Portrayal of Queen Isabella II in Galdós' *Episodios* and *Novelas contemporáneas.*" *"La Chispa '81": Selected Proceedings.* edited by Gilbert Paolini, 277–86. New Orleans: Tulane University Press, 1981.

Rodgers, Douglass M., ed. *Benito Pérez Galdós: el escritor y la crítica.* Madrid: Taurus, 1979.

Rodríguez, Alfred. *An Introduction to the "Episodios Nacionales" of Galdós.* New York: Las Américas, 1967.

Ronell, Avital. "Why I Write Such Good Translator's Notes." *Glyph Textual Studies* 7, 229–32. Baltimore: Johns Hopkins University Press, 1980.

Saussure, Ferdinand. *Course in General Linguistics.* Edited by Charles Bally and Albert Sechehaye. Translated by Wade Baskin. New York: McGraw-Hill, 1966.

Seymour-Smith, Martin, ed. *Novels and Novelists: A Guide to the World of Fiction.* New York: St. Martin's, 1980.

Shklovksy, Victor. "La construction de la nouvelle et du roman." *Théorie de la littérature.* Edited by T. Todorov. Paris: Seuil, 1965.

Smith, Gilbert. "Hermeticism and Historical Fiction: *La estafeta romántica* of Galdós." Paper presented at the Southeastern Conference on Romance Languages and Literatures, Rollins College, Winter Park, Fl., February 1983.

Snow, C. P. *The Realists: Portraits of Eight Novelists.* London: Macmillan, 1978.

Spires, Robert C. *Beyond the Metafictional Mode: Directions in the*

Modern Spanish Novel. Lexington: University of Kentucky Press, 1984.

Stamm, James R. *A Short History of Spanish Literature.* New York: New York University Press, 1984.

Stern, J. P. *On Realism.* London: Routledge & Kegan Paul, 1973.

Tierno Galván, Enrique. "Aparición y desarrollo de nuevas perspectivas de valoración social en el siglo XIX: lo cursi." *Revista de estudios políticos* 42 (1952): 85–106.

"Translation." *The Compact Edition of the Oxford English Dictionary.* 2 vols. Oxford: Oxford University Press, 1971.

Urey, Diane F. *Galdós and the Irony of Language.* Cambridge: Cambridge University Press, 1982.

Verdicchio, Massimo. "A Reader like Phaedrus." *Diacritics* (Spring 1984): 24–35.

White, Hayden. *Metahistory: The Historical Imagination in Nineteenth-Century Europe.* Baltimore: Johns Hopkins University Press, 1975.

————. *Tropics of Discourse: Essays in Cultural Criticism.* Baltimore: Johns Hopkins University Press, 1978.

Wolhfarth, Irving. "The Politics of Prose and the Art of Awakening: Walter Benjamin's Version of a German Romantic Motif." *Glyph Textual Studies* 7, 131–48. Baltimore: Johns Hopkins University Press, 1980.

Index

Alberique, 193
Alfonso XII, 103, 188, 194–95
allegory, 112, 150, 161–62, 202, 217, 219–26, 248–49n.8
Alter, Robert, 7–8, 250n.19
Amadeo de Saboya, 175, 199, 217
Ansúrez, Diego, 101
Ansúrez, Lucila, 102–24, 129, 144, 160, 176, 190, 211, 240n.15, 244n.4, 244n.6, 245n.7, 246n.15
Antoñita, 102
Araceli, Gabriel, 101, 162–63, 167, 172, 224–25, 229–31
Aransis, Guillermo de, 131, 139
Aristotle, or Aristotelian, 3, 116, 251n.20
Arratia, Don Sabino, 59, 241n.25
Arratia, Zoilo, 31, 53–54, 57–58, 68, 82, 86, 241n.25
Aumale, Duque de, 95
Avalle-Arce, Juan Bautista, 238n.4
Azorín, *Doña Inés*, 9

Balzac, Honoré de, 3–4, 218, 249n.10; *Comédie humaine*, 177; "Sarrasine," 155
Baroja, Pío, 9
Barthes, Roland, 154–56, 164, 180, 206, 239n.11, 241n.24, 247n.18, 249n.9, 249n.14, 253n.42, 253n.43
Baudelaire, Charles, 168
Baudrillard, Jean, 17
Benina, 138–39, 248n.23
Berberina, 107
Berkowitz, H. Chonon, 148, 152
Blanquat, Josette, 188
blindness: Galdós's, 188–90, 192; Tito's, 168, 186–88, 190, 208
Bly, Peter A., 11, 239n.8, 242n.33

Bourbon Restoration, 4, 13, 151, 194–95, 202
Bravo, Leonarda, or "Leona la Brava," 156, 159, 187
Brentano, Clemens, 26
Brizard, Isaac, 131–33
Bueno, Javier, 188

Cabeza, 193
Cabrera, Ramón, 32, 36, 84
Calabria, Don Florestán, 156, 159
Calderón de la Barca, Pedro, 179
Calpena, Fernando, 19, 29, 31, 33, 47–73, 82, 86, 87, 99, 101, 163, 167, 219, 226, 233, 235, 240n.23, 241n.25, 241n.27, 241–42n.30
Calpena, Pilar, 162, 194
Candelaria, or Penélope, 156
Cánovas del Castillo, Antonio, 181, 184–86, 195, 198, 202–3, 225
Cardona, Rodolfo, 243n.38
Carlist War (First), 13, 16, 29, 37, 53–54, 57, 59, 98, 110, 194
Carlos María Isidro de Borbón, Infante don, 16, 21–22, 59–60, 72, 195
Carlos V, 195
Carlota, Infanta doña Luisa, 72, 88–91, 120
Carlyle, Thomas, 233
Carrasco, Bruno, 81, 85, 92–93
Carrasco, Eufrasia, 85–86, 93, 98, 102, 104–7, 112–13, 118–21, 138, 142, 144, 195, 246n.16
Carrasco, Lea, 85–86
Carrasco, Leandra, 75–98, 176, 214, 233
Carrillo, Gómez, 188

Carroll, David, 249–50n.17, 250n.18, 251n.22
Casalduero, Joaquín, 33–34, 38, 108, 148, 167, 243–44n.1, 244n.3
Castelar, Emilio, 140–41, 144
Castro-Amézaga, Demetria, 52–53, 63–65, 68, 82, 85, 241n.23, 241–42n.30
Castro-Amézaga, Don Alonso, 52
Castro-Amézaga, Gracia, 52, 68, 241–42n.30
cause and effect, 16, 18, 21, 24, 81, 87–88, 90, 99, 155, 182, 207
Celestina, or celestinism, 35, 106–7
Centurión, Don Mariano, 81, 97–98, 133–35, 139, 248n.24
Cervantes, Miguel de, 3, 9, 33, 92, 217–19, 228; *Don Quijote*, 33, 51, 56, 92, 121, 164; Quijote figure, 59, 92, 98, 122, 158; quixotic, 101, 121–22
Chamberlin, Vernon, 189
Chilivistra, or Silvestra, 156, 159, 162, 193, 207–9, 213, 220
"Churi," 54–55
Cide Hamete Benengli, 217, 219
Clavería, Carlos, 177–78, 189, 231–33, 243n.34, 251n.22
Clavileño, 82
Clío, 71, 125, 143
Coleridge, Samuel Taylor, 26, 161, 220
Conejo, Casiana, 156, 161–62, 168–69, 187
Convenio de Amorebieta, 191
Convenio de Vergara, 59–60, 76, 191, 194
Culler, Jonathan, 151–52, 163–64, 170–71, 207, 212–13, 220–22, 247n.18, 249n.10, 250n.19

De Bolla, Peter, 246n.13
Delfina, 193, 209, 220
Dendle, Brian, 12, 20, 23–24, 28, 48, 78, 82–83, 128, 148, 163, 170, 171–72, 183, 188–89, 213, 238n.3, 239n.14, 239n.20, 244n.1, 245n.8, 247n.18, 247n.19, 248n.25, 252n.28
De Man, Paul, 168–69, 222–24, 226, 249n.8, 250n.19
Derrida, Jacques, 51, 74, 99, 173, 175–76, 179, 183, 222–23, 243n.39, 250n.18, 250n.19, 250n.20, 251n.23, 252n.27, 252n.29, 253n.40
"desamortización," 61–62, 127–29, 134, 137–40
Desposorios, Sor Catalina de los, 102, 106, 117
Dickens, Charles, 4
Donata, 102, 106, 158, 193, 203, 209
Don Juan: figure, 164, 197; motif, 32, 35–36, 101
Don Quijote. See Cervantes
Dostoevski, Fyodor, 3
Ducazal, Felipe, 193
Dulcinea, 121
Dumas, Alexandre (père), 95, 189

"Efémeras," 40, 183–85, 187, 199, 211, 251n.24
"la Eloísa," 194
Emparán y Baraona, María Ignacia, 102, 104–6, 113–14, 118, 120, 122
Enguídanos, Miguel, 148, 152, 252n.26
Enrique de Borbón, Don, 193
"el Epístola," 33, 54, 59
epistolary form, 54, 61, 65, 178. *See also* letters
epistolary novel, 7, 63, 99
Espartero, Baldomero, 16, 30–31, 53–61, 76–78, 124, 127, 130, 242n.30
Estevañez, Nicolás, 160

Fago, José, 19–33, 35–56, 48, 63, 82,

86, 92, 99, 118, 176, 226, 233, 239n.4, 242n.31
fantastic characters, 40, 157–58. *See also* "Efémeras"; Graziella; Liviano, Tito; Malaena
fantastic journeys. *See* journeys
fantastic mode, 40, 42, 175, 180–84, 187–88, 207, 223, 226, 251n.22
Fernando VII, 16, 198–99
Flaubert, Gustave, 229, 249n.10; *L'Education sentimentale*, 163, 170; *Salammbô*, 222
Floriana, 158, 165, 179, 211
Foucault, Michel, 173–76, 183
Francisco de Asís, Infante don, 87–88, 90, 93, 95, 115, 117–18
Franco, Nicolás, 88
Frank, Manfred, 26, 37, 73–74, 80, 98–99
free indirect speech or style, 23, 36, 239n.8
Freud, Sigmund, 17, 251n.22
Frye, Northrop, 164

Galán, Baldomero, 30–31
Gambito, 117, 246n.15
García Fajardo, José (Pepe Fajardo or "Beramendi"), 101, 103–23, 139, 163, 167, 172, 176–77, 211, 231, 233, 235, 244n.3, 245n.12, 246n.15, 246n.17
García Fajardo, Segismundo, 193–94, 202–3, 207, 253n.38
Generation of 1898, 9, 232
Gide, André, 7
Gilman, Stephen, 6, 8, 147, 153, 192, 217–18, 228, 251n.21, 253n.39
Goethe, Johan Wolfgang von, 178
Gogorza Fletcher, Madeleine de, 243–44n.1, 251n.21
Goldman, Peter B., 245n.11
González Bravo, Luis, 81
Gracián, Bartolomé, 106, 120, 245n.7
Graziella, 159

Greimas, A. J., 206
Guasa, Mateo, 43
Gullón, Germán, 225
Gullón, Ricardo, 9, 147, 240n.15, 251n.24

Halconero, Vicente, 151, 159, 162–64, 171, 175, 177–78, 190, 193–94, 196, 203, 207, 211–12, 214–15, 221–22, 235, 249n.12, 252n.25, 253n.38
Hegel, G.W.F., 46, 70, 251n.20
Heidegger, Martin, 251n.20
Hercules, or herculean, 166, 241–42n.30
Hermosilla sisters, 102
Hillo, Don Pedro, 50–51, 67
Hinterhäuser, Hans, 12, 170, 220, 244n.2
Historia lógico-natural, 115–16
Hoffman, E.T.F., 251n.22; *Prinzessin Brambilla*, 168–70

Ibero, Fernanda, 151, 159–63, 193–94, 209–13, 221, 252n.25, 253n.39
Ibero, Santiago (father), 52–53, 60, 68, 70, 77, 82, 86, 101, 163, 167, 241–42n.30
Ibero, Santiago (son), 101, 122, 163, 209–11
Idiáquez, Juana Teresa, 68–72, 85, 90, 233
"intra-historia," 232–33
irony, 55–56, 75–77, 79–82, 86–87, 91–93, 98–99, 109–11, 115, 123, 148–50, 167–69, 202–3, 243n.34, 248n.23, 249n.8
Irving, Washington, 189
Isabel II, 13, 16, 48, 77, 80–81, 86–88, 90–91, 93, 95–98, 101–24, 127–30, 134, 136, 140, 142, 145, 177, 199, 231, 234, 242n.31, 245n.12
Iser, Wolfgang, 249n.9

"el isleño," or "el gaunche," 166,
191, 217–19, 224, 226, 230–31
Iturrigalde, Facunda, 190

Jakobson, Roman, 179
Jameson, Fredric, 249n.9
Jiménez, Juan Ramón, 251n.24
journey, motif: 13, 16–19, 40, 47, 75,
83; as textual process or book, 19,
25–26, 61, 80, 99–100
journeys, of characters: 16, 18–19,
26, 28–29, 32–33, 37, 48–49, 52,
54, 57, 75–76, 82–83, 86, 93, 97,
143, 242n.30; endless, 26–27, 29,
36, 39, 78, 82, 93, 98–100;
fantastic, 36, 39–40, 82, 150, 157,
179, 184, 214; of reader, 16, 19,
33, 98
Joyce, James, 229; *Finnegans Wake*,
222
July Revolution, 103

Kercheville, Francis, 251n.22
Kermode, Frank, 212
Krause, Karl, or Spanish Krausism,
70
Kronik, John W., 8–9
Krzywicki-Herbert, George, 242n.32

LaCapra, Dominick, 246n.13
Lamennais, Felicité de, 70
Lamartine, Alphonse de, 178
Laurent, Auguste, 177
Lentricchia, Frank, 250n.19
letters, as documentation: 63–74;
functions of, 49–50, 53–55, 57–66,
68, 178, 197, 240–41n.23; reading,
54–55, 61–62
letter writer, 53–55, 57–58, 61, 64–66
Lévi-Strauss, Claude, 17, 41–42, 64,
206
Liviano, Tito, 36, 40, 149–50, 154–
60, 163–69, 171–72, 175, 178–88,
190–94, 196–209, 211–22, 224–37,

231, 233–35, 251n.21, 252n.28,
253n.39
Loaysa, Pilar de, 50–52, 54, 57, 61–
62, 64–65, 68–69, 72, 85, 233,
241n.23
Locus Solus (Raymond Roussel), 222
Luco, Marcela, 32–36, 38, 40, 42, 45–
46, 51, 85, 239n.12
Lukács, Gÿorgy, 8, 11, 92, 123, 175,
249–50n.17

Macherey, Pierre, 248n.7
Malaena, 40, 82
Maltrana, Juan Antonio de, 65–67,
72, 198
Mara, 102
María Cristina de Borbón, 16, 21, 59,
72, 76, 88–89, 102, 113, 117, 120
Mariclío, or Madre Mariana, 144,
150, 156–59, 166, 168–69, 178–79,
182–83, 185, 196, 201–3, 207–8,
213, 215–19, 224, 226, 240n.15
Maroto, Rafael, 53, 56–60
Marx, or Marxism, 17, 250n.19
Mazaltob, 102, 106
Mendizábal, Juan Alvarez de, 49, 60–
64, 66, 75, 78, 143–44, 231
Merino, Martín, 103
metafiction. *See* self-conscious novel
Michelet, Jules, 177, 232
Miedes, Ventura, 104–6, 114, 119,
121–22, 176, 186, 211, 233, 235
Milagro, Rafael del, 81, 97–98
Milagro, Rafaela del, 86, 158
"Ministerio relámpago," 103, 105,
108–9, 112–14, 117–20, 245n.10
Monsalud, Salvador, 101, 163, 172
Montes de Oca, Manuel, 77
Montesinos, José, 12, 148, 181, 220,
228
Montoro, David, 156
Montpensier, Antonio, Duque de,
193
Moreau, Fredéric, 163–64

Muñoz, Fernando, 88

Narváez, Ramón María, 77, 81, 83–
84, 120, 127, 130, 134–36,
243n.36, 246n.16
Negretti, Aurora, 31, 52–54, 57–58,
61, 63, 68, 82, 85
Nicéfora, 158–59, 161–62, 180, 193,
209, 220
Nietzsche, Friedrich, 21–22, 28, 38–
41, 67, 82, 233–34, 241–42n.30;
"antiquarian history," 22, 38–39,
45, 186; critique of historical
objectivity, 46–47; "monumental
history," 22–23, 38
Nocedal, Ramón, 134

Obdulia, 161, 165
O'Donnell, Leopoldo, 124, 127, 129–
30, 136–40, 143–45, 186, 243n.34
Olózaga, José de, 80
Olson, Paul R., 245n.11

"Paca la Africana," 193
Paredes, Dominiciana, 102, 106, 158,
240n.15, 245n.7
Parker, Andrew, 250n.19
parody, 7, 76, 94–95, 98–99, 114,
119, 149–50, 156, 167–68, 178,
189, 198, 202, 242n.30, 249n.8,
252n.35
Pasamonte, Ginés de, 224
Pascal, Roy, 239n.8
Patrocinio, Sor María, 106, 109, 113,
117
Paúl y Angulo, Francisco, 162, 193,
253n.38
Pavía, Manuel, 195, 202
Pavlovskii, Isaak Ia., 189
Pepe *el empalmado*, 156
Pérez Galdós, Benito: *El Abuelo*, 8;
Amadeo I, 147–48, 154, 159, 164–
65, 179, 182, 188, 190, 193–94,
199–200, 203–4, 217, 219, 225,

252n.33; *El amigo Manso*, 8; *Los
Ayacuchos*, 19, 48, 52, 63–64, 87,
241n.30; *Bodas reales*, 19, 48, 74–
100, 104, 109, 134, 164, 167, 177,
185, 189, 195, 201, 214, 242n.31;
El caballero encantado, 183,
251n.21; *La campaña del
Maestrazgo*, 19, 30–48, 71, 84, 95;
Cánovas, 147–48, 152, 156, 166,
168, 181, 184–85, 187–88, 194,
196, 198, 202–4, 215, 234; *Celia en
los infiernos*, 189; *La corte de
Carlos IV*, 225; *Los duendes de la
camarilla*, 106, 120, 245n.7;
España sin rey, 147–48, 158, 180,
195–96, 209; *España trágica*, 147–
48, 152, 159, 162, 175, 178, 190,
193–95, 202; *La estafeta
romántica*, 19, 48, 52, 54, 63–72,
241n.28; *Gerona*, 240n.15; *Juan
Martín "el Empecinado,"* 232;
Misericordia, 8–9, 138; *Novelas
contemporáneas*, 5, 12, 139, 228,
231; *Novelas de primera época*,
228; "La novela en el tranvía," 8;
Luchana, 19, 30–31, 52, 54, 232;
Mendizábal, 19, 48–53, 60–64, 73,
85, 241n.27; *Montes de Oca*, 19,
48, 76–77, 85; *Narváez*, 13, 103–
23, 185, 243n.36, 246n.15,
246n.16, 246n.17, 252n.35;
O'Donnell, 13, 123–46, 159, 197,
247n.20; *De Oñate a la Granja*,
19, 48, 52, 73, 75–76; *Prim*, 115,
127; *La primera República*, 147–
48, 157, 165, 179, 202, 213;
Trafalgar, 76, 167, 229–30,
240n.15, 242n.33; *La de los tristes
destinos*, 111, 115, 122, 127;
Vergara, 19, 33, 49, 52–60, 63–64,
66, 73, 85; *Zumal-acárregui*, 19–
34, 48, 85, 87
Pez, Manolita, 102, 130, 137,
248n.24

Poe, Edgar Allan, 251n.22
Polish Messianism, 70
Poniatowsky, José, 69–70
Prim, Juan, 78, 115, 124, 151, 175,
    180, 190, 195, 212
Prometheus, 166
Proteus, 154
Proust, Marcel, 218, 229; *A la
    recherche du temps perdu*, 155

Regalado García, Antonio, 12, 148,
    152, 172, 183, 245n.11
Revolution of 1868, 13, 103–4, 197,
    199
Ribbans, Geoffrey, 115–16, 148, 152,
    154, 190, 217–18, 231, 233,
    245n.10, 245n.11, 247n.20,
    248n.25
Riva Guisando, José de la, 132–33,
    137
Rodríguez, Alfred, 5–6, 12, 19, 28,
    36, 39, 54–55, 136, 148, 160, 169–
    72, 181, 239n.11, 239n.12,
    239n.14, 243n.35, 243n.1,
    246n.17, 247n.21, 247n.22,
    248n.1, 248n.12, 253n.39
romanticism, 13, 16–18, 32, 38–39,
    42, 53, 55, 58, 68, 81, 85, 94–96,
    98, 251n.22; romantic idealism,
    16, 34, 38, 54, 58; romantic
    writers, 46, 189, 228
Romarate, Don Wifredo, 158–60,
    180–81, 193–94, 207, 209, 212,
    252n.25, 253n.38
Ronell, Avital, 51–52
Rousseau, Jean-Jacques, 224,
    250n.19; *Julie*, 226; *La Nouvelle
    Heloïse*, 177–78, 222, 226

Sagasta, Práxedes Mateo, 200–201,
    206
Salamanca, José, 247n.20
Salmerón, Nicolás, 179–80
Santapau, Manuel (Nelet), 31–47, 82,

86, 90, 92, 98–100, 176, 233,
    251n.21
Santiuste, Juan (*Confusio*), 101, 115–
    16, 119, 121–23, 127, 136, 139–45,
    154, 167, 230, 235, 244n.3,
    248n.25
Sanz, Elena, 225
Saussure, Ferdinand de, 10, 179
Schelling, Friedrich, 70
Schopenhauer, Arthur, 233
Schlegel, Friedrich, 168
Schleiermacher, Friedrich, 73
"Seda," 54–55
self-conscious (metafictional or self-
    referential) novel, 7–9, 124,
    250n.19; *self-conscious textual
    strategies*, 11, 74, 80, 87, 122, 159,
    161, 224, 228–30, 232
Serrano, Francisco, 127, 206
Seymour-Smith, Martin, 3–4
Shklovsky, Victor, 152
Smith, Gilbert, 64, 241n.28
Snow, C. P., 3, 8
Socobio, Cristeta de, 85, 87–91, 95–
    100, 235
Socobio, Serafín de, 87
Socobio, Valeria de, 102, 106, 129,
    142
Socobio, Virginia de, 102
Spires, Robert, 8
Stamm, James, 3
Starobinski, Jean, 168
Stern, J. P., 8

Tarfe, Manolo, 138, 140, 142–44,
    247n.20, 248n.24
Theirs, Luis Adolphe, 177
Tierno Galván, Enrique, 249n.14
Tito. *See* Liviano, Tito
Tolstoy, Leo, 229
Trafalgar, Battle of, 4
translation, 17, 49, 50, 55, 60, 65–66,
    80, 95–96, 98–99, 117, 189–90,
    221, 226; definitions and functions

of, 47–48, 50, 52, 68–74, 219,
240n.19; translated text, 51–52,
86; translator, 51–61
translations of Galdós's works
(recent), 237n.4
"las tres Parcas/Ecuménicas," 158
"turno pácifico, 196, 208

Ulibarri, Don Adrián, 20, 24, 27, 29,
48, 91, 98
Ulibarri, Saloma, 19–20, 24–33, 43,
51, 63, 100, 118, 238n.4, 242n.31
Unamuno, Miguel de, 7, 232; *Niebla*,
9; *Paz en la guerra*, 232
"Unión liberal," 126–27, 137–38,
143, 243n.34
Urdaneta, Don Beltrán de, 31–47, 53,
63, 69–73, 78, 82, 86, 90, 95–96,
99–100, 120, 176, 186, 197, 199,
201, 215, 230, 233, 235, 239n.14
Urdaneta, Valvanera, 64–68, 72, 85,
190
Urdaneta Iiáquez, Rodrigo, 33, 65,
68–72
Urríes, Don Juan de, 151, 180, 193,
195–97, 210

Valcárcel, Teresa, 88
Valle-Inclán, Ramón del, *Tirano
Banderas*, 9
Verdicchio, Massimo, 250n.19
Vicálvaro, 127
Villaescusa, Colonel, 127, 130, 135–
36, 247n.22
Villaescusa, Teresa, 102, 106, 124–46,
157, 186, 209–11, 247n.20,
247n.21, 247n.22, 248n.24
Voltaire, François-Marie Arouet, 233

Weiner, Jack, 189
White, Hayden, 10–11, 79, 125, 173–
74, 241–42n.30, 246n.13
Wohlfarth, Irving, 240n.18
woman as text, 25, 28, 32–33, 52,
197, 240–41n.23

Yohar, 102

Zahón, Jacoba, 52
Zorrilla, José, 200–201, 206
Zumalacárregui, Tomás, 19–30, 36,
239n.8